RAMBLE

CALIFORNIA

A Wanderer's Guide to the Offbeat, Overlooked, and Outrageous

BY

ERIC PETERSON

speck press

golden

Published by Speck Press
An imprint of Fulcrum Publishing
4690 Table Mountain Drive, Suite 100 • Golden, Colorado 80403
303-277-1623 • speckpress.com

ISBN: 978-1-933108-20-9

This publication is provided for informational and educational purposes. The information herein contained is true and complete to the best of our knowledge.

Library of Congress Cataloging-in-Publication Data

Peterson, Eric, 1973-
  Ramble California : a wanderer's guide to the offbeat, overlooked, and outrageous / by Eric Peterson.
    p. cm.
  Includes index.
  ISBN 978-1-933108-20-9 (pbk.)
  1. California--Guidebooks. 2. Curiosities and wonders--Colorado--Guidebooks. I. Title.
  F859.3.P48 2008
  917.9404'54--dc22
                    2008031484

Printed and bound in China

10 9 8 7 6 5 4 3 2 1

Book layout and design by Margaret McCullough
California map provided by Marge Mueller, © Gray Mouse Graphics
Pages 4, 9, 13, 26, 43, 46, 63, 75, 87, 97, 100, 112, 115, 116, 117, 135, 138, 142, 149, 151, 159, 165, 166, 170, 171, 188, 189, 190, 191, 194, 199, 203, 205, 209, 220, 221, 222, 237, 239, 240, 241, 257, 259, 260, 261, 262 and the cover © Shutterstock, page 16 © Richard Carroll, page 32 © Glenn Cormier, page 12 © Tom Michele Grimm, page 110 © Musée Mécanique, page 36 © Phillipe the Original, page 168 © Treebone Resort, all others © Eric Peterson. For specific information about individual photographs, please contact the publisher.

To Dad.

**It's been great traveling with you.
And I'm damn glad we avoided that three-car
collision on I-5 in LA.**

THANKS TO:

Ruthie, Mom, Mitch, Olivia, Sam, Arin, Brad, Aunt Jean and
Uncle Mark, Jen and Lance Van Court, Susan Hill Newton, Derek Lawrence,
Margaret McCullough, the Yosemite Bug, Evergreen Lodge, Kenny Karst,
Brooke Swayne and SoCal Surf School, Jon Peterson and Surfin Fire,
Steve Bailey, Katherine Jarvis, Robert and Caleb and Jah in Chico,
Dave Koterwas, Scott Durango Redick, Vlad Bozic, Jenny Franklin,
Hilary Townsend, Kate Buska, Valerie Arias, Leslee Gaul, Daniel Watman,
Eric Rimmele, Megan Rodriguez, Captain Dutch Meyer,
and Beth Bruegman.

CONTENTS

INTRODUCTION 6

CHAPTER 1: Los Angeles
and Southern California 12

CHAPTER 2: Going Wrong in Hollywood 46

CHAPTER 3: Sand and Surf and a Fence
into the Ocean 64

CHAPTER 4: San Francisco
and Northern California 88

CHAPTER 5: Stress, Dread, and Rock and Roll . . . 116

CHAPTER 6: A Beer Drinker in Wine Country . . 138

CHAPTER 7: Central California: The Coast
and the Valley 150

CHAPTER 8: Grow Trip 172

CHAPTER 9: The High Sierra and Vicinity 190

CHAPTER 10: In Muir's Bootprints 206

CHAPTER 11: The California Desert 222

CHAPTER 12: The Desert, Man 240

RAMBLE MANIFESTO 262

APPENDIX: INFO, ETC. 267

INDEX 270

INTRODUCTION

I took a walk in Marina del Rey and found a metaphor for
all of California. The walk was perhaps a three-mile loop.
First I saw the Ritz-Carlton and marina-front apartments
and commuters on bicycles. Then slums of dinky, beat-up
rentals. Then I turned a corner into a brand-new development of two-story, single-family homes, probably a million
a pop. One of them was having a Democratic Party caucus
in the garage.

I followed the labyrinth of new streets into what should
have been a dead end at the back gate of a massive new apartment tower, but the back gate was unlocked. Cars zipped into
the off-street parking spaces as I walked out the front entry. I
could tell that walking out of this complex was beyond rare.

I was greeted by strip malls, neon, the blare of internal
combustion engines—a nearby highway with sidewalks
merging into a highway in the distance merging into a super-
highway on the horizon merging into a megasuperhighway
just beyond the horizon. The only other pedestrians looked
like they had just teleported here from various third world
countries. We are all next to anonymous amid the endless
swirl of cars and lights.

The metaphorical and literal end of the road, California is aptly nicknamed the Golden State because this is one of the places where gold matters most. This is where the economic tide of the entire West ebbs and flows, rushing out from LA and San Francisco, flowing inland to Vegas, Phoenix, and Lake Tahoe, surging into Utah, Colorado, and the Pacific Northwest, and barely trickling into Kansas and North Dakota before the tide changes and the boom goes bust as the wave recedes, the origin cities crashing last and crashing the hardest, if only because they surged laughably high with the initial wave.

Then all is calm until the next wave of economic mania rushes in.

Equal parts impending seismic-induced doom, idyllic beach resorts, endless suburbs, and drug-fueled orgy of excess, this state is infinitely diverse. Its population, topography, and rate of mutation are astounding. So is its ballyhooed economic might and endless flow of fresh fruit, software, and entertainment increasingly oriented to those with ADD or ten-year-old boys—or those who share characteristics of both.

And it just might be the greatest state for road trips, with its skyscraping mountains and human-made mountains in family fun theme parks and mountainous skyscrapers and of course the western state line that is the Pacific Ocean. A loop around California melts from seaside paradise into urban squalor into desert squalor into lush greenery then back into urban squalor and seaside paradise again. And there's so much to see in between.

A California road trip is one of my favorites. I love rising with the sun and racing it all day long across mountain and desert, ultimately losing somewhere around Barstow but making it to LA on time for dinner with my sister and her family. I love driving up the coast and visiting old friends. I love exploring the inland wilderness and alpine areas, and desert. And I love going home to Colorado.

I look at California as one body: 30 million individual cells coursing through its circulatory freeway system, a hyperactive and continuously growing body without a singular set of DNA, chaotic and fascinating and scary and lovable.

Love it or hate it, California *is* America to much of the world. It's the country's face and front door, its heart and soul, and its worst intentions, the ultimate hyperparable of the United States in its most untied state.

And no matter how cynical my words read, I do love California.

— *Eric Peterson*

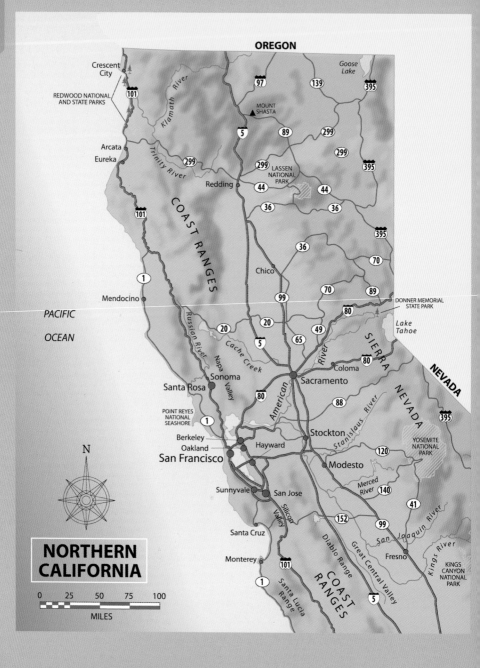

OREGON

Crescent City

REDWOOD NATIONAL AND STATE PARKS

Klamath River

Goose Lake

97

139

395

MOUNT SHASTA

5

89

299

Arcata

Eureka

Trinity River

299

299

299

395

LASSEN NATIONAL PARK

Redding

44

44

COAST RANGES

36

36

395

36

70

Chico

70

89

99

80

DONNER MEMORIAL STATE PARK

Mendocino

1

Russian River

Cache Creek

20

20

20

Lake Tahoe

PACIFIC

OCEAN

5

65

49

Napa Valley

American River

SIERRA

Coloma

Santa Rosa

Sonoma

Sacramento

80

88

Stanislaus River

NEVADA

POINT REYES NATIONAL SEASHORE

1

Stockton

YOSEMITE NATIONAL PARK

Berkeley

Oakland

San Francisco

Hayward

Modesto

120

395

N

Sunnyvale

San Jose

Merced River

140

Silicon Valley

152

99

41

San Joaquin River

Santa Cruz

Diablo Range

Great Central Valley

Fresno

Kings River

Monterey

101

COAST RANGES

KINGS CANYON NATIONAL PARK

1

Santa Lucia Range

5

NORTHERN CALIFORNIA

0   25   50   75   100

MILES

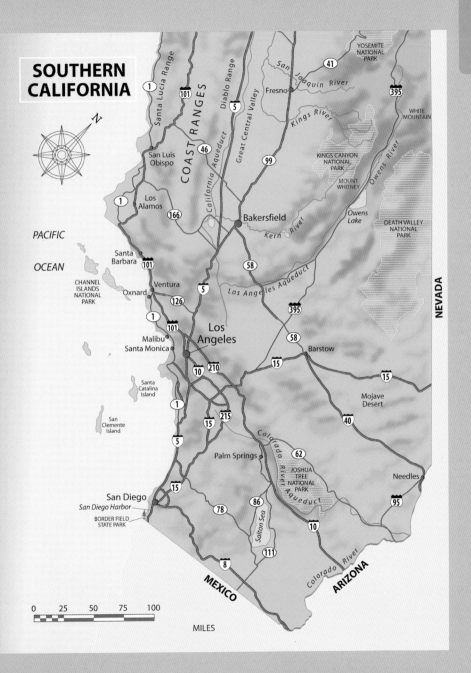

SOUTHERN CALIFORNIA

N

PACIFIC

OCEAN

Santa Lucia Range

Diablo Range

COAST RANGES

California Aqueduct

Great Central Valley

San Joaquin River

YOSEMITE NATIONAL PARK

Fresno

Kings River

WHITE MOUNTAIN

Owens River

1

101

41

395

San Luis Obispo

46

KINGS CANYON NATIONAL PARK

MOUNT WHITNEY

1

Los Alamos

166

5

99

Owens Lake

DEATH VALLEY NATIONAL PARK

Bakersfield

Kern River

Santa Barbara

101

CHANNEL ISLANDS NATIONAL PARK

Ventura

Oxnard

58

Los Angeles Aqueduct

126

5

1

101

395

Los Angeles

58

Barstow

Malibu

Santa Monica

Santa Catalina Island

10

210

15

15

San Clemente Island

1

Mojave Desert

15

215

40

1

5

Colorado River Aqueduct

Palm Springs

62

JOSHUA TREE NATIONAL PARK

Needles

San Diego

San Diego Harbor

15

78

86

Salton Sea

10

95

BORDER FIELD STATE PARK

8

111

Colorado River

MEXICO

ARIZONA

NEVADA

PACIFIC OCEAN

0   25   50   75   100

MILES

LOS ANGELES AND SOUTHERN CALIFORNIA

INTRODUCTION

Somewhere amid the maddening unpredictability of traffic and the undying predictability of the tides is the fabled California cool, an invention surely made on or near the beach among the wet suits and bikinis and joints and bonfires.

But the big, big, big, *huge* money of California isn't in the beach. That money is in importing Chinese products as fast as the containers can be unloaded. Thus, the only waterfront property in LA proper is dedicated to the industrial netherworld of Los Angeles Harbor. Luckily, there are great beaches to be found both north and south. Unluckily (but perhaps deservedly), the whole region suffers from brown-air syndrome.

Beyond the sea, money is just about everywhere in Southern California—the only exception being where it's most needed. This is an economy so big and diverse it encompasses Disneyland and pornmakers in the San Fernando Valley, as well as the odd corporate entity that specializes in adult videos featuring costumed dwarves. This is also the

STATS & FACTS

- The world's first movie theater opened in Los Angeles on April 2, 1902.

- Los Angeles's original full name is El Pueblo de Nuestra Señora la Reina de los Angeles de Porciúncula, that is, The Town of Our Lady the Queen of Angels of the Little Portion. It is impossible to explain what "Little Portion" means in one sentence, but it has very little meaning nonetheless.

- Sierra Madre's Lavender Lady is the world's largest blooming plant, a wisteria vine with branches 500 feet long.

- The Hollywood sign, erected in 1923, was originally a real-estate ad that read Hollywoodland. By 1973, the sign was falling apart—one *o* had toppled downhill and an arsonist had burned an *l*—prompting a $250,000 reconstruction financially spearheaded by movie stars. The letters stand fifty feet tall, stretch some 450 feet across, and collectively weigh more than twenty tons.

- The Port of Los Angeles and the Port of Long Beach are the country's busiest and second busiest seaports, respectively.

home of Hollywood, where dreams are made into plastic and sold to the world, surrounded by the definitive futuristic megacity awash in the by-products of its own explosive growth, in turn surrounded by deserts and orange groves converted to suburbs until the real-estate profits and drinking water dwindle to zero.

The weather—more often than not 70 degrees and sunny—attracts all sorts of professionals, especially stars (music, movies, and porn), the members of said stars' posses, and said stars' agents. The favorable climate also appeals to a wide range of addicts, criminals, and lunatics who do not like the cold.

This means people-watching in California is no mere diversion—it's a full-time job. In Southern California, common specimens include disillusioned also-rans and strung-out never-weres; less common are the rich and famous, a group far outnumbered by the poor and desperate. Demographically speaking, Los Angeles is home to one of the most ethnically diverse populations on the planet. The suburbs have street signs in Vietnamese, and the kids develop new languages that have more to do with age than race.

More conservative than Los Angeles but not quite as conservative as Orange County, San Diego prides itself on being less of a mess than LA, but with the same great weather plus a naval shipyard and an ever-more-militarized international border a few miles away. The San Diego–Tijuana metropolitan area, which has roughly the population of the Bay Area, is the perfect marriage of the first and third worlds...well, except for the three-layer barbwire fence and border patrol agents between the spousal cities.

Regardless, whether you're cruising for hookers on Hollywood Boulevard or hiding out in Imperial Beach, Southern California has something for everybody and is pretty much anything and everything you want it to be—maybe too much of something, anything, everything.

Read:

- Ramona by Helen Hunt Jackson
- What Makes Sammy Run? by Budd Schulberg
- Red Wind by Raymond Chandler
- The Player by Michael Tolkin

Listen:

- Pet Sounds by The Beach Boys
- Straight Outta Compton by N.W.A.
- LA Woman by The Doors
- Loud and Plowed and...LIVE!! by The Beat Farmers

Watch:

- Pulp Fiction
- Blade Runner
- Chinatown
- Sunset Boulevard
- Colors

To-Do Checklist:

- Impersonate the paparazzi
- Puke at Disneyland
- Party all night
- Sleep all day
- Surf in between

BIG THINGS AND OTHER ROAD ART

Cabazon Dinosaurs
Adjacent to I-10, Main St. exit, Cabazon
www.cabazondinosaurs.com

There's nothing that says "I'm almost to Los Angeles" like the Cabazon Dinosaurs, with the colossal *Tyrannosaurus rex* (Mr. Rex) and *Apatosaurus* (Ms. Dinny) sidling up to I-10 in the California desert. Famous for their cameo in *Pee-Wee's Big Adventure*, Mr. Rex and Ms. Dinny are the product of the late Claude Bell, who worked on the twin dinos until his passing in 1989. Once threatened with demolition, the dinosaurs are now in the hands of a creationist organization that sells antievolution books and gifts right out of Ms. Dinny's prodigious belly.

Watts Towers
1765 E. 107th St., Los Angeles
213-847-4646

Watts does not get the tourists it should. While most of LA's visitors skip South Central in favor of Anaheim, they're missing out on a series of towering spires that put Sleeping Beauty's castle to shame.

The Watts Towers are seventeen distinct structures crafted by Italian immigrant Simon Rodia between 1931 and 1955. Supported by a skeleton of steel pipes, the towers are clad in a multihued mosaic of tiles, broken pieces of pottery, seashells, glass shards, and other salvaged materials. The tallest measures ninety-nine feet, six inches. Like Florida's Coral Castle and Colorado's Bishop Castle, it's hard to fathom that this is all the work of just one man who shunned scaffolding, power equipment, bolts, and blueprints.

In 1955, Rodia picked up stakes and essentially abandoned his life's work. His shack burned down, leading the city of Los Angeles to condemn the property and order his sculptures razed. But a group of locals came together to save these masterpieces of folk art. Since then, the towers have served as a community arts center founded by the late director Noah Purifoy, a highly regarded outsider artist whose works are on display in the desert outside Joshua Tree.

Farmer John Murals
3049 E. Vernon Ave., Vernon
323-583-4621
www.farmerjohn.com

In Vernon, a largely industrial town just southeast of downtown Los Angeles, Farmer John has been in the pig business since the 1930s. While the odor surrounding Farmer John's pork processing plant is a bit funky—and its interior could well be a horror show—the murals all over its facade are something

else: a vibrant scene of greased pigs and scarecrows and vivid green pastures. Hollywood set artist Les Grimes painted the murals from 1957 to 1968, and the company has since restored them, making this exterior artwork a worthwhile detour from the museums and their typically pleasant interiors.

Old Trapper's Lodge
On the campus of Pierce College
6201 Winnetka Ave., Woodland Hills

From a different, less politically correct time, outsider artist John Ehn's sculptures originally wrestled, leered, and re-clined in Burbank. But now the pieces are semiretired in a shady corner behind the ag building on the campus of Pierce College. Ehn's vibrant and odd cast of characters, most of them seemingly unhinged or unbalanced and from a West more weird than wild, first populated the grounds of his Old Trapper's Lodge motel and apartment. After Ehn passed away

in the 1980s, his family sold the land to the Burbank Airport and the concrete statues were relocated to Pierce College.

Venice Beach Public Art
Various locations
www.venicechamber.net

A massive mural of onetime Venice resident Jim Morrison looms over Speedway near 18th Avenue. In addition to the Lizard King mural, down near Main and Rose streets, just a few blocks from Venice Beach proper, there are two landmarks of oddball architecture. The first are Frank Gehry buildings fronted by a three-story pair of binoculars by sculptor Claes Oldenburg. The second is the nearby Venice Renaissance adorned by a large clown in a tutu. That's right—a large clown in a tutu. The perpetually moving statue, fittingly called *Ballerina Clown*, is the work of Jonathan Borofsky.

Chicano Park Murals
Under the I-5 cloverleaf,
Barrio Logan, San Diego
www.chicanoparksandiego.com

Leftist artists have created an amazing outdoor gallery in what could be a concrete wasteland below a web of overpasses. Instead, the park is alive with color and creativity and serves as a postindustrial canvas for artists with wildly different messages and visions: murals range from Quetzalcoatl, the winged serpent god, to pro-labor statements, to leering "cosmic clowns."

Queen Califia's Magical Circle
**Kit Carson Park,
about twenty miles inland
from San Diego in Escondido
www.queencalifia.org**

A true public art masterpiece, this walkable work of tile and
sculpture is the only work in the United States by the late
artist Niki de Saint Phalle, a contemporary of Christo and
the new realists. The Magical Circle features a menagerie of
slightly psychedelic beasties and colorful characters inter-
locked in an environment that somehow makes perfect sense
when you're inside of it.

Dr. Seuss Collection and Trees
La Jolla, San Diego

Dr. Seuss lived and worked in La Jolla, and a library on the
campus of the University of California at San Diego is named
for him. The Theodore Geisel Library features an archive
and a gallery of the good doctor's work. Not far away, in
Ellen Browning Scripps Memorial Park, above La Jolla Cove,
the oddly bent "Dr. Seuss" trees supposedly inspired Geisel's
depictions of whimsical flora.

The Velaslavasay Panorama: Effulgence of the North
**1122 W. 24th Ave., Los Angeles
213-746-2166
www.panoramaonview.org**

Before movies, there were panoramas. Sometimes there was
a plot, but most of the time there was only a 360-degree painting of a faraway land, say the Sahara Desert or the Great White
North. The nineteenth-century phenomenon disappeared

with the twentieth-century advent of the motion-picture era but is staging a comeback in the twenty-first century. Near the University of Southern California campus, the hypnotic *Velaslavasay Panorama* is perched on the second floor of a historic West Adams theater. It is a two- and three-dimensional re-creation of the Arctic, complete with subtly shifting lights and a soundtrack of wind and creaking ice. I can safely tell you that it's better than most modern Hollywood flicks.

R.I.P.

Hollywood Forever Cemetery
Screenings are held on Saturday nights in the summer
6000 Santa Monica Blvd., Los Angeles
www.cemeteryscreenings.com

I take a swig of my beer and survey the scene. A thousand or so people are crowded onto a wide-open green next to a big white building. It's a bustling outdoor party with picnics and pizzas and booze. It's also Saturday night in the middle of a cemetery. The big white building is about to serve as a screen for the movie *Carrie*.

"Who's buried here?" I ask a compatriot.

"Rudolf Valentino," comes his answer. "Douglas Fairbanks. And the girl Fatty Arbuckle supposedly murdered."

I remark that it is an unusually festive scene to see in a normally solemn and silent place like a graveyard.

"It's a party in their honor, the people who are buried here," my friend replies. "I think they'd want us to be here, having a good time and enjoying life."

A few minutes later, *Carrie*'s opening locker room sequence begins flickering on the structure in front of us. The crowd cheers. I lean back and enjoy the movie, the perfect film for this perfect moment in time.

DEARLY DEPARTED STARS

There are so many famous dead people buried in and around LA that it boggles the mind why the paparazzi chase the living ones to no end. The dead stars don't dodge the flashbulbs or take a swing. No, they are generally more than willing to pose for a picture—that is, if you can find them. Many LA–area graveyards are so vast it's nearly impossible to locate a specific grave without a map. And to make matters worse, some crypts are private and some cemetery offices are none too helpful to wandering tourists. As a primer, here are three of the most popular celebrity cemeteries and their most famous departed residents.

Forest Lawn Memorial Park
1712 S. Glendale Ave., Glendale
323-254-3131
www.forestlawn.com

Humphrey Bogart, Jimmy Stewart, George Burns,
Gracie Allen, Larry Fine, Chico Marx, Clark Gable,
Ted Knight, L. Frank Baum, Walt Disney, Spencer Tracy,
Douglas Fairbanks, Mary Pickford

Pierce Brothers Westwood Village Memorial Park
1218 Glendon Ave., Westwood
310-474-1579

Marilyn Monroe, Dean Martin, Natalie Wood, Bob Crane,
Jack Lemmon, Walter Matthau, Don Knotts, Donna Reed,
Truman Capote, Roy Orbison

Holy Cross Cemetery
5835 W. Slauson Ave., Culver City
310-670-7697

Béla Lugosi, Lawrence Welk, Spike Jones, John Candy,
Rita Hayworth, Bing Crosby, Sharon Tate

Henry Charles Bukowski, 1920–1994
Green Hills Memorial Park
27501 S. Western Ave., Rancho Palos Verdes

The writer and poet who personified LA's gutter, Henry
Charles Bukowski drank and wrote and womanized and bet
on the ponies and worked odd jobs when absolutely necessary. Fittingly, his semiautobiographical novels and poems

were usually about drinking, writing, womanizing, betting on the ponies, and working odd jobs when absolutely necessary. It seems Bukowski didn't have to try too hard— he pretty much did whatever felt good and didn't apologize for it. Perhaps that's why his gravestone bears the inscription Don't Try.

Skeletons in the Closet

1104 N. Mission Rd., Los Angeles
323-343-0760
www.lacoroner.com

For that special morbid someone, the resident gift shop at the LA County Coroner is going to hit the jugular. This little shop offers plenty of LA Coroner–branded merchandise, such as T-shirts, leather binders, beach towels, business-card holders, as well as more-general death-related toys and games. The beach towel, complete with the official logo of a chalk body outline, is the top seller.

VICE

Porno Grauman's

Outside the former TomKat Theater
(now Pussycat/Studs)
Santa Monica Blvd., Santa Monica

Highlighted by the handprints and footprints—but alas, no dickprints or boobprints—of porn legends John Holmes, Linda Lovelace, Marilyn Chambers, and Harry Reems, this porn theater, which now swings both ways, is the Grauman's

Chinese Theatre of the skin-flick industry. Tucked into a busy retail district in a mostly Russian neighborhood, the current Pussycat/Studs venue has a much different clientele than the surrounding businesses, but the immortality in concrete gets paid very little mind.

Jumbo's Clown Room
5153 Hollywood Blvd., Hollywood
323-666-1187
www.jumbos.com

Open since 1970, Jumbo's Clown Room is a great dive featuring exotic dancers, who are considerably more real than the LA norm, as well as no nudity, no cover charge, and cheap drinks. This allows for guilt-free lechery and leering, but also makes for a great low-key hangout (even a good date spot for the right special someone who's not easily offended). And the girls—who come in all sorts of sexy shapes and sizes—are quite talented.

Los Angeles Nightlife

Hollywood dives run the gamut from the authentic dive that is the Frolic Room (6245 Hollywood Blvd., 323-462-5890) to the nearly pitch-black faux dive and *Jackass* hangout that is the Burgundy Room (1621 1/2 N. Cahuenga Blvd., 323-465-7530), to kickass Polynesian dives like the Tiki-Ti (4427 Sunset Blvd., 323-669-9381, www.tiki-ti.com), which has been pouring Cobra Fangs and about eighty-four other tropical drinks since 1961. If your ears are craving live music in la-la land, indie rock is the staple at sci-fi-inspired Club Spaceland (1717 Silver Lake Blvd., 323-661-4380, www.clubspaceland.com), acoustic singer-songwriters are the focus at the Hotel Cafe (1623 1/2 N. Cahuenga Blvd., www.hotelcafe.com), and the Troubadour (9081 Santa Monica Blvd., www.troubadour.com) and the Whisky a Go Go (8901 W. Sunset Blvd., 310-652-4202, www.whiskyagogo.com) are two of the most storied rock clubs in the country. Open since 1957 and 1964, respectively, legends like Tom Waits and Led Zeppelin have graced the stages at these joints.

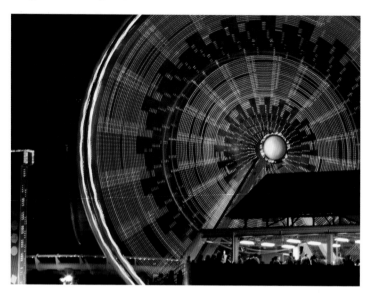

San Diego Nightlife

Most of the see-and-be-seen crowd hits the nightlife district known as the Gaslamp Quarter, which is lined with bars and restaurants. As for imbibing outside of the Gaslamp, there are numerous classic seaport dives in San Diego. In Little Italy, The Waterfront (2044 Kettner Blvd., 619-232-9656, www.waterfrontbarandgrill.com), the city's oldest operating bar—in business since 1933—offers a vintage-meets-kitsch nautical vibe and a double tall of local color. Nearby, The Casbah (2501 Kettner Blvd., 619-232-HELL, www.casbahmusic.com) is a punk-rock institution, with loud live music at least six nights a week. Just off the Embarcadero and marked by a sign reading "*Top Gun*: Sleazy bar scene filmed here in 1985," Kansas City Barbecue (610 W. Market St., 619-231-9680, www.kcbbq.net), a similar holdout hole-in-the-wall, is plastered with bras, stickers, and naval regalia.

HUH?

Necromance
7220 Melrose Ave., Los Angeles
323-934-8684
www.necromance.com

The best place to buy dead things in LA—hell, the best place to buy dead things in California—Necromance is one of those stores people either love or hate. If you don't like stuffed beavers, human skulls, splayed cobra skins, boar trophies, bug rings, and rabbit- and gator-foot keychains, the place will probably not be your cup of tea. But if you do like any or

STAR MAPS

- In the original 1931 *Frankenstein*, the monster chucks the little girl into Lake Sherwood in Ventura County.

- In *Pulp Fiction*, Butch runs over Marcellus Wallace in the crosswalk over Fletcher Drive at Atwater Avenue in Glendale. There is no Jack Rabbit Slim's. The 1950s-themed diner was a movie set in a Culver City warehouse.

- Daniel-san's apartment in *The Karate Kid* is at 19223 Saticoy Street in Reseda.

- In 1946, Howard Hughes nearly died when he crashed his experimental XF-11 aircraft into a mansion at 808 Whittier Drive in Beverly Hills.

- A cave in Griffith Park's Bronson Canyons served as the Batcave on TV's *Batman*.

- The Cunningham's house from *Happy Days* can be found at 565 N. Cahuenga Avenue in Hollywood.

- The departure point for the "three-hour tour" in *Gilligan's Island* was Alamitos Bay in Long Beach.

- What served as Korea in TV's *M*A*S*H* is now Malibu Creek State Park, open to the public, in Calabasas.

- The climax of *Blade Runner* takes place at the Bradbury Building at 304 S. Broadway in downtown LA. The movie was set in 2010, but the building dates back to the nineteenth century.

- Hugh Grant picked up Divine Brown at the corner of Sunset Boulevard and Courtney Avenue and was subsequently arrested for lewd conduct at Curson and Hawthorn avenues.

all of the above dead-animal products (as well as desiccated bats in glass frames, freeze-dried rats, the penis bones of minks and raccoons…), I heartily recommend a stop.

Wacko/Soap Plant

4633 Hollywood Blvd.,
Los Angeles
323-663-0122
www.soapplant.com

This colorful, aptly named store —except for the soap-plant thing— Wacko / Soap Plant, established in 1976, is a long-standing retail trove for off-kilter books, bobbleheads, action figures, religious knickknacks, original outsider art, and just about anything else your eccentric Angeleno could possibly want. Personally, I bought a ball that looks like a baby's head that cries and wails when you bounce it; a bargain at $3.50.

L. Ron Hubbard

The Scientologists are to Hollywood what the Mormons are to Salt Lake City. The hyperreal backdrop is perfect for proselytizers pushing a religion based on science fiction. Not to get down on any one religion—I typically check "none of the above"—but Scientology is one of the most outlandish, involving alien ghosts in every living cell and

Tom Cruise as a pseudo pope and eternal salvation for the world if and only if every last person converts to, yep, Scientology. Good luck with that.

If you're especially interested, forty-five-minute guided tours covering Scientology founder L. Ron Hubbard's life are available for free at 6331 Hollywood Boulevard, and stress tests are available for free along the sidewalks of Hollywood.

Or just go ahead and convert.

Bunny Museum
1933 Jefferson Dr., Pasadena
626-798-8848 for appointments
(necessary except for holiday
open houses)
www.thebunnymuseum.com

If you have 25,000 bunnies in your house and you exchange new bunnies with your spouse every day, you must have

nothing but bunnies everywhere, all throughout your house. And lest we forget the huge ivy-covered bunny out front and the Garden of Broken Dreams out back that holds the remains of your sadly broken bunnies. (Your neighbors love you, yes?)

Welcome to the world of Candace Frazee and Steve Lubanski in Pasadena. Their house—aka the Bunny Museum —features bunny dolls, bunny figurines, stuffed bunnies, live pet bunnies, freeze-dried formerly live pet bunnies, bunny magnets, bunny salt and pepper shakers, and all sorts of other bunny paraphernalia—perhaps enough to make you sick.

Museum of Jurassic Technology

9341 Venice Blvd., Culver City
310-836-6131
www.mjt.org

Words don't do every museum justice. This is one of them. Exhibits delve into cat's cradles, Russian space dogs, and melting dice. Go see for yourself. And give yourself plenty of time.

Whaley House

2476 San Diego Ave., Old Town San Diego
619-297-7511
www.whaleyhouse.org

Before New Town—the site of modern downtown San Diego—there was Old Town, awash in Wild West thuggery and end-of-the-world ambience. Thus, there was plenty of murder; thus, there are plenty of ghosts.

Most of the haunting in Old Town centers on the Whaley House, which was built in 1856 and is the most haunted house in the whole country, according to the supernatural experts at the Travel Channel. (No, I don't know how they quantify haunting.) Head docent Patricia Petersen believes the claim. "I've seen things move. I've heard things. I've smelled cigar smoke. I've watched children play with a dog that wasn't there—we have a ghost dog!"

Lizard People below Los Angeles
**Under Los Angeles, from Dodger Stadium
(1000 Elysian Park Ave.)
to the LA Central Library (630 5th St.)
www.reptilianagenda.com**

There is an ever-expanding mythology of cold-blooded,
evil-eyed folk who created an unknown subterranean me-
tropolis on the other side of the blacktop from downtown
Los Angeles. Below the urban surface, there are hundreds
of tunnels, some of them preindustrial, some postindustrial,
yet others ancient, and nearly all of them are sealed off by
chain-link fencing. According to Hopi legend, Lizard People
have long occupied this underground city; the Lizard People
used some sort of magical acid to melt the bedrock into
livable honeycomb. In the 1930s, a mining engineer named
G. Warren Shufelt surveyed LA using an odd pendulum device
in a black box and found evidence of an ancient city below it
that could have once been home to some 5,000 Lizard People.
He theorized that the Lost Land of the Lizard People was

hundreds of feet underground in the shape of a massive lizard and that the Lizard People created the world's first history books by inscribing their slithering words on fabled gold tablets. However, his attempt to dig a shaft to find their lost treasure proved fruitless. Shufelt further theorized that the Lizard People survived a massive meteor shower about 4,000 years ago, but natural gas permeated the fractured bedrock in the shower's aftermath and suffocated the city.

In more recent times, true believers have further claimed that the US Government took control of the lost underground city during the Cold War and that the secret entrance was someplace in the bowels of the LA Central Library. Yet other true believers hold that the Lizard People remain in firm control of everything from Hollywood to Disneyland to Washington, DC.

Hemet Maze Stone

**In Maze Stone Park,
three miles north of Hwy. 74 off California Ave.,
unincorporated Riverside County**

Riverside is full of intriguing legends, including Wetzel's Riverside Monster (a reptilian hominid who may or may not be related to the Lizard People who live under downtown LA) and the Mount Rubidoux attack midgets—don't ask. But the only concrete evidence I could find of a mystery was this ancient labyrinth of petroglyphs double wrapped in a barbwire-topped chain-link fence.

The exact purpose of the boulder's maze, inscribed by the Cahuilla people an estimated 3,000 years ago, remains cloudy. At least fifty other stones have been found in the vicinity, many of them bearing traces of ancient red paint and visible from far in the sky.

Some 150 miles to the southeast are the Blythe Giants, locally known as the Intaglios and visible only from the sky, figures of hunters and serpents ranging in size from 75 feet to 165 feet and of similarly hazy and ancient origins.

GRUB

Randy's Donuts
805 W. Manchester Ave.,
just off I-405, Inglewood
310-645-4707
www.randys-donuts.com

One of those rare attractions straddling the elusive line between the Grub and Big Things and Other Road Art categories, Randy's Donuts is known for the enormous donut on top of its roof. This particularly big donut—twenty-two feet across—is one of the last remnants of a now-defunct chain called the Big Donut Drive-In that built numerous supersized donuts in LA in the 1950s. While it has earned celebrity status thanks to appearances in such movies as *Mars Attacks!*, this is a heck of a donut joint. I am salivating just thinking of a lemon jelly. In the immortal words of Homer Simpson, "Mmm...donuts."

Barney's Beanery

8447 Santa Monica Blvd., Hollywood
323-654-2287
www.barneysbeanery.com

A Hollywood mainstay since 1920 and a Route 66 fixture near its western terminus, this barroom and eatery, wallpapered in license plates and movie posters, remains a great spot to feed yourself in LA today. While the menu has its premiums—Dom Perignon and a hot dog at $195—it is, for the most part, lowbrow. Chili has been the house special since W. C. Fields's day, and I've heard from unreliable sources that Fields enjoyed that Dom –hot dog combo back during the silent era. There are also

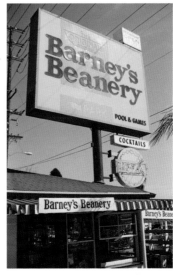

Barney's locations in Santa Monica (1351 3rd St. Promenade, 310-656-5777) and Pasadena (99 E. Colorado Blvd., 626-405-9777).

Jerry's Famous Deli

12655 Ventura Blvd., Studio City
818-980-4245

This legendary deli for Tinseltown deal-making is also notable for one special employee who kept showing up well after his deal was made. The late alt-comic and self-described "song-and-dance man" Andy Kaufman got his break as immigrant mechanic Latka Gravas on *Taxi*, but he still kept his day job at Jerry's busing tables. Never wanting to give fate a chance to say, "I told you so," Kaufman's best joke

perhaps was keeping a minimum-wage job as his star rose higher in the Hollywood sky. And he never cashed his paychecks; instead he taped them to the wall.

But besides the bizarro comedy lore, Jerry's makes a fat sandwich, with more than enough meat, and the matzo ball soup deserves some sort of Oscar. There are eight Jerry's in metro LA, but the Studio City location is the original where Kaufman taped his keep to the wall.

Phillipe the Original
1001 N. Alameda, Los Angeles
213-628-3781

Several restaurants stake claim to the invention of the French dip sandwich, but none so convincingly as Phillipe the Original. Open since 1908 (and at its current location since 1951), this place hasn't changed much over the years, from the sawdust on the floor to the pickled pig's feet to of course the array of French dip sandwiches on the menu. You can get beef,

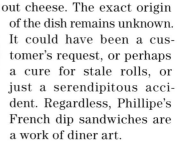

lamb, pork, ham, or turkey, single- or double-dipped, with or without cheese. The exact origin of the dish remains unknown. It could have been a customer's request, or perhaps a cure for stale rolls, or just a serendipitous accident. Regardless, Phillipe's French dip sandwiches are a work of diner art.

Croce's
802 5th Ave., San Diego
619-233-4355
www.croces.com

A long-standing jazz club and upscale eatery owned by Ingrid
Croce, the widow of late folk legend Jim Croce, is my pick in
the Gaslamp Quarter. "I opened it in 1985 as a tribute to Jim,"
Ingrid tells me as I gobble a delectable jalapeno-bedecked
grouper filet. "There was nothing downtown then." Today,
there are more than 200 restaurants lining the neighborhood's
sixteen square blocks.

Torrey Pines Gliderport
2800 Torrey Pines Scenic Dr., La Jolla
858-452-6802
www.flytorrey.com

In La Jolla, the outdoor cafe at Torrey Pines Gliderport is a great place to eat and people-watch—and the people are flying, or at least trying to. The menu is short, but the food is terrific. The wraps and the tortilla soup hit the spot while watching paragliders launch from the adjacent seaside cliff.

SLEEPS

Queen Mary
Moored at 1126 Queen's Hwy., Long Beach
562-435-3511
www.queenmary.com

A legendary transatlantic vessel that was auctioned to the highest bidder after serving as both civilian and military transport, the *Queen Mary* is on the West Coast because the highest bidder was the City of Long Beach. Now the boat is its own private hotel/entertainment complex/shopping mall, and it's haunted to boot. And that, too, is pretty well as commercialized as it could get, with ghost tours and all sorts of Halloween hullabaloo. But it's a more than worthwhile lodging: guest rooms are vintage staterooms, full of lacquered wood and historic details, and there are remarkable views of downtown Long Beach and the adjacent industrial netherworld.

In Los Angeles

For those on a budget, I like the clean and colorful rooms at the Vibe Hotel (5920 E. Hollywood Blvd., Hollywood, 333-469-8600 or 866-751-8600, www.vibehotel.com) and Banana Bungalow (603 N. Fairfax Ave., West Hollywood, 323-655-2002 or 877-666-2002, www.bananabungalow.com). Both offer bunks in hostel rooms for around $20, as well as private rooms for about $75 nightly. Also in West Hollywood, the Farmer's Daughter Hotel (115 S. Fairfax Ave., Los Angeles, 800-334-1658, www.farmersdaughterhotel.com) is a step up in terms of price and stars, funky but unpretentious, and the home away from home for most *Price is Right* contestants.

In San Diego

In Ocean Beach, Crystal Pier Hotel (4500 Ocean Blvd., 800-748-5894, www.crystalpier.com) allows you to sleep over the ocean (it's surprisingly loud). For a few bucks more, Tower23 (723 Felspar St., 866-TOWER23, www.tower23.hotel) is a slick and modern oceanfront hotel designed in symbiosis with the ocean but not right on top of it.

MISC.

Border Field State Park and Border Meetups
At the intersection of the United States,
Mexico, and the Pacific Ocean
www.parks.ca.gov

At the otherwise picturesque intersection of the United States, Mexico, and the Pacific Ocean, Border Field State Park is bisected by an ugly, dilapidated fence. The fence in turn bisects a historical granite monument marking the border. There was no fence until the 1970s. Now there are several walls in the vicinity and a phalanx of armed guards on the US side. And the US side of the granite monument is weathered and

icky, while the Mexican side is much more manicured. Open space predominates north of the border, while the Tijuana bullring and the touristy beach area known as Playas are south of the fence.

Spanish teacher Daniel Watman organizes a monthly border meetup (www.bordermeetup.org) at Friendship Circle, the round concrete pad around the marker. It started as a language exchange between his San Diego–based students and friends in Tijuana. "It turned out to be really impacting and it was even cooler than I expected," he says. "A lot of my students got to be friends with my friends in Tijuana, exactly what I wanted…people breaking down barriers and stereotypes. I started thinking of other things to bring people together at the fence."

Watman has since organized such events as poetry readings, yoga sessions, surfing events, salsa dancing lessons, and birthday parties, with the fence the only barrier between attendees on both sides.

Disneyland Resort
Anaheim
www.disneyland.com

"Are you in good health?" asks Olivia, my nine-year-old niece. We're waiting in line for the Hollywood Terror Tower, which she says is the scariest ride at Disney's California Adventure, the theme park that opened next door to Disneyland in 2001.

"I like to think I am," I respond.

"Do you barf easily?"

"No, not really. I recently had a nine-year no-barf streak."

Soon we are wearing seatbelts and free-falling. I scream at the top of my lungs. Olivia is stoic, fearless.

Back on the pavement, she appears energized by the experience, not nauseated. "That was awesome," she says. I agree.

We're on night one of a three-day Disney vacation. Since I don't have kids of my own, I borrowed my sister Arin's: Olivia and her six-year-old brother, Mitch.

We ride two more coasters—Mulholland Madness and the loop-de-loop California Screamin' before calling it a night. Back in our room, the kids and I tell stories and laugh until I call lights out just before midnight.

We still make it into the park before the official opening at 9 AM, a perk of staying at the Grand Californian, and in short order ride the dizzying Mad Tea Party teacups, the interactive Buzz Lightyear Astro Blasters, and the twisting and turning Indiana Jones Adventure. Time and time again, I see Mitch and Olivia's faces shift to blissful mirth.

But it's only two hours in and I'm wearing down rapidly. Can I survive an entire day?

Later we ride Pirates of the Caribbean—another one that Mitch refuses to ride—and Space Mountain (twice!) before hitting the pool at the Grand Californian Hotel, more time at California Adventure, and finally dinner in downtown Disney. I feel like I've walked fifteen miles and am mentally jellified, strung out on thrill rides.

There is some talk of making it back to Disneyland for the nightly parade and fireworks, but Uncle Eric starts snoring the moment he hits the bed at the hotel. At just 8:45 PM, Mitch and Olivia chatter for a spell but give up on me and get into their pajamas before it gets too late. I'm more exhausted than I was after surfing near San Diego, backpacking in Yosemite, or biking across Los Angeles.

Exploring Disneyland with two kids might just be the most extreme sport in California.

Channel Islands National Park
Off the Los Angeles Coast
www.nps.gov/chis

The five northernmost links in the Channel Islands chain, of which the better-known Santa Catalina is the southernmost seventh, this park is known as the "Galapagos of North America" for its unique evolutionary pathway that wrought the diminutive (and endangered) island fox, island jay, and other pint-sized counterparts of mainland species. The park—a mere sixty miles from downtown Los Angeles—also features the world's largest sea cave, Valdez Cave, which is big enough for a dinghy to make a U-turn inside. Farther from the coast, San Miguel Island is one of the world's most prolific havens for marine mammals. During prime season, as many as 35,000 seals and sea lions come ashore at the island's Pont Bennett.

Santa Catalina Island

As the song goes, "twenty-six miles across the sea" from the LA coast, ferries leave from Newport Beach, Long Beach, LAX, and other points.

By far the most developed of the Channel Islands chain—and not part of the national park—Santa Catalina is what LA would be like if you got rid of the cars and the sprawling urban-suburban-exurban galaxies and respectively replaced them with bikes and golf carts and a little seaside village. Just like the mainland, it's got great weather, a laid-back vibe, and plenty to see and do. But unlike the mainland, there's no smog or traffic jams. In other words, it's pretty much paradise. Take a ferry out for a day and rent a bike and explore, or spend a night or two and really, truly get away from it all.

GOING WRONG IN HOLLYWOOD

3 DAYS, 100 MILES (MUCH OF THAT ON FOOT ON HOLLYWOOD BOULEVARD)

Caked with lore, splendor, and rot, Hollywood is an adjective, a way of life, an industry, a fantasy, and ultimately an actual place. Some people buy a one-way bus ticket, others a round-trip flight, yet others—like myself—arrive from points east in their respective cars. Still others apparently change in a phone booth and fly in to save the day.

· · · · ·

En route to LA, I sleep a night at the Rendezvous, a colorful retro motel in Palm Springs, renovated for the twenty-first century. My room is the Pretty in Pink suite, a Marilyn Monroe–themed accommodation. I am assured the star once slept here herself, and that she still makes regular appearances.

"People see her here all the time," says Betty as she checks me in, "if they're pure at heart." She tells me that she has most definitely seen Marilyn's ghost herself. "Usually you see her looking back across the pool from here," she says, pointing at my open door from the far side of the palm-pillared courtyard.

I see nothing.

· · · · ·

Twenty-four hours later I'm checked into a new room, this one at the Vibe Hotel in Hollywood, and stepping out onto the street. The Hollywood sign, the Capitol Records building, and a menagerie of eccentrics greet me.

The first thing that strikes me is the sidewalk star of Tod Browning, the director of *Dracula* and *Freaks.* Then a rosy-cheeked fat lady on a folding chair spits not fifteen feet away from that of Sir Laurence Olivier's. I take a snapshot of the star of Roscoe "Fatty" Arbuckle, one of Hollywood's great tragedies. Arbuckle was a huge silent film star and comic genius whose career went down in flames on false rape charges.

Then a man who has no nose, just an inward-pointing scar, squeals with glee as I pass him by, smiling and pointing at Will Rogers's star. I try to smile back but almost

certainly fail. A smile without a nose looks much different than what you see on T-shirts bearing round, yellow nose-less smiley faces.

I continue west on Hollywood Boulevard, pausing to take a picture of John Belushi's star, then stopping to browse a maps-of-the-stars bin at a souvenir shop. I'm not sold on any of them. I need an angle for this story but don't think it's going to come from a sleazy $5.99 map telling me where Robert Blake and O. J. offed their respective ex-wives.

As I exit the store, the guy without a nose is right there, still grinning. He's barely in my field of vision as I continue down Hollywood Boulevard. My smiling walking partner and I pass a guy with one leg and one stump, crutches in his arms like an askew broken crucifix, haphazardly dragging himself with his hands, his stump sliding over Basil Rathbone's star. The man with no nose slows to engage the one-legged man, and the pair slowly fades away.

Two icons of Hollywood Blvd.: neon and palm

After dancing around a puddle of puke near Gene Autry's star and passing a Roman gladiator and a slimmed-down Barney the Dinosaur, I'm in front of Grauman's Chinese Theatre. Sensory overload—Marilyn and Snoopy and Chucky the psychotic doll and tourists and the world premiere of a Martin Lawrence movie across the street.

I stop and pull out my map, thinking of finding a spot for a beer or two. A man dressed as Superman, bearing a resemblance to an older and narrower Christopher Reeve, approaches.

"Need some help finding something?" he sticks his chest out and asks.

I at first try to shake him off but quickly realize he's probably a gold mine.

"I'm also an actor," he tells me. Duh. "This is my *waiter* job."

Again I'm tempted to walk away but realize I should press on. "How much can you make doing this?"

"It depends on how well you play it," he tells me. "If you're good, you can make $200 or $300 a day. Chucky does real well."

He tells me his name is Christopher Dennis and that in 1991 he was one of the first three "ambassadors of Hollywood" to start working Hollywood Boulevard (along with a she–Charlie Chaplin and Elvis), interacting with tourists and posing in their pictures for tips. Some of the more aggressive entertainers, who chased down non-tippers, gave the industry—which now has mushroomed to eighty-five "ambassadors" or so—a bad name. Same goes for cartoon characters taking off their animal heads to light a cigarette.

When the fuck did Hollywood become an unauthorized Disneyland of the bizarre, with costumed characters wandering around the street, copyright holders be damned? It was a gradual transition that exploded full force in 2005, Christopher tells me.

I take his picture but decline to tip him. Nonetheless, he takes me into the Virgin Records next door and shows me a documentary called *Confessions of a Superhero*, profiling him and three other wannabe actors whose "waiter" gigs are hanging around on Hollywood Boulevard dressed in tights.

"Have any of you guys made it?"

"Yes," Christopher informs me. "I brought a girl, Trisha, in as Supergirl. She posted her photos on her MySpace page and the *Smallville* producers saw it and they brought her in for an audition. She didn't get it, but she got on the reality show *Who Wants to Be a Superhero?* And she moved up from that: she's going to be in the May issue of *Playboy*. She might even end up on as one of Hugh Hefner's girlfriends on that reality show—he's going to be taking on five girls instead of three."

No shit.

I double back east, passing a Spider-Man with an embarrassing bulge and a fanny pack, then follow a guy carrying a gray cat that stares at me over his left shoulder, and ultimately take refuge at a pub called the Pig 'n Whistle.

Another icon of Hollywood Blvd.

"Why is Hollywood littered with so much human wreckage—famous, infamous, anonymous?" I ask the bartender, a North Carolinian named Heather wearing a black camisole.

"I don't know if it's the weather or the celebrity factor or what, but it's definitely something," she answers. "You should have been in here earlier. We had a bunch of crazies. We had the Dollhouse Guy. He wears a dollhouse on his head."

I sit there and drink my beer, and a couple of minutes later an older, raven-haired guy with a sports jacket, T-shirt, and tie sits on the barstool next to me and orders coffee with "a lotta milk and a lotta sugar," and tells me he got thrown out of the joint earlier.

"Why?" I ask him.

"I was wearing a dollhouse on my head," he responds. "I can't think of any other reason."

He tells me his dollhouse is a symbol: nobody should be homeless.

"I have a plan," he explains. "If it is executed properly, there will be no more mortgage companies."

Then the manager approaches. "Weren't you the guy yelling at me, telling me to go fuck myself earlier?"

Dollhouse Guy gets up and runs out.

Heather passes me by on the bar. "See what I'm talking about?"

Before I close my tab, she tells me of another patron. "He was completely nonlinear. It wasn't even subjects and verbs." She tells me that LA is unique; New York keeps its wackos in check or institutionalized.

"Giuliani cleaned up Times Square," I respond, "but Hollywood's still Hollywood."

On my way back to the Vibe, stripes of streetlight and darkness take turns on the passing sidewalk stars: Pat O'Brien, Chris Farley, Jonathan Winters...

Near Marion Ross's star I step in some dog shit. Then some other guy actually slips on the same dog shit. "Fuck!" he screams. "*Fuck!*"

I pass Hollywood Toys & Costumes. A bunny suit beckons in the window. Should I buy a costume and do the whole Hollywood ambassador thing with Superman? I have two more days.

· · · · ·

I go out for a predinner drink that snowballs into two and a couple of hours at Jumbo's Clown Room, an infamous no-nudity cabaret where Courtney Love once flashed flesh.

"How far would you go for fame?" I scribble in my little notebook. "Would you kill your spouse right before your record release party?"

The names on the board include Pixie Presley and Apple Messiah. Onstage is a dread-locked blond named Mary with a lot of cleavage and a little bit of cellulite.

Mary dances. She winks at me as she spreads her legs. I give her a dollar. Later I ask her why Hollywood attracts both superstars and lowlifes.

"You get these highs and you get these lows," she responds. "Like this place:

The aptly named Dollhouse Guy

there's some darkness here, but there's also a lot of light."

All of the girls are very gracious, thanking me for my meager tips. One of them, I note in my book as my buzz increases, has "an ass like Chinese calligraphy."

But I soon wander back into the glowing Hollywood night and find myself eating an incredibly spicy noodle dish at a Thai joint, Ganda, before acquiring a twelve-pack of Tecate and a sleeve of lemon cookies for the room.

I fall asleep in my clothes.

Scaring away graffiti crows

· · · · ·

In the morning I look up Tod Browning and Fatty Arbuckle on Wikipedia and realize just how tragic these guys were.

Browning was ostracized by the industry after *Freaks* and eventually became a recluse who attended his brother's funeral in a separate room. Arbuckle was blacklisted—his films were actually banned—after the case of a party where young starlet Virginia Rappe ended up dying. While Fatty was found not guilty after two mistrials, rumors that he violated her with a champagne bottle or crushed her when he pounced on her destroyed his career. He had a bit of a comeback a decade later, then died of a heart attack.

I do a fifty-mile sightseeing loop around LA, visiting (in order) Skeletons in the Closet, the gift shop at the Los Angeles county coroner's office; the Farmer John murals in Vernon; the Watts Towers; Randy's Donuts; the Museum of Jurassic Technology; and the old TomKat Theatre before I make it back to Hollywood for a late lunch.

At Barney's Beanery I have chili loaded with cheese and oyster crackers and salsa and onions. "Los Angeles, California," reads the menu. "A sort of siren's lair from which songs of opportunity, notoriety, fame, and fortune have beckoned adventurous dreamers for generations, all with one thing in common: they had to eat."

Me, too. I'm back on the case, trying to explore the underbelly of Hollywood. Maybe Tod Browning or Fatty Arbuckle ate chili here; surely Belushi did. A live police chase is on the television above the bar.

Next to me, a burly guy with a rhino tattoo on his right bicep asks for the chase on the other TV. "It's the most exciting thing on."

We sit there and crack wise as a desperate, mostly low-speed chase unfolds, running a course through residential neighborhoods, industrial back alleys, and the occasional freeway. We take pleasure in watching a meltdown, a car crash, a shooting star burning white and going dim.

"We need a big screen," someone behind me says.

"I might go watch it at home," says the guy with the rhino tattoo.

"But you could miss the spectacular finale on the way there," I warn.

We sit there transfixed, expecting the catastrophic collision at every intersection, the potential calamity at every turn.

My friend with the rhino tattoo goes to the bathroom and misses the not-so-grand finale: the guy finally turns into a dead end and makes a weak effort to back up into one of his pursuers before accepting defeat and surrendering to the armada of cops blocking his only exit.

The booze beckons

"What happened?" Rhino tattoo is back. "Shit, I leave for one minute to take a piss and I miss everything."

I bid rhino tattoo good-bye and make a couple of stops at the weirdest Hollywood shops—Necromance, a purveyor of dead things from rabbit feet to cobra skins to stuffed beavers, and Wacko/Soap Plant, full of great books and art and action figures—before returning to my room that is dimming as the day nears sunset, traffic noise persistent. I have heartburn.

After a Tecate or two, my heartburn subsides. I go out for a stroll and try to find a seat at the Pig 'n Whistle, but every last barstool is occupied. I walk on and buy a new pair of Converse low-tops, which I had been in desperate want of for my California research. Then, after listening to a guy screaming gibberish amid the tourist traffic, I wind up

Wacko's plastic menagerie

at the bar in the Roosevelt Hotel for an $8 Heineken. I order some food and gobble up an entire bowl of wasabi-crusted edamame to try and make up the difference.

I walk by Grauman's Chinese in hopes of seeing my buddy Superman, but he's nowhere in sight. But then there's Marilyn— and Supergirl! Is it the one who might be Hefner's fifth chick? Maybe, just maybe. I don't know.

There are also two Captain Jack Sparrows in close proximity, one posing for a picture and the other sulking off down the sidewalk. Tough night.

Then suddenly out of nowhere, there's Dollhouse Guy, and he's in full dollhouse regalia. I feel like I've bumped into an old friend. We exchange greetings.

"Some of these characters do pretty well," he tells me. "But I don't do it for money."

"Yeah, your costume is a political statement, right?"

"Yeah, except tonight I need $10 to get my car out of parking, so I might pose for some pictures and make some money. It's totally unregulated," he adds. "You don't need a permit or anything. You just go out there and do your best."

I take his picture and try to give him seventy-five cents, but he refuses.

He tells me his name is Juan.

I backtrack to drop off my old shoes at the motel. En route, I stop at the Hollywood & Highland Center, a plush indoor-outdoor shopping center with stairways tiled with quotes of actors recounting their arrival in Hollywood and how they got their big break. Funny, none of the quotes are about not making it or, worse yet, going nuts.

Back at my room, I drop off my shoes, have a beer, and write a bit before re-embarking into the Hollywood night. I land at the Burgundy Room, supposedly a hangout for the *Jackass* guys but now pretty much empty. A guy with a knit cap that reads Fuck Off shows up and starts fielding calls on his cell. Then his buddy shows up. Then a couple of way-too-dramatic actress types show up—it's always easy to spot them, especially in Hollywood. Then a tattooed guy with a shaven head who downs shots like it's a race and for the most part leaves his conservative-looking date at the bar with me. We sit there in silence while he smokes or talks on his phone or whatever out front.

I feel I already know this bar, so I finish my second beer and leave.

I walk back to the Vibe, taking note of all of the blank stars on the sidewalk, just waiting, beckoning for a name. I also take note of how abruptly the Walk of Fame ends, and how it becomes ordinary sidewalk in front of a Toyota dealership.

Last of all, I ponder the option of hoofing it back to Jumbo's for last call or Ganda for more spicy Thai, but logic and exhaustion get the better of me. I fall asleep in my clothes once again.

· · · · ·

My leisurely, nearly aimless morning, while not quite up to Hollywood standards—I leave the motel at 9:30 AM—takes me up into the Hollywood Hills and into Forest Lawn Memorial Park in Glendale, the final resting place for countless stars: Humphrey Bogart, Sammy Davis Jr., Clark Gable, Carole Lombard, W. C. Fields, Ted Knight, Walt Disney, and many, many more. But the cemetery is vast, so vast that the only grave of a "star" I actually see is that of L. Frank Baum, the author of *The Wizard of Oz*.

But every other marker I see is an unknown entity, a name I don't know, stories untold. Did they seek fame? Did they want to be movie stars? Did they wear dollhouses on their heads? Did they almost make it? Were they considered as the fifth in a porn baron's harem for a reality show?

Forest Lawn is a quiet and peaceful place in the midst of urban chaos. No costumed freaks wander amid the crypts and markers. And, also unlike the sidewalk lining Hollywood Boulevard, none of the markers are blank, nor do they beckon.

I return to my room for a bit of work. While talking on the pay phone outside of my room, Supergirl and a Jack Sparrow emerge from a nearby doorway and slink down the stairs, presumably en route to their day job in front of Grauman's.

Why aren't the Disney and Warner Brothers lawyers waiting for them there with restraining orders?

· · · · ·

I meet my friend Feldman for lunch at Jerry's Famous Deli in Studio City. I take his advice and go for a bowl of matzo ball soup with rye bread and a coffee; he gets a pastrami sandwich.

"They give you so much meat here," says Feldman, removing half of his sandwich's pastrami and putting it aside to box up and take home for another sandwich later. "That's how us Jews do it," he says.

We talk about the costumed characters and whether they infringe on any copyrights. Feldman doesn't think so since they work for donations. I wonder whether Disney would send a henchman to dispatch of somebody dressing up like Mickey Mouse, especially if that somebody was especially depraved.

"I guess it's better for your panhandlers to dress up like Snoopy or Superman than to just be standing there with a sign that says I Need Money," I add. Feldman agrees.

We talk about his pending fatherhood, my travels, and Dollhouse Guy.

After lunch, we part and I make my way up the valley to Woodland Hills and the funky folk art environment known as Old Trapper's Lodge, once in the middle of nowhere and now on one of the last chunks of pasture on the campus of Pierce College. I take a few snapshots of this handcrafted rogues' gallery surrounded by peace and quiet, just a few miles but a world away from Hollywood Boulevard.

· · · · ·

Traffic coagulates but doesn't quite scab at the 101 and the 405, and I decide to drop off my car in Hollywood for an oil change. Another break from the street and the sidewalk at the Vibe. The clock is ticking. Should I get a costume? Should I drop acid? Should I freak out? Let me ponder that for a minute...

· · · · ·

A few minutes later I'm waving to two cavemen riding horses below a highway overpass.

A few more minutes later I find myself in Hollywood Toys & Costumes. The selection is astounding—frog suits, gorilla suits, superheroes—Supergirl is just $59.99—pirate dreadlocks for $49.99, Jesus...

I walk up to the cashier with a cheap ($7.99) bunny mask. Easter's right around the corner, and I can't rationalize spending much. At least it's a legitimate business expense for tax purposes. As I get to the front of the line, my heart starts beating pretty fast.

Apprehensively walking back to Grauman's Chinese, I see Snoopy and several pirates and a guy painted silver, then I'm blocked by two men in suits at a velvet rope. The theater is closed to the public tonight because of the premiere of *10,000 BC*. Thus the mounted cavemen.

I retreat to the pirates and Snoopy and mill around, mask in bag.

"Stress test?" asks an unshaven hipsterlike Scientologist.

"No, thanks."

I finally pull the mask out, rip off the price tag, and put it on. A passing guy looks at me as if I'm out of my mind.

I take the mask off. I can't do this.

I muster enough courage to put the mask back on and walk a hundred feet. I feel utterly ridiculous. The abstract nature of the cheap bunny mask doesn't help, especially amid the brand-name characters. I must look psychotic. Acid definitely would not have helped.

I take the mask off again. This is much harder than it looks.

But the night is still young.

I walk east, past pointy mannequin nipples, karate kids running laps in an 800-square-foot store, and skate punks brown-bagging it. A half hour and a knock on my door later, I greet my friend Bailey in the bunny mask. Before heading out for drinks and dinner, I recount my inability to wear it on the sidewalk by Grauman's. We talk further about who these costumed freaks really are.

"They're just one step above panhandlers," I argue.

"But it's an important step," Bailey adds, mentioning that there was a big hubbub when Chewbacca shook down some tourists for a tip. "Apparently you can dress as Chewbacca and you can ask people for a donation when dressed as Chewbacca, but you can't harass people dressed as Chewbacca."

As we walk east to Thai town for dinner, Bailey tells me of a band he had played in for a few gigs, Horace 8 and the Werewolves. "I was a Werewolf," he volunteers.

Apparently, Horace 8 was only Horace 8 because there was no infinity key on his computer—he just turned it sideways.

"He wanted to be Horace Infinity, but he settled for Horace 8?" I ask, incredulous.

"That pretty much sums up the whole experience," says Bailey, detailing a band that withered from a four-piece to a three-piece to a two-piece in three gigs before Bailey left Horace 8—a tattooed thirtysomething who didn't think rehearsals were necessary— as a solo act.

After dinner at Feldman's worthy recommendation Sanamluang, we happen to be right across the street from Jumbo's. So we make it in there for a last drink. Or two.

"You've got to understand, LA loves a stage, and when you put on a costume and go hang out in front of Grauman's, that is a stage," says Bailey. "In some ways it's no different than these girls here, dancing for dollar tips."

I agree. Silence.

"How do you think it would work if there was a guy onstage behind her in a bunny mask doing the cha-cha?" I muse. "Do you think that would go over well?"

Not too surprisingly, Bailey laughs but doesn't think it would go over well at all. He says that the stage for oddball costumes does not extend this far east on Hollywood Boulevard. Once the sidewalk loses its stars, a bunny mask pretty much amounts to probable cause.

We stroll back to the motel. Bailey heads home.

It's just me and the mask.

I pull it out of the sack and look at it. It looks back at me with cutout pupils. I put it on and admire myself in the bathroom mirror. I practice some poses, but the look is a bad trip no matter what. Keep your kids away from that man. Call security. Call the cops. Call anybody. Call mommy.

I decide the mask just isn't safe for public consumption. Maybe it's just an excuse for my stage fright, but also it's no Hollywood ending. Clock nearing midnight, I hit the streets in search of one.

Call the authorities

· · · · ·

At Hollywood and Highland, two guys push and pull a shopping cart containing what turns out to be another guy. I cross the street. A well-dressed man takes a picture of Ricky Martin's star—Ricky Martin has a star?—but Grauman's is desolate. No thrilling conclusion there.

I start walking the mile back east to my room. About halfway back, a man dressed entirely in black and wearing black sunglasses at night makes a move as if he's going to attack me. I recoil and then he tries to hug me. "C'mon man," he says in a thick, slurred accent. "Don't be scared."

What the fuck?

Not more than a block later, an odd dude with puffball hair and glazed eyes ambles into my path and sort of points at my crotch without making the slightest hint of eye contact. I dodge him as well.

I quickly realize my chance for a plot twist, a major surprise ending, just passed—twice. But you can't really end on a nonsensical fight or an anonymous love scene. No, I keep walking.

Ahead I see something on one of the stars: a bundle of white roses, a burning candle, an upside-down pill bottle, an open bottle of champagne. It's Belushi's star, twenty-six years to the day after he overdosed at the Chateau Marmont in West Hollywood. I pause in the anomalous peace of the Hollywood night for a good long while.

The Frolic Room is pretty much empty at last call, but above the bar Belushi's signed head shot smiles down at me with cocked eyebrows. I toast him with my beer.

"Artists are fragile," says the guy on a neighboring bar-stool in a moment of clarity. "They love the adoration, but when the contempt starts, they can't handle it."

That's the happiest ending I can muster.

The End.
Roll credits.

Where to go...

Rendezvous
1420 N. Indian Canyon Dr.,
Palm Springs
760-320-1178
www.ballantinesoriginalhotel.com

Vibe Hotel
5922 Hollywood Blvd., Hollywood
866-751-8600
www.vibehotel.com

Grauman's Chinese Theatre
Hollywood Blvd. and
Highland Ave., Hollywood
www.manntheatres.com/chinese

Pig 'n Whistle
6714 Hollywood Blvd., Hollywood
323-463-0000
www.pignwhistle.com

Hollywood Toys & Costumes
6600 Hollywood Blvd., Hollywood
323-464-4444
www.hollywoodtoysandcostumes.com

Jumbo's Clown Room
5153 Hollywood Blvd., Hollywood
323-666-1187
www.jumbos.com

Ganda
5269 Hollywood Blvd., Hollywood
323-466-4281

Skeletons in the Closet
1104 N. Mission Rd., Los Angeles
323-343-0760
www.lacoroner.com

Farmer John Murals
3049 E. Vernon Ave., Vernon
323-583-4621
www.farmerjohn.com

Watts Towers
1765 E. 107th St., Los Angeles
213-847-4646

Randy's Donuts
805 W. Manchester Ave.,
just off I-405, Inglewood
310-645-4707
www.randys-donuts.com

Museum of Jurassic Technology
9341 Venice Blvd., Culver City
310-836-6131
www.mjt.org.

Barney's Beanery
8447 Santa Monica Blvd., Hollywood
323-654-2287
www.barneysbeanery.com

Necromance
7220 Melrose Ave., Los Angeles
323-934-8684
www.necromance.com

Wacko/Soap Plant
4633 Hollywood Blvd., Los Angeles
323-663-0122
www.soapplant.com

The Hollywood Roosevelt Hotel
7000 Hollywood Blvd., Hollywood
323-466-7000

Hollywood & Highland Center
6801 Hollywood Blvd., Hollywood
323-817-0200

Burgundy Room
521 1/2 N. Cahuenga Blvd., Hollywood
323-465-7530

Forest Lawn Memorial Park
1712 S. Glendale Ave., Glendale
323-254-3131
www.forestlawn.com

Jerry's Famous Deli
12655 Ventura Blvd., Studio City
818-980-4245

Old Trapper's Lodge
On the campus of Pierce College,
6201 Winnetka Ave., Woodland Hills
818-719-6401

Sanamluang
5176 Hollywood Blvd., Hollywood
323-660-8006

The Frolic Room
6245 Hollywood Blvd., Hollywood
323-462-5890

SAND AND SURF AND A FENCE INTO THE OCEAN

6 DAYS, 300 MILES (ABOUT 50 MILES BY BIKE AND MUCH LESS BY SURFBOARD)

PART I

Some cities are like hives, tightly tunneled orbs of perfect community, everyone doing their part, their processes honed, a concrete and clockwork machine with human cogs.

The cities on the Southern California coast are not like hives as much as they are like constant tides of ants—most of them behind the wheel—scurrying back and forth across a nearly endless smorgasbord of fresh, sweet fruit. A nonstop parade of near-neon chunks of yellow pineapple and glistening red cherries and gently green honeydew arcs.

· · · · ·

I wake with the sun and drive south on the Silver Strand, the scenic route between the industrial haze of the naval harbor and the seemingly infinite blue of the Pacific. Parking my car on a side street in Imperial Beach, fifteen miles south of San Diego and the final surfing mecca before Mexico, there are five haggard-looking individuals smoking

outside a beachfront bar. I walk past them onto the beach and meander to the pier for a look at surfers catching surprisingly large waves.

A born landlubber, I'm taking a surfing lesson in less than an hour. Despite this being my first try at the sport, I'm not particularly scared but not really sure what to expect—except that these guys make it look far easier than it actually is.

Instead of backtracking on the beach, I loop back to my car on the streets, probably the most desolate of any town on the California coast. Soon I'm on a much less desolate street, clogged I-5, en route to Oceanside, forty-five miles north and known for its surf, its historic Spanish mission, and its proximity to the marines at Camp Pendleton.

My instructor, Brooke Swayne, greets me with a smile and a wet suit. She tells me that she's an instructor with her husband's company, SoCal Surf School, which runs surf camps for kids in addition to giving individual lessons. She also tells me that she's found Christ and that the surf camps do not allow instructors to smoke or cuss in front of the campers.

Dolphins forever

Before getting into the water, Brooke has me practice popping up from my belly onto my feet. It goes well, but of course we're still on dry land. Then Brooke gives me the safety lesson, telling me to keep my board perpendicular to the shore, showing me how to rotate it between swells, and describing the contingency plan for all sorts of surfing mishaps. She throws in a few other tips about how to speed up and slow down, how to read the waves, and how to paddle.

Then she tells me to use the force. "You have to trust the board," she says. "It's going to sound contradictory after everything I told you, but just clear your head."

We wade out into the surf, jumping over smallish waves and diving under their bigger brethren. Then the moment of truth arrives. I plop my belly on the middle of the board and wait for a good wave. It arrives quicker than expected. I start to pop up to my feet but don't even come close to catching the wave.

A few seconds later, I figure out which way is up and reel in my stray board. I paddle my way back out for another shot and again fail. And again. And again. Each and every time the pop-up is the hitch in my surfing giddyup and each and every time the end result is me flailing uncontrollably as I fall off my board. But also each and every time the wave is slightly different, and so is my failure.

During a break, Brooke points out linebacker legend Junior Seau's beachfront house and tells me how he stands out like a sore thumb surfing here, a 250-pound Samoan on a longboard.

I ask her why Oceanside is a surfing mecca.

"We have surf year-round," she says. "It's just a banquet of things." She also offers me some constructive criticism. "You're fighting yourself out there."

Then she tells me an anonymous quote she especially likes about controlling waves: "You can't stop the waves, but you can learn to surf."

We go back out, but the tide wanes before I can paddle, pop up, and truly surf while keeping a clear head. But I feel good about my effort. I learned a lot, including that I curse uncontrollably while surfing. I probably have no future as a surf camp counselor.

As the lesson ends, Brooke tells me that surfing is her escape. "When you live in Southern California," she says, "surfing is a way to get away. When you're surfing, you can't think of anything else. It's purifying."

She leaves me to my own devices, which are pretty pathetic for a beach bum, as I have no towel, nor do I have

flip-flops. I go to a beach store and find the former but not the latter (I opt for a blue towel emblazoned with Oceanside over the American Beach Club one bearing the rear view of three women wearing star-spangled thong swimsuits).

Then I wander around downtown Oceanside amid the bars, the military surplus stores, the adult bookstores, the comic book stores, and the barbershops, all of which are bustling with marines. I drop in at the California Surf Museum for a look at a rusted old motorized Jet Board, the result of the Bloomingdale heir's "distaste" for paddling, and a 155-pound redwood longboard from the 1930s, before eating at the surf-themed Longboarder Café across the street. The spicy turkey chili and mug of microbeer do me good.

I check into my room at the Wyndham, a block from the Oceanside pier, and find myself mildly irritated at various mildly irritating situations. But around 4:30 PM I am getting back into the ocean during high tide, paddling a rented surfboard and wearing a rented wet suit, and those mildly irritating situations wither away to nothingness in the face of the waves, which again batter and beat me as I vainly attempt to ride them.

But the crisp orange light of the setting sun reflecting on the never-ending liquid undulation is one of the prettiest sights I've ever seen. Incompetently thrashing around on a surfboard, I somehow feel at one with the ocean, maybe for the first time in my life.

Purified of all banal stresses and walking back to turn in my rentals, I overhear a passerby telling his girlfriend, "But it depends on how you fail: you can fail with style or you can fail with disgrace," without realizing it would resonate between my ears. I laugh out loud when the guy at the surf shop tells me, "Didn't drown. You came out ahead." I pay him $15 and I'm still ahead.

Back in my room, I call my parents to report on the day.

"What are you doing?" Mom asks.

"I was just surfing. If you want to call it that."

My dad—who grew up in Southern California but never surfed on a board—describes a childhood trip to Oceanside.

"That was one of the most fun times I ever had. I was about eight years old."

I tell him about the odd marine-based economy of comic books, nudie magazines, and buzz cuts.

"Camp Pendleton," he responds, "makes Oceanside, which is one of the greatest beach towns in California, one of the roughest."

Alone in my room, the ocean receding in the blackness, my fatigue hits high tide and nothing—not a shrimp burrito, not booze, not TV—can keep me awake.

· · · · ·

The storm rolled in sometime during the night and is whipping the palms relentlessly when I get up. Rain and surfing go together like oil and water—and oil is one of the more appetizing things that washes into the sea from the Southern California storm water drains. A good rain can keep surfers at bay for several days as the tide chews up and disperses all of the gunk and slime and filth.

So I decide to make a day out of sightseeing in San Diego County. Before leaving Oceanside, I brave the wet wind and make my way down the Oceanside Pier. At 1,954 feet, it's the longest wooden pier on the West Coast. I want to take Brooke's quote to heart. Sometimes rambling in foreign places during crummy weather can be trying. But it's desolate and beautiful and alive in the water. The birds seem especially active, enjoying a smorgasbord of food disturbed and distracted by the storm.

Saying good-bye to the pier and the full-bellied birds, I saddle up the Saturn, the first stop being Queen Califia's Magical Circle, a fantastical public art masterpiece located twenty miles inland in Escondido. The gate is padlocked. I guess it's closed because of the rain. It looks incredible, but I can't see much. Whatever. A half hour lost.

I make it back to the coast before noon to check out La Jolla Cove and get a good look at the wind-warped trees that helped inspire Dr. Seuss's flora. It's raining, but my jacket is more than adequate. My second destination here: the historic kitsch of the Cave Store, a dusty souvenir shop with a tunnel down into the cave below. But from the looks of it, is inexplicably closed in defiance of its posted hours. I get a cup of coffee and a banana-nut muffin at a nearby café and consume both while taking pictures of the hundreds of birds and the tide pools and the living, breathing ocean below.

Then I call my friend Daniel Watman, a local Spanish teacher and social/environmental/political activist. We'd met for a couple of beers two nights before at Croce's in the Gaslamp Quarter in downtown San Diego.

Daniel has organized about thirty border meetups over the last few years, during which he brings together groups at Border Field State Park, which since 1972 has been separated from Tijuana, Mexico, by an ugly, semi-dilapidated fence. Interestingly, Daniel's meetups come from both sides of the border and participate in activities together—such as salsa dancing classes, gardening events, and language exchanges—in spite (or perhaps because) of the fence bisecting the event.

We arrange to meet up at a trolley stop in Chula Vista. After a failed search for a perhaps mythical, perhaps demolished munchkin house in the hills of La Jolla and a failed retrieval of a possibly lost camera at the Hotel Del Coronado, I'm fifteen minutes late picking Daniel up at the trolley stop. No big deal. I can't control the munchkins or my camera or the waves or the weather.

He navigates me south on I-5 to Dairy Mart Road, two miles north of the border. We exit and drive west. After a quick stop to look at the new fencing—the feds are shoring

Raven knows best

up the border into an ultra-militarized triple fence despite
considerable opposition and despite the fact that single and
double fences have done little to stop illegal immigration
borderwide—we head down the road to Border Field
State Park.

José and Daniel

Because of flooding, we have
to park in a lot and hoof it a half
mile or so on a trail, then another
half mile on the beach to make it
to the border, ominously marked
by the fence that, despite its
many man-sized holes, extends
about fifty feet into the surf.
Other than this police-state
nightmare, it's a spectacular
setting featuring an undeveloped coastline on the north
side of the fence and a bustling
neighborhood and beach and
bullfighting arena on the
south side.

Daniel tells me more
about his meetups. "The
whole idea is to make connections across
cultural barriers," he says. "One time we did a surfing event.
People surfed out from both sides. We met out where the
fence line would have been and just hung out."

He says each border patrol agent operates differently,
running the gamut from mellow to aggressive. One agent
threatened someone who momentarily stuck their head
through the fence with a $500 ticket. Others let Daniel cross
into Mexico there because it's not technically illegal to
cross into Mexico there, only to cross back.

At the fence I'm snapping pictures and a guy with a
shaven head and a goatee approaches from the beach in
Tijuana. Daniel talks with him. He's José from LA. He speaks
English and says he is an American citizen. He asks if either
of us has a smoke. He says he could use a shot of booze,

wouldn't mind going surfing either. He won't let me take his picture, except he will let me shoot his handshake with Daniel. Seems like a nice enough guy.

"Nice meeting you, José," I say, bumping fists with him through the fence.

"Take care."

He walks south on the lonely beach.

Daniel leads me up the hill to the 1851 Italian marble monument marking the US–Mexico border following the Mexican-American War. The marble monument marked the border in the middle of a wide-open bluff for 120 years until Pat Nixon showed up to commemorate the new border fence. The monument is now essentially part of the fence. Daniel tells me Nixon said during the ceremony, "I hope this fence won't be here very long."

Through the fence we meet Loba, the friendly little mutt owned by the caretaker of the garden on the Tijuana side of the park. I scratch her nose through the fence, something she really seems to enjoy.

Daniel and I are heading back down the hill when Loba illegally crosses into the US through a gap in the fence to run in her massive undeveloped backyard. She sprints up and down the beach, sniffing this and rolling in that and playing and having fun, oblivious to the fact that she has just crossed an ever-more-militarized international boundary without so much identification as a dog tag.

But Daniel and I decide it is not a good idea for Loba to follow us all the way back to the parking lot, so we charge back the other way to get her heading in the right direction. Once she's far ahead of us, we stealthily make our escape.

Up ahead we see a border patrol agent on foot and another on an ATV. The latter guy pulls up to us and asks what we're doing. We tell him. He seems a bit sarcastic but otherwise doesn't bother us.

The second agent is more inquisitive. As the three of us walk together, we tell him that I'm a travel writer and Daniel organizes the border meetups at the park. He seems dubious of Daniel's meetups. "Why?" he asks, incredulous.

We're soon met by yet another border patrol agent; this one drives a truck and is much more confrontational. He takes my driver's license. He asks for Daniel's ID; he tells him it's in my car.

"What's the problem?" I ask. "It's not like we crossed the border or anything."

He refuses to answer or give me back my license but offers us a ride back to the parking lot in the back of his truck, which we warily accept.

When we make it back to the Saturn, a pair of San Diego cops waits next to it. Daniel gives the aggro agent his passport, and he calls in our info on his walkie-talkie.

A few minutes later a California Department of Fish and Game agent shows up.

"They're bullshitting us," the alpha border patrolman tells him. "They saw us and they totally ran the other way."

I realize they probably saw us chasing Loba off without seeing Loba herself and explain what we were doing. He still doesn't believe me. What a dick.

They variously accuse us of breaking imaginary rules, of crossing mud laced with E. coli, of taking pictures without a permit,

Maintenance issues abound

and of smuggling. I wonder if they watched us with a hidden camera and thought José might just have handed us some contraband that we chucked into the wetlands on our walk back, but I'm not sure they're that competent. After all, we were told on several occasions that they didn't see us go in—although one of them changes his tune at some point.

After fifteen minutes, I'm on the verge of losing my temper.

After thirty minutes, they let us go.

"No big deal," the fish and game warden says. I silently disagree.

In all, at least six guys on this huge case, certainly at a cost of several hundred dollars to the taxpayers, accomplishing absolutely nothing in the process. Good work if you can get it—and at the time of writing, the border patrol is hiring.

An hour later, Daniel and I recount the scenario, laughing over pupusas at Restaurante El Salvadoreño. He tells me how they harassed him one day when he tried to hang a bedsheet painted with the slogan Friends Not Fences on the fence at the park a few years before. An agent stopped him then brought out his supervisor. Mexicans on the other side realized what was going on and told Daniel to throw the banner over and they'd hang it on their side, so he did just that.

Loba gets ready to make a break for it

The agents did not like this move. "They were just livid. They said, 'It turns out, it's not illegal, but the park's closed.' They kicked me and some Italian tourists out."

I shake Daniel's hand as I drop him off at his house an hour later.

Then I make a beeline to Kansas City Barbecue—the place where they filmed the bar scene in *Top Gun*, as the sign says—and watch the final two minutes of the Super Bowl. The Giants win.

"Right there, you fuckin' homo!" yells a bartender as he gives Tom Brady the bird on the TV. Then, to Bill Belichick, "Fuck you, you fuckin' cheater!"

The guy next to me says, "Relax, Chris, you won."

"I didn't win," he says. "Nobody won."

"Justice prevailed," I interject.

From there I head north to my room at the Four Seasons Resort Aviara in Carlsbad, just five miles south of

Oceanside. Because the resort has a surf concierge on staff, I assume it will be a prominent development a stone's throw from the Pacific, but after searching the coast vainly for fifteen minutes, I stop for directions and realize the hotel is actually a few miles inland. This upsets me. After three beachfront nights, I'm getting pretty hooked on the ocean.

I finally laugh when I realize the ridiculousness of my line of thought. "It is the fucking Four Seasons, after all," I laugh to myself, chilling out and riding the wave.

I'd handled the day's unexpected situations quite nicely up to this point, outsmarting the idiot border agents and bouncing from place to place to place like I knew the area inside out. After checking in and nursing a beer at the bar, it strikes me that if Mexico is corrupt, so is America—and so am I.

Taking my second beer back to my deluxe suite, I write for another couple of hours before climbing into the enormous and majestic bed. All is well, or at least well enough. I've got another surf lesson in the morning.

I hope Loba got back home okay.

· · · · ·

I get a call from Tony, the PR rep for the Four Seasons, in the morning. Surfing is off.

"After it rains, there's some really nasty stuff in there."

I agree. I don't want or need E. coli.

Then Marco the concierge calls. Surfing is back on. Apparently the water tested okay.

Over breakfast with Tony, he tells me of his first (and, as it turns out, only) surfing experience. "I'm from Cleveland. When they got me out there, it wasn't pretty."

The Four Seasons Aviara's full-time surf concierge is named Ross, a twentysomething from Philly who recently transferred from the Four Seasons Resort Scottsdale. He surfed the Jersey Shore as a kid and is happy to be on the West Coast.

"It's almost this tribe around the world that just loves being in the water," he tells me on the ride to the beach in the official surf concierge van. He also tells me he's been studying both nursing and physical therapy while handling his hotel duties.

At Ponto State Beach, Ross turns me over to Jon Peterson (an *h* away from my father's namesake), the proprietor of Surfin Fire and a full-time firefighter in Encinitas.

We work on my pop-up and he likes what he sees. On dry land, I'm starting to tune in to a clear mental picture of what I want to do.

Out on the water, however, it's a different story. I stand up too quickly and lean back without using my hands enough. The end result only differs in terms of the direction I fall off of the board. We go back to shore for remedial pop-up lessons and again J. P. says he's impressed with my moves. But in the water I revert to the guy flailing his arms as he tumbles off the board on the front end of a tiny wave.

To my credit, conditions are poor. "It's ugly out here," says J. P., "like a dishwasher. The waves suck."

J. P. helps propel me into waves and I fall down. I paddle with waves and fall down. Once after taking a spill in knee-deep water, the surfboard bonks me dead-on in the fleshy part of my nose.

"How you doing?" J. P. asks as we walk back up the beach in between stints on the surf.

My frustration breaks. I smile. "I'm trying to stay positive."

Later J. P. tells me it's been a tough week because two young employees died in separate accidents, one in an avalanche, the other in a car accident. "I guess when it's your time to go, it's your time to go," he says.

Finally, I'm imagining myself and the wave and listening for the wave and it all comes together. "Stick it!"

I somehow do stick it and ride the wave, nimbly jumping off the board as it glides to a stop near shore.

"That'll keep you coming back," J. P says.

I go back to my bad habits and wipe out many more times before sticking one more. The tide is going back out; we call it a day.

"You're a surfer now," says Ross on our way back to the resort.

"I don't know if I'll call myself a surfer yet," I retort.

PART II

The sun is swooping down into the ocean, the San Diego suburbs disappear into the wide-open acreage of Camp Pendleton and rematerialize as I drive north to my sister Arin's house in Orange County. Upon arrival, I incite a near panic in my niece, Olivia, my nephews, Mitch and Sam, and my dog-in-law, Moose. Everyone is very excited to see Uncle Eric. We have a great time talking, playing, doing homework, and reading bedtime stories. All of it makes me see my all-too-banal bumps in the road for what they really are.

The next morning is spent planning part two of my beach journey: a two-day, fifty-mile ride on a beach cruiser from Marina del Rey to Newport Beach. The route spans two counties—Los Angeles and Orange—and passes through or near plush suburbs, low-income neighborhoods, military installations, and protected wetlands. The Ritz-Carlton in Marina del Rey agrees to let me rent a cruiser for the journey and also leave my car there for the duration. I take them up on the offer and drive fifty miles north to the marina.

After a bewildering two-hour walk through the marina and the surrounding mix of luxury apartment towers, dinky old duplexes, and strip malls, I meet my old college friend Kat in Venice for dinner at Baby Blues Barbecue. Over a huge plate of ribs, chicken, mashed sweet potatoes, and collard greens, I tell Kat my full plan. An LA resident for the better part of a decade, she thinks I'm out of my fucking mind.

"Do you know how far it is to Long Beach?"

"About thirty miles," I tell her. "And another twenty or so to Newport Beach."

She looks dubious. "Call me if you get into trouble."

Later that night we meet another old college friend, Bailey, at Kat's place. Her husband, Ross, is just wrapping up an acting rehearsal. We talk over a few beers and Ross agrees that I am out of my mind. Bailey, the only LA native at the house, is more optimistic.

Likewise, the valets at the Ritz alternately think I'm nuts and heroic as I get ready for departure the following morning. The main hitches, everyone agrees, are the big bump on the coast, Palos Verdes, and the industrial netherworld surrounding LA and Long Beach harbors. Because nobody on duty ever rides much past Redondo Beach, exactly how a lone rider on a cruiser should navigate those areas is a bit of a question mark. Brian, the surfer valet, is the only one who shares Bailey's positive outlook. "It's going to be a great ride," he tells me.

Just before 9 AM it begins. I circle the marina on a bike path that takes me to the oceanfront. I'm one bug in a million, a much smaller percentage on a bike. The comparison to millions of ants traversing an endless fruit buffet seems especially apt now.

Before long I'm passing directly under the ants in the planes taking off from LAX. A few minutes later, I'm cruising down Manhattan Beach. I don't have a lock and need to pee but lose the urge when a dreadlocked bum emerges from the public restroom before I can fully dismount. Also, my tires have been low on air from the get-go, so I'm on the lookout for a bike shop.

I find a good one, the Hermosa Cyclery, in Hermosa Beach. They fill my tires, sell me a lock, give me a map, and offer all sorts of tips for pedaling over Palos Verdes and around the harbors.

John, a transplant from Kansas City, gives my bike a once-over and fills the tires from the air hose. "It's amazing with a bike and the buses and trains around here how easy it really is to get around. I don't drive. I don't have a car."

From Hermosa I glide into chichi Redondo Beach. It's only 11 AM, but I feel the need to keep up my momentum with the hump of Palos Verdes dominating the immediate horizon. So after a quick snapshot of the commemorative bust of George Freeth—"the man who could walk on water" (no messiah, but according to the plaque the country's first lifeguard and first surfer, which is somewhat messianic anyway)—at the pier, I start cranking up the first of several hills from the beach and pass a tall black guy in a silver suit on the way up. He jokingly jeers my competitiveness and we strike up a conversation up top.

His name is Robert, he's a former major league pitcher, and he had too many beers the night before. "Gotta sweat it out," he tells me.

I ask him if he rides the beach regularly. He says he does, especially to clear out the cobwebs, explaining, "It keeps me tied down to reality."

Soon two older women walk their dogs past our position on the edge of a parking lot. "Good morning, ladies," Robert's voice booms. "Beautiful day—California, can't beat it. I don't know how those East Coasters do it." The women amiably concur.

Minutes later, I'm working my way up an even bigger hill into Palos Verdes proper, past million-dollar homes—scratch that, make it five-million- and ten-million-dollar homes—to a Mediterranean-style strip mall fronted by a Poseidon fountain for a snack of a Snickers and VitaminWater. Semisatisfied but feeling slightly pressed for time, I continue meandering up and over the peninsula, which includes several more lung-busting inclines broken up by even more beautiful views of the coast below and the blue infinity to the west.

"This sucks," I think to myself on one of the uphill stretches. "Why the fuck did I do this?"

Then the terrain flattens. "Is the uphill worth the downhill?"

Once I start to zip down the hill, my train of thought quickly answers, "This is great."

I pass a sign warning Land Is Constantly Moving. A motorcyclist honks. Mexican construction workers build mansions and Mexican gardeners tend the yards of the ones that have already been built. A guy on his lunch break decries the surf far below and tells me, "You're still quite a way from Long Beach."

Crossing the bridge in San Pedro

On my descent off the Palos Verdes peninsula into San Pedro and Los Angeles proper, the landscape of multimillion-dollar homes changes to a landscape of million-dollar homes, then—at sea level—the urban-industrial landscape of San Pedro, the old neighborhood at the LA Harbor. While I wouldn't necessarily want to be cruising here after sunset, it's not bad at 2 PM, bustling with humanity and a pleasant albeit somewhat third world vibe.

My treads work the sidewalks and curbs of San Pedro until the road—25th Street—ends, sending me northward on Gaffey. Confusion reigns when I come to a pedestrian bridge graced with an official "Come Back to San Pedro Soon" sign and scads of unofficial graffiti. I cross it once—pedaling hard to get up and over—but don't like what I see, so I return to my starting point. Unfortunately, three minutes of exploration reveals that the hill below is bordered by LA Harbor and a highway, blocking me from my endpoint in Long Beach. So I crank the cruiser over the bridge one more time and resume my northbound route.

An obese man straddling a mobility scooter at a nearby crosswalk grunts, "Anaheim," in response to my query regarding the best way to divert around the harbors into Long Beach, and I'm soon cruising east again, although with a gritty industrial landscape to my right instead of the Pacific. The multilane road crosses three busy bridges (with bike lanes, fortunately) as I make my way into Long Beach. When I finally see the downtown skyline at about 3 PM, it's like a beacon of hope.

Soon I am cruising up to the dock where the *Queen Mary* is permanently moored. The legendary and allegedly haunted cruise ship now serves as a hotel, museum, and drinking-and-eating emporium. I check in to my small, vintage stateroom and quickly wipe some of the sweat and spent fossil fuels from my person, and then take a taxi to the Aquarium of the Pacific, the anchor of downtown Long Beach's recent billion-dollar makeover. The sharks and the sea lions get top billing, but it's the psychedelic jellyfish and hyperactive octopuses that captivate me the most.

Passing a hectic cathedral on Ash Wednesday, I walk a mile or so to the Museum of Latin American Art, which is also excellent, featuring a wide range of works by artists from Mexico, Colombia, and other countries. But now I'm in need of a liquid painkiller after my ride, so I spot a vintage watering hole, the V Room, and grab a barstool next to an elderly gentleman who looks half asleep behind his glass of white wine and snifter of brandy.

I order a PBR and take several quick gulps. A second guy, clearly buzzed, approaches and introduces himself as Ray and tells me he's a Vietnam veteran and a Mexican by heritage. I tell him I'm half Norwegian.

"I can see it in your face," he responds. "You're a fucking Viking. Fucking Vikings discovered America."

Then he goes on a bit of a rant. "I was in Vietnam, and Joe"—pointing to the somnambulant grayhair next to me—"was in World War II fighting for Germany. I would have shot his ass and he would have shot mine, but here we are."

Ray goes outside to smoke, and Joe livens up a bit and tells me he's lived in the area for thirty years. "I still don't know all the highways. Unbelievable."

Then he goes in a different direction. "We were wrong," he tells me of the Nazis. "We were wrong. Maybe not all Germans, but enough." He takes a contemplative sip of brandy and makes a horizontal motion with his hand.

Ray returns and grins. "You know who did the best 'America the Beautiful?'" he asks Joe and I. "Ray Charles. He fucking nailed it." Then he gets a faraway look in his eyes. "We are Americans," he says. "I don't care who the fucking president is, I love my country."

A princely jellyfish

Finishing my second can of PBR, I bid Ray and Joe good-night. I stop at an Irish pub and devour a plate of fish-and-chips before taking the free bus back to the *Queen Mary* for a nightcap and a much deserved night's sleep.

The ride up is definitely worth the ride down.

Feeling a bit of soreness in the morning, but nothing debilitating, I see a story in the paper about wave machines

being installed in London on the Thames, quoting a source, "This is not surfing except in its most limited sense." Another story covers an aquarium octopus that plays with a Mr. Potato Head for an hour a day.

After breakfast, a busboy asks me if I'm a swimmer.

"Well," I tell him, "I can swim."

"You're not an Olympian?" He appears to be serious.

Maybe I already have this California beach thing down pat.

I get back on the cruiser and make my way to the bike trail along Belmont Shores. After finishing the previous day with miles and miles of nonbeach cruising, it's nice to be back on the coast again with the cool salty breeze and the living tide.

I divert around Alamitos Bay—where the SS *Minnow* took off on its fateful three-hour tour on *Gilligan's Island*—and cross from LA County into Orange County. After riding through the streets of Seal Beach and around the Naval Ammo Depot on the Pacific Coast Highway, I finally arrive at the ideal boardwalk trail in Huntington Beach. It's a dream trail, smooth and flat and running to the horizon and beyond, above big crashing waves and the surfers who ride them.

I lock the cruiser up near the Huntington Pier and get advice—go to Newport, rookie—and lunch of fish tacos and a pint of pale ale at The Longboard Restaurant & Pub on Main Street. The local paper at the bar has a story about the controversy surrounding Trestles, a legendary surf spot at San Onofre State Beach (between Los Angeles and San Diego), and a new Orange County toll road that wanted to pass through park boundaries. The California Coastal Commission quashed the route, a victory for the "Save Trestles" camp, and county officials said they would consider their options.

After lunch and a visit to the International Surfing Museum (a bit bigger, but not altogether different, from its counterpart in Oceanside), I bike the last stretch of beach trail to Newport, my final endpoint. I alternate between pedaling and cruising, watching the surfers in the ocean

with envy and plotting how I can get out there one more time.

After checking into the swank Newport Beachwalk Hotel, everything comes together. Tom, the hotel's general manager's husband—the second retired pro ballplayer I meet on the trip—is impressed with the story of my ride and not only offers to take me surfing in the morning, but also to give me and the bike a lift back to Marina del Rey afterward. I can't believe my good fortune.

At sunset, I have a few glasses of wine with Jane and Tom and a British guest, Sebby, a barrister studying for her American bar exam in a few weeks. "Newport Beach is as good as it gets," she tells me. "It's stuck in a time warp, the 1980s. Here people accept me for who I am. In Chelsea, I don't know anybody—I don't come from the right stock."

I head to a cool bar and grill, The Blue Beet, for pork chops and beer, striking up a conversation with Joey, a stockbroker who commutes eighty-one miles every day to and from Manhattan Beach. I tell him I just biked down fifty miles from Marina del Rey.

He spends three hours a day in his car. "That's when I get my best work done. That's when the madness happens." Then he tells me that one of the circular apartment towers next to the Ritz where I started is where Howard Hughes holed up in the penthouse for three years.

I ask him if he surfs; he actually wakeboards. "I don't like to paddle," he cackles. "Fuck that. It's pure laziness."

I tell him about the Bloomingdale heir's Jet Board at the California Surf Museum. He likes the idea of a motorized surf-board, especially one that runs on gasoline. "I love to burn fuel," waxes Joey, a native Southern Californian. "I just love it. People in New York don't have cars. People in San Francisco maybe have one car. People in LA have three cars."

Joey takes off and I finish my beer and leave the Blue Beet, quaffing one more beer at the Beach Ball, a sleazy bar on the main drag. Then I turn in.

I meet Tom in the lobby in the morning. He's got a wet suit and board for me, no rental required. The water is cold,

but the sky is blue and the waves are mellow. I catch a few momentarily but always fall off backward or "pearl" and nosedive forward.

"It's a perfect day," says Tom between shimmering waves. "Sometimes you see dolphins out here."

As if on cue, a group of dolphins surface a couple of hundred feet away, happily cresting in the surf over and over again.

Tom shivers and advises, "Surfers always try to ride their last wave all the way in to shore."

He gives me a push. I'm patient with my pop-up, and keep my hands down. I'm one with the wave. I'm surfing. I'm wiping out.

Tom wades in.

"Well, I rode it most of the way in," I sheepishly tell him.

"That counts."

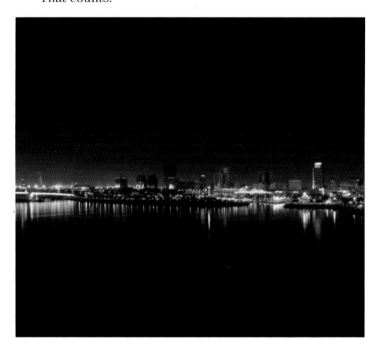

Where to go...

SoCal Surf School
Oceanside
760-889-8984
www.socalsurfschool.com

California Surf Museum
223 N. Coast Hwy., Oceanside
760-721-6876
www.surfmuseum.com

Longboarder Café
228 N. Coast Hwy., Oceanside
760-721-6776

Wyndham Oceanside Pier Resort
333 N. Myers St., Oceanside
877-999-3223
www.wyndham.com

Queen Califia's Magical Circle
Kit Carson Park, Escondido
www.queencalifia.org

Dr. Seuss trees
Ellen Scripps Browning Park
above La Jolla Cove, La Jolla

Cave Store
1325 Coast Blvd., La Jolla
858-459-0746

Border Meetups
Border Field State Park
Where the Pacific Ocean, the
United States, and Mexico
intersect
www.bordermeetup.org
www.parks.ca.gov

Restaurante El Salvadoreño
2851 Imperial Ave., San Diego
619-231-8254

Kansas City Barbecue
610 W. Market St., San Diego
619-231-9680
www.kcbbq.net

Four Seasons Resort Aviara
7100 Four Seasons Point,
Carlsbad
760-603-6800
www.fourseasons.com/aviara

Surfin Fire
Carlsbad
760-438-0538
www.surfinfire.com

Ritz-Carlton, Marina del Rey
4735 Admiralty Way,
Marina del Rey
310-823-1700
www.ritzcarlton.com

Baby Blues Barbecue
444 Lincoln Blvd., Venice
310-396-7675
www.babybluesbarbq.com

Hermosa Cyclery
20 13th St., Hermosa Beach
310-374-7816
www.hermosacyclery.com

Queen Mary
1126 Queen's Hwy., Long Beach
562-435-3511
www.queenmary.com

Aquarium of the Pacific
Long Beach Waterfront
562-951-1629
www.aquariumofpacific.org

Museum of Latin American Art
628 Alamitos Ave., Long Beach
562-437-1689
www.molaa.org

V Room
918 E. 4th St., Long Beach
562-437-4396

**The Longboard
Restaurant & Pub**
217 Main St., Huntington Beach
714-960-1896

International Surfing Museum
411 Olive Ave., Huntington Beach
714-960-3483
www.surfingmuseum.org

Newport Beachwalk Hotel
2306 W. Oceanfront Blvd.,
Newport Beach
800-571-8749
www.newportbeachwalkhotel.com

The Blue Beet
107 21st Pl., Newport Beach
949-675-2338
www.thebluebeet.com

Beach Ball
2116 W. Oceanfront
Newport Beach
949-675-8041

SAN FRANCISCO AND NORTHERN CALIFORNIA

INTRODUCTION

Cradled in green and surrounded by sea, with its fog and skyscrapers and a distinctive red bridge, from afar San Francisco looks like paradise. And to many of its residents from within, it is a paradise, of individuality and freedom and eccentricity.

But somehow this paradise is simultaneously Bill O'Reilly's hell on Earth and one of the country's most beloved, historic, vibrant, and bizarre cities. Of the two, I wholeheartedly take the latter.

Not that San Francisco is perfect. While many residents disagree—or at least point out its superiority to Los Angeles— there certainly are a few faults, pun intended. And there is also a serious homelessness problem, a serious parking problem, and a serious pretentiousness problem. As far as comparing San Francisco and LA, it's apples and oranges, or maybe antiquated clusterfucks and futuristic supermesses.

At 6 million people, the metro Bay Area is not nearly as overrun with humans as is Southern California, but there is no denser urban core in the West than Frisco, and only

Manhattan tops it nationwide. It statistically follows that it is far and away the best place in the country to catch a contact high by merely walking the streets.

San Francisco is the weird urban heart of a weird mossy wilderness with a climate that's aptly perfect for growing high-grade wine grapes and high-grade marijuana. These two cash crops are nestled in the midst of some of the best Sasquatch

STATS & FACTS

- The famous Lombard Street—the most crooked street in the world besides Wall Street—zigzags down 200 feet in elevation over the course of a quarter-mile of switchbacks at an average grade of about 15 percent.

- Anton LaVey founded the Church of Satan in San Francisco in 1966. There is little left (church HQ moved to Hell's Kitchen, NYC, and most church landmarks have been demolished) but the Nine Satanic Statements remain applicable while in the city, especially my favorite: "Satan represents vital existence instead of spiritual pipe dreams!"

- About a half-million detectable earthquakes shake California every year.

- California produces 17 million gallons of wine a year—about thirty-four gallons per seismic tremor, to help soothe the nerves.

- In service since 1901, the Centennial Bulb in Livermore is the world's oldest known working lightbulb. See the light for yourself at Fire Station 6 at 4550 East Avenue.

habitat in the lower forty-eight, full of immense trees, immense ferns, immense boulders, and plenty of rugged coastline.

Like the wine-and-weed pairing, inland volcanism goes nicely with the coastal seismic activity. In the southernmost part of the Cascades, Mount Lassen erupted hundreds of times leading up to its climactic blast in May 1915, less than a decade after San Francisco burnt to a crisp in the wake of a quake measuring somewhere around 8.0 on the Richter scale.

Today, the damage done to the city is all but invisible, thanks to layer upon layer of the man-made. Reopening the Bay Bridge after the 1989 Loma Prieta quake, which registered a relatively minor 6.9 on the Richter scale (only 5 percent of the power of the 1906 mother), took only a month.

STATS & FACTS (CONT.)

- Hundreds of thousands of monarch butterflies fly thousands of miles to Pacific Grove and other coastal communities to rest, mate, and ultimately die. The big mystery is how the new generation knows where to migrate after hatching, especially considering that there are five generations a year.

- In San Francisco's Haight-Ashbury district, the Grateful Dead called the Victorian at 710 Ashbury Street home before their hippie icon days. And Charles Manson called an apartment at 636 Cole Street home before his murderous messiah days.

- The Potter Schoolhouse at 17110 Bodega Lane in Bodega was the primary location for Alfred Hitchcock's classic ornithophobic thriller *The Birds*.

- Goat Rock near Jenner is the site of the finale of teen action schlock classic *The Goonies*.

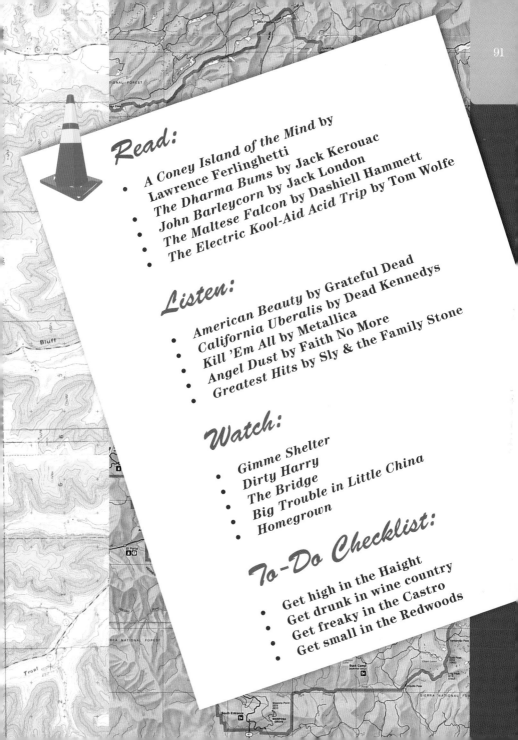

Read:

- A Coney Island of the Mind by Lawrence Ferlinghetti
- The Dharma Bums by Jack Kerouac
- John Barleycorn by Jack London
- The Maltese Falcon by Dashiell Hammett
- The Electric Kool-Aid Acid Trip by Tom Wolfe

Listen:

- American Beauty by Grateful Dead
- California Uberalis by Dead Kennedys
- Kill 'Em All by Metallica
- Angel Dust by Faith No More
- Greatest Hits by Sly & the Family Stone

Watch:

- Gimme Shelter
- Dirty Harry
- The Bridge
- Big Trouble in Little China
- Homegrown

To-Do Checklist:

- Get high in the Haight
- Get drunk in wine country
- Get freaky in the Castro
- Get small in the Redwoods

The devastated zone around Lassen, on the other hand, still bears the mark of the 1915 natural disaster with fallen forests, steaming geothermal vents, and the otherworldly scar the lava made going down the mountain.

The reborn, seemingly impervious city of San Francisco sitting atop a possible apocalypse and the surrounding wild land, lakes, and rivers left where Mother Nature put them is a taste that's easily acquired but hard to kick.

BIG THINGS AND OTHER ROAD ART

Cartoon Art Museum
655 Mission St., San Francisco
415-227-8666
www.cartoonart.org

With animation cells from *The Simpsons*, R. Crumb originals, and a chronological history of one of the most American of art forms, the Cartoon Art Museum is one of only a few museums of its kind anywhere. Special exhibitions cover artists and themes that span from female cartoonists on love and sex to Edward Gorey to the sexualization of superheroines.

Defenestration
6th St. and Howard St., San Francisco
www.defenestration.org

Surreal public art coming from a decaying building in SoMa (the south of Market neighborhood), Defenestration is just what it sounds like. For those lacking a cerebral dictionary, the word's definition is "to throw out of a window." Thus, the former skid-row hotel now features dozens of chairs, lamps, clocks, and other objects in midthrow out of the windows. The message relates to the surrounding urban squalor, our throwaway culture tossing aside not only objects and buildings, but people as well.

Cornerstone Gardens
23570 Arnold Dr., Sonoma
www.cornerstonegardens.com

The creation of multiple rock-star landscape architects, Cornerstone Gardens has gardens that range from traditional to unusual to downright bizarre. A walk here winds past a blue tree and beds of vivid whirligig flora, past politically charged gardens detailing the importance of the Mexican migrant worker to California agriculture, and even past an offbeat mini-golf course made from all of the traditional artificial surfaces seen in landscaping. One of the gardens, *The Garden of Visceral Serenity* by Yoji Sasaki, invites visitors to sit in a patina-covered metal box and contemplate. Which I did. I recommend you do the same.

Paradise Ridge Winery
4545 Thomas Lake Harris Dr., Santa Rosa
707-528-9463
www.paradiseridgewinery.com

Atop the ridge of its namesake, this winery's commanding view of Sonoma Valley is just one perk. The wine is another. Yet another is the remarkable sculpture garden that rotates every year alongside a collection of permanent and semi-permanent installations. The work ranges from whimsical to abstract, reflecting the taste of the winery's owner, Dr.

Walter Byck, who named the garden for his late wife, Marijke. Sculptures range from antiwar mask walls to found-object whales to foreboding metal eagles, but they change every year. I was the first person to accurately guess that the electric plugs sprouting from the flowerpot is named *Power Plant*.

Wave Organ
On the Pacific Ocean,
just east of the San Francisco Yacht Club
www.exploratorium.org

An extension of the nearby Exploratorium that's both free and extends into the sea, *Wave Organ* is a piece of musical sculpture. But no human plays this instrument—that's left to the fingertips of the Pacific Ocean and the rhythm of the moon. A tip: go at high tide. That's when the organ's music is loudest.

R.I.P.

Captain Courageous, 1963–1983
Roadside memorial in Klamath

A disastrous flood hit the Klamath River in 1964, sweeping a young steer from his pasture in Klamath Glen into Crescent City Harbor—sixteen miles as the crow flies, perhaps double that by the river's route, on a cresting storm surge filled with flotsam and jetsam—where townsfolk were surprised to see him treading water the next morning. After he struggled to land with human help, Captain Courageous lived a full life on the North Coast before his less eventful passing at the ripe old age of twenty.

Norton I, Emperor of the United States and Protector of Mexico, 1819–1880
Woodlawn Memorial Park, 1000 El Camino Real, Colma

The patron saint of itinerant San Francisco eccentrics, Joshua Norton was a failed businessman who went off the deep end and proclaimed himself emperor. Although he had no power and lived in a low-rent boardinghouse, Norton wandered the streets dressed in colorful military regalia, inspecting the infrastructure and the uniforms of police officers, issuing odd decrees, and passing currency bearing his image to many businesses that, strangely enough, accepted it as if it was United States currency.

Now a collector's item, Norton's money has actually done better than the greenback in recent years. And his decrees weren't all the ramblings of a madman. In fact, he was

sometimes visionary: he demanded a bridge and a tunnel across the Bay to Oakland long before they existed. City leaders in San Fran even wanted to name a new twenty-first-century span of the Bay Bridge after Emperor Norton, which city leaders in Oakland flatly rejected.

Colma
Just south of San Francisco
650-997-8300
www.colma.ca.gov

Starting with the gold-fueled population boom in 1849, San Francisco has had a tough time disposing of its dead. As more and more people lived in the city, more and more also died in the city. With real estate a scarce commodity, in 1902 San Francisco's leaders banned the burial of dead bodies within city limits.

This policy paved the way for Colma. Founded in 1924, Colma is now home to a population of 1.5 million people, as the saying goes, but only 1,100 are breathing. Today, 73 percent of Colma's land area is cemetery land. There are sixteen cemeteries in town. Everybody who was anybody in San Francisco is buried here, including Joe DiMaggio (Holy Cross Cemetery), Levi Strauss (Home of Peace Cemetery), Wyatt Earp (Hills of Eternity Memorial Park), and William Randolph Hearst (Cypress Lawn Memorial Park).

VICE

The Emerald Triangle: Humboldt, Mendocino, and Trinity Counties

Three Northern California counties, Humboldt, Mendocino, and Trinity, comprise the Emerald Triangle, named for the color of its chief cash crop: marijuana. The region is considered the largest producer of marijuana in the United States, and is undoubtedly a prime supplier of the state's $1 billion medical marijuana industry.

While the value of the region's ganja industry is not known, a Humboldt State University professor has been quoted estimating Humboldt County's weed industry alone at upward of $500 million a year. Multiply that range by three and we're talking about a billion-dollar industry at minimum, an industry at least in the same general ballpark as Hollywood's modest movie trade. To its credit, the Emerald Triangle has produced its own share of hits, often with catchy names like Trainwreck and Strawberry Cough.

The Emerald Triangle's weed economy was initially underpinned by a favorable climate and the large workforce of hippies in the general vicinity, but both of these factors have become less integral over time. Police choppers drove most of the growing indoors during the Reagan years, and peace-loving hippies have by and large been replaced by gun-toting capitalists. Trespassing is not recommended.

Based on an ingrained cultural tolerance for really good marijuana and an economy that depends on it, the Emerald Triangle is just about the closest thing to the Netherlands on American soil. Just be discrete.

Heinold's First and Last Chance
48 Webster St., Jack London Square, Oakland
510-839-6761
www.heinoldsfirstandlastchance.com

In business continuously since 1883, this watering hole is a historic and literary landmark thanks to its association with writer Jack London, Oakland's favorite son, who used to drink here. The walls are plastered with photos and relics from the restless, short-lived life of London, the ceilings papered with dollars and other currency, some of it blackened from

kerosene and cigarette smoke of the past. Today, the cigarettes are no more, but the bar and floors are still slanted like something in an Escher piece, just as they have been ever since the 1906 earthquake. The tilt is significant enough that it's surprising the beers don't just topple down the bar. The crooked joint might just be the alcoholic cousin of San Francisco's zigzagging Lombard Street.

Beat Bars

The trinity of old beatnik places around the legendary City Lights Bookstore in San Francisco's North Beach neighborhood are still going strong. Best known is Vesuvio (255 Columbus Ave. at Jack Kerouac Alley, 415-362-3370, www.vesuvio.com), which opened in 1948 but traces its legacy to the time Neal Cassady stopped for a drink on October 17, 1955. The bar lives up to its reputation: it's loaded with character and characters, and a slideshow of vintage nudes plays above the bar. Across the street, and lower profile, Tosca (242 Columbus Ave., 415-986-9651) opened well before Vesuvio, in 1919, getting around that pesky prohibition by serving a coffee-looking cocktail of steamed milk, chocolate, and brandy, still the house specialty today. The absolutely vintage place

was a favorite of Hunter S. Thompson's and allows smoking on Sunday due to a loophole in the ban. Almost next-door is the Specs' Twelve Adler Museum (12 Adler St., 415-421-4112), and it's definitely the odd child of the trio, clad in assorted oddities and ephemera and featuring the same bohemian vibe it did when it opened in 1968.

For an unbelievable view, a martini list 100-drinks long, and a swank if touristy vibe, the Top of the Mark (999 California St., 415-616-6916, www.topofthemark.com) is on the nineteenth floor of the InterContinental Mark Hopkins Hotel atop Nob Hill. Atop something much less swank—the Stockton Street tunnel—the aptly named Tunnel Top (601 Bush St., 415-986-8900) is a funky joint with a killer jukebox, classic oddball San Francisco decor, and walls that double as screens for projected films. In Oakland, Yoshi's (510 Embarcadero Jack London Square, 510-238-9200, www.yoshis.com) is the Bay Area's standby club-slash–sushi bar and Japanese restaurant. The stage has been graced by the likes of Dizzy Gillespie and Branford Marsalis, and the sushi is some of the state's best.

Good Vibrations's Vibrator Museum
1210 Valencia St., San Francisco
415-974-8980

Featuring about five to ten sex toys on display at any given time, this museum of rotating historical anomalies of the vibrating or eggbeating or penetrable kind is a short but sweet entrée into one of the oldest, biggest, and best sex-toy stores—excuse me, sexuality boutiques—in the nation, selling everything from Jackrabbits to assless chaps and literally everything in between. According to the in-house experts, vibrators were invented by American doctors in search of a better way to treat females with maladies ranging from wrinkles to tuberculosis. Clitoral massage was standard medical practice circa 1900 in order to induce a therapeutic hysterical paroxysm, better known today as an orgasm.

STAR MAPS

- In *Dirty Harry*, Clint Eastwood's character shoots and tortures serial killer Scorpio in Kezar Stadium in Golden Gate Park and later kills him at a rock quarry (now shopping mall) just south of the Larkspur exit on I-101.

- *Star Wars* creator George Lucas was raised on a walnut farm in Modesto.

- Francis Ford Coppola serves as an honorary ambassador to Belize from his home base in San Francisco.

- The 1960s officially ended at the Free Festival at Altamont Speedway between Tracy and Livermore on December 6, 1969.

- Mendocino stood in for Cabot Cove, Maine, in the TV show *Murder, She Wrote*. Jessica Fletcher wrote books and solved weekly murders from the 1888 Victorian at 45110 Little Lake State that is now the Blair House Inn (www.blairhouse.com).

HIGH-TECH STAR MAPS

- Birthplace of Google, an office on the main drag at 165 University Avenue in Palo Alto; birthplace of Apple, the  attached garage at 2066 Crist Drive in Los Altos; the granddaddy of them all, the birthplace of Hewlett-Packard, in the garage at 366 Addison Avenue in Palo Alto.

Tribute to Prostitutes Plaque
Corner of W. Church St. and S. State St., Ukiah

A property owner who learned that his new buy was the site of an infamous brothel, which operated around the turn of the nineteenth century to the twentieth century, installed a very official-looking unofficial plaque mounted to a rock and reads "To the ladies of the night who plied their trade upon this site." This is the one of a select few roadside attractions I've encountered honoring the world's oldest profession.

HUH?

Bigfoot Hotspots

Legend of Bigfoot
2500 I-101, Garberville
707-247-3332

Redwood National and State Parks
707-464-6101
www.nps.gov/redw

Willow Creek-China Flat Museum
Hwy. 299, downtown Willow Creek
530-629-2653

Bluff Creek
Six Rivers National Forest, Hwy. 96
530-627-3291
www.fs.fed.us/r5/sixrivers

While you never know when and where the next Bigfoot sighting will occur, there are some more-reliable ways to learn about the big fella in Northern California.

Near Garberville, a hunk of wood carved into a happy Sasquatch fronts the Legend of Bigfoot, a souvenir stand hawking T-shirts, wood carvings, toothpick holders, and a healthy selection of Bigfoot paraphernalia.

Off the North Coast, Jedediah Smith State Park was the location of a sighting; the sighters in question included a former Playboy playmate and the Bigfoot in question allegedly sported an erection.

Inland, the Willow Creek-China Flat Museum is known for its Bigfoot wing. The Bigfoot collection includes newspaper articles, plaster casts of feet and hands and hips, photographs, and artwork (including a portrait influenced by Renoir or van Gogh, and a diorama influenced by neither). Of special note are two display cases dedicated to the impact of Sasquatch on popular culture, with numerous children's books, toys, and a trio of Bigfoot-inspired board games. The volunteers at the museum's front desk tend to be overly enthusiastic, middle-aged women, and hardcore believers.

To the north is Bluff Creek, on which Roger Patterson shot the famous Bigfoot film in 1968, albeit a good twenty miles from the road. You can hike down a precipitous bank to the confluence of Bluff Creek and the Trinity River. The area is alive. There are tadpoles in the river and snails in the creek. Lizards scramble on the rocks. There are also plenty of blackberries (Bigfoot's favorite!).

But it is so rugged that there was really no way to explore the vicinity on foot. So maybe the big fella is just sitting there in the woods watching you.

Winchester Mystery House

525 S. Winchester Boulevard, San Jose
408-247-2101
www.winchestermysteryhouse.com

In 1884, a soothsayer warned Sarah Winchester: "When you finish building your house, you will die." Winchester took it to heart. Luckily, she was one of the Winchester Rifle Company Winchesters, so it was not a financial concern to hire guys to perpetually build stairways to nowhere and rooms too small for the smallest of people.

It follows that Sarah Winchester's house was under construction from the day her fortune was told in 1884 to her death in 1922. The finished product, featuring 160 rooms, 47 fireplaces, 950 doors, and 10,000 windows, has been a tourist trap ever since it was auctioned off as Winchester requested in her will. (I'm not sure if her spiritual advisor foresaw that development.)

But the tour, which runs about $20, is an interesting exploration of the woman's tortured and superstitious psyche, driven by guilt for those killed by Winchester guns and mourn-

ing for a dead husband and child. Obsessed with the number thirteen, the house is not for triskaidekaphobes (those scared of the number in question) because many closets have thirteen coat hooks, many staircases have thirteen steps, and many stained glass windows have details that come in thirteens. As my tour guide Wayne put it, "A daisy has twelve petals, but a perfect one has thirteen."

826 Valencia

826 Valencia St., San Francisco
415-642-5905
www.826valenica.org

As the sign near the door indicates, 826 Valencia is San Francisco's only independent pirate-supply store, carrying a wide range of common pirate gear—eye patches, peg legs, skull-and-crossbones flags, pirate dice—as well as some very arcane finds: a huge tumbler of buried treasure, a vat of lard, a jar of feathers, a drawer of sea salt, and even a fish theater. The proprietor of the place is actually writer and publisher Dave Eggers, who runs a nonprofit writing center in the back. Other branches include 826 New York City, home of the Brooklyn Superhero Supply Co.

Paxton Gate

824 Valencia St., San Francisco
415-824-1872
www.paxtongate.com

Perhaps the mutant cousin of Necromance in LA, Paxton Gate specializes in unique gardening products and dead things. You'll find carnivorous plants, Japanese pruners, and Slovakian watering cans, as well as framed butterflies, skulls of all sizes and descriptions, dogfish sharks in jars, apothecary jars, and jackalopes. But what stands out is the store's specialty: artistic taxidermy made of a dead mouse or two. The ones that involve one dead mouse are characters: Mexicans in sombreros, punk rockers with Mohawks, and other stereotypes. Costing more than $200, the extra-special ones are made of two mice stitched together to make one believable two-headed mouse.

The Saint John Will-I-Am Coltrane African Orthodox Church

1286 Fillmore St., San Francisco
415-673-7144
www.coltranechurch.org

When a church has ministers of sound, I take notice. And when one has John Coltrane as its patron saint, I might just convert. Welcome to the Saint John Will-I-Am Coltrane African Orthodox Church.

"It's very open," explains Senior Warden Clarence Stephens. "Come as you are."

By that, Stephens means you can wear jeans and a T-shirt to the services. He also means you can bring any instrument and join in with the band during Sunday services, usually held from around 12:30 to 3 PM. The place is standing-room only; the room is full of musicians creating an utterly holy racket of improvisational jazz from the soul.

Telos, the Last/Lost City of Atlantis
Under Mount Shasta

There's just something about Mount Shasta. According to some, the extinct Southern Cascades volcano is a mile above a domed city called Telos. Also according to this same some, Telos is the last refuge for those who fled the sinking city-state of Atlantis some 12,000 years ago and who now number about 1 million.

But others say it's an energy vortex, or an incarnation of the sun on Earth, or the home to the same race of Lizard People that live beneath the streets of downtown LA, or even home to perhaps the same attack midgets or dark dwarves who respectively terrorize Mount Rubidoux or Point Lobos. Others still report UFOs and Sasquatch. I personally don't know who to believe.

A friendly hitchhiker named Steven told me that a Mount Shasta crystal pusher (of the New Age variety, not metham- phetamine) told him to look at it and visualize what he wanted and it would appear. Steven took his advice. He visualized a couple of attractive hippie chicks to keep him company on a cold night, and up they walked. So go figure.

Mystery Spot
466 Mystery Spot Rd., Santa Cruz
831-423-8897
www.mysteryspot.com

A "gravitational anomaly" that might just be a hoax, the Mystery Spot is an oddly angled piece of architecture where the laws of physics allegedly do not apply. The house is atop the Mystery Spot, an inexplicably off-kilter chunk of land 150 feet across, supposedly discovered by surveyors in 1939 and perhaps owing its oddity to buried spacecraft, a magma vortex, or dielectric biocosmic radiation (I support the third theory). You won't believe your eyes—unless you stop and think about it for a couple of seconds.

GRUB

Oysters

Drakes Bay Family Farm
17171 Sir Francis Blvd., Inverness
415-669-1149
www.drakesbayoyster.com

Hog Island Oyster Company
Bar: 1 Ferry Building, San Francisco
Farm: 20215 Hwy. 1, Marshall
www.hogislandoysters.com

Tomales Bay Oyster Company
15749 Hwy. 1, Marshall
415-663-1242
www.tomalesbayoysters.com

There are few better places for fresh oysters than the Point Reyes area north of San Francisco. A pair of oyster farms— Hog Island Oyster Company and the eponymous Tomales Bay Oyster Company—calls Tomales Bay home, and nearby Point Reyes is home to Drakes Bay Oyster Farm. The stalwart bivalves are not only fresh in these parts, but according to Drakes Bay owner Kevin Lunnie, they provide a critical ecological service—filtering the water clean—that can't be handled by the decimated natives. And they're carbon sinks and ultra-productive protein providers. And they're so good with horseradish and hot sauce. And they're aphrodisiacs.

Goats

Harley Farms (tours available by reservation)
205 North St., Pescadero
650-879-0480
www.harleyfarms.com

No, you don't eat the goats. (Unlike oysters, they're not alleged aphrodisiacs.) You pet the goats—and let the babies chew on your clothes and shoes. You eat the cheese.

There is no better place for a full-fledged goat encounter and cheese eating than Harley Farms in Pescadero. Around twenty baby goats are delivered by goat-stork on a good spring day and they absolutely love to mob humans who venture into

their pen. Around 200 older goats hang out in the pasture and are less prone to butt your gut or chew on your shorts. They are also the ones responsible for producing the milk that produces the delectable cheese sold in the store on-site.

SLEEPS

In San Francisco, you've got plenty of good options for bedding down for every size pocketbook. On the rock-star end of the spectrum, you can't beat the Phoenix Hotel (601 Eddy St., 800-248-9466, www.jdvhotels.com), a midcentury classic renovated in high style for the twenty-first century that features jungle sounds piped into the vibrant pool courtyard populated with surreal sculpture. Moving down the spectrum to excellent value in North Beach is the San Remo Hotel (2237 Mason St., 800-352-7366, www.sanremohotel.com), where you get classic Victorian hotel rooms for under $100. And more toward the broke-college-student end of San Francisco's lodging spectrum are several hippified hostels: the Red Victorian (1665 Haight St., 415-864-1978, www.redvic.com), an aptly named red 1904 Victorian; the Green Tortoise (494 Broadway, 800-867-8647, www.greentortoise.com), with a sister hostel in Seattle and sleeper bus tours of the West; and the Pontiac Hotel (509 Minna St., 415-863-7775, www.pontiachotel.com), where a private room can be had for as little as $35. Beyond that, I recommend the floor on a friend's apartment.

Scattered about in Northern California, other solidly offbeat and affordable picks include the Curly Redwood Lodge (701 Redwood Hwy. S., Crescent City, 707-464-2137, www.curlyredwoodlodge.com), a mom-and-pop gem with a facade and woodwork cut from one massive redwood; the Calistoga Inn (1250 Lincoln Ave., Calistoga, 707-942-4101, www.calistogainn.com), a European-style hotel atop a microbrewery; and Railroad Park Resort (100 Railroad Park Rd., Dunsmuir, 530-235-4440, www.rrpark.com), featuring vintage railcars renovated into comfy guest rooms.

MISC.

Musée Mécanique

Pier 45, Shed A, Fisherman's Wharf, San Francisco
415-346-2000
www.museemecanique.org

An offbeat attraction that melds robotics and entertainment and history and amusement, this stalwart San Francisco museum-meets-arcade is an awesome look back at how people used to waste their time 100 years ago. The mechanical offerings range from the dirty movies of a century past, girlie-show Cail-o-Scopes, to music-making orchestrations, to mechanical dioramas depicting everything from royal ballrooms to opium dens, not to mention manic mechanical monkeys, pinball and vintage arcade games, robotic fortune-tellers, and a whole mess of other weird robots that will probably haunt your bad dreams forever.

Black Panther Party Landmarks in Oakland

An audacious, intelligent, angry, sometimes violent political movement was born in the northern reaches of Oakland in 1966 when Huey Newton and Bobby Seale met as fellow students on the campus of what is now Merritt College. They came up with a socialist platform called the Ten Point Program, demanding equality and opportunity, and sold Little Red Books. Hounded by J. Edgar Hoover and FBI counterintelligence and stymied by murder trials of Newton, Seale, and other members, the Black Panther Party died in the 1970s. Newton was shot and killed outside a crack house in Oakland in 1989. Seale remains active in community outreach work.

In 1967, the Panthers organized an armed escort for schoolchildren at the intersection of 55th and Market streets after speeding cars had killed several kids. Eventually a stoplight went in, a landmark to the Panthers' push for change. Other landmarks include the nearby Ebony Lady Salon at 5500 Market Street—in 1966, the North Oakland Anti-Poverty Center—where the Ten Point Program was written, and, a couple of blocks away at 5624 Martin Luther King Jr. Way, the party's first office.

Redwood National and State Parks

Far northwestern California
707-464-6101
www.nps.gov/redw

A walk in the woods in the Redwood Forest has a way of putting things in perspective. Here are the planet's tallest trees, topping out at more than 350 feet tall. Not only are these trees big, they're ancient. Many of them took root before Columbus arrived in the New World, and the oldest are more than 2,000 years old. In 2006, researchers discovered "Hyperion" (at an undisclosed location in the park), the tallest living thing in the world at 379 feet tall. Apparently pesky woodpeckers kept the tree from hitting the 380-foot mark.

But pondering these superlatives is nothing in comparison to actually hiking one of the park's trails and seeing these skyscraping treetops for yourself. Once beyond the roadside, the dense forest is a world away. Thanks to the shadows of the canopy, along with the cool ocean air, the area is a respite from the inland heat all summer long. And the area's denizens are remarkably diverse: you might see banana slugs, Roosevelt elk, and gray whales—all on the same hike.

Point Reyes National Seashore
About thirty miles north of San Francisco
415-464-5100
www.nps.gov/pore

A triangle of beautiful coastline, pastoral farmland, and New Age vibe, Point Reyes National Seashore is only a scenic, hour-long drive north from San Francisco but a world away. Inhabited by human beings for thousands of years, this peninsula—the windiest spot on the West Coast—juts out into the Pacific Ocean and offers a haven for life in air and sea and land, and peacefully coexists with farming and ranching operations that have been feeding San Francisco for a century and a half.

But don't get too comfortable. Point Reyes is on the Pacific plate, separated from the rest of California by the San Andreas Fault. The entire peninsula jumped twenty feet northward in the 1906 earthquake.

Lassen National Park
About fifty miles east of Redding
530-595-4444
www.nps.gov/lavo

Mount Lassen was the Mount St. Helens of its time, blowing its top dozens of times after waking up in a bad mood in 1914. Its biggest belch came on May 22, 1915, when it spewed forth a mushroom cloud six miles high amid an eruption that markedly changed the landscape. Forests burned down, lakes were created, and the mountaintop cratered.

While the volcano has been quiet for almost a century, the area's geothermal activity can be seen in the form of steaming vents and bubbling mud pots. In other words, the hot spot is still there—and still hot. But until it wakes up in another pissy mood, the mountain is a great place to hike and otherwise take in the outdoors.

Mendocino
150 miles north of San Francisco

As hippie chic as it gets, Mendocino is a former logging town that went into rot before bohemian artists planted roots here in the 1960s and slowly but surely turned it into one of the best places to get away in Northern California. With an oceanfront location amid riparian headlands and art galleries both upscale and funky, "Old Mendo"—the idealistic hippie colony—is slowly getting eaten away by "New Mendo," with luxury travelers and constant waves of the new rich fleeing San Francisco.

Not that the psychedelic edge has been entirely worn away—this is still right in the middle of the state's most fertile marijuana farmland. On a recent visit, an unshaven fellow was openly selling hash at Dick's Place (45080 Main St., 707-937-5643). Yes, I bought some, and, yes, it was good.

Before or after you wander Mendo's web of streets and trails and beaches, stop in Fort Bragg, about ten miles north up the coast. There you'll find Triangle Tattoo & Museum (365B N. Main St., 707-964-8814, www.triangletattoo.com), an operating tattoo parlor where the walls are loaded with photos and other artifacts relating to tattoos throughout time, including Maori tattoos, freak-show tattoos, and patriotic tattoos, not to mention a top-notch brewery in North Coast Brewing Company (455 N. Main St., 707-964-2739, www.northcoastbrewing.com).

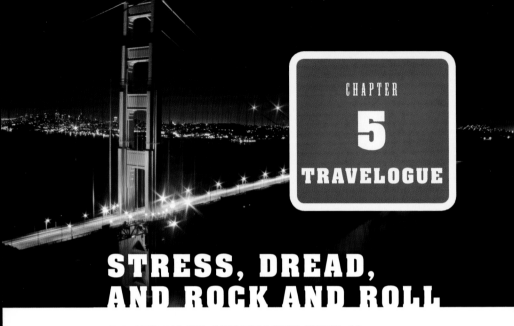

STRESS, DREAD, AND ROCK AND ROLL

5 DAYS THAT STRETCHED INTO 10, 300 MILES OR SO

There is a certain electricity I feel in the grooves of her fingertips. After a couple of beers at the Maiden Pub in Big Sur, I somehow end up talking to this girl, one of two sisters from Xenia, Ohio. She plops in my lap for a snapshot. She's blond, built, and pretty. And she's not my girlfriend.

I bid her goodnight and drive off to the Esalen Institute for its legendary night baths at 1 AM, the only time the oceanfront hot baths are open to the public. I disrobe in the coed locker room in front of an attractive woman. I jump into a tub and relax.

A few minutes later, a naked couple plops into my tub. Her nipples twinkle in the moonlight. The bath is so very, very relaxing, but they start to cuddle and, considering that they are naked, could use some privacy.

Back in my room at the Big Sur River Inn, I lustily fall asleep with the blond from Ohio on my mind. I doubt I will ever see her again in my life. It was an innocent flirtation, I tell myself, nothing more.

· · · · ·

The unholy trinity of sex, drugs, and rock and roll beckons like a three-horned succubus in a denim miniskirt and fluorescent lipstick. Especially when you're a teenager. Or in San Francisco.

For a good long part of many people's lives, drugs and booze serve as diversions while plotting how to have sex with someone. The irony is that if you do too many drugs, the sex is no good. But that's where rock and roll enters the picture. It just sounds better and better and better the more fucked up you get. If you are the one making the noise, it feels better and better, too, the more you drink and drug, the all-too-common irony being—not unlike the sex—that to others it sounds progressively worse.

· · · · ·

A few nights later, I am with my girlfriend, Ruthie, the blond from Ohio occasionally dancing through my thoughts. We have a wonderful, romantic getaway in Sonoma County and all that it entails: wine, goats, cuddling, hot lovin', bickering, a radioactive octopus play set.

Then I drop her off at the airport in Oakland. I kiss her good-bye and head to Jack London Square.

Overheard on the square: "I flatlined for four minutes, man."

Later, my college buddies Vlad and Scott (aka Scott Durango Redick, or SDR for short) meet me at my room at the Waterfront Plaza Hotel in Oakland. "Spitzer's banging a much hotter chick than Bill Clinton was," I note as we look at the call girl's pictures from St. Tropez.

Later, over a sushi dinner at Yoshi's, I tell Scott Andrew Redick his adopted name of Scott Durango Redick is, acronym-wise, the same as sex, drugs, and rock and roll.

Durango and Vlad

Newly bearded and swarthy, part-time drummer and full-time adman, SDR doesn't realize the concept, but he immediately embraces the idea. He's just moved to San Francisco for a new job and started seeing an attractive, hip woman a mere five days after relocating. Vlad, an emergency room surgeon and connoisseur of ADD drugs, is in the midst of a yearlong gig in the area.

We make our way to Heinold's First and Last Chance Bar, open since 1883 and crooked from the 1906 earthquake. Too much beer.

I watch a vintage peep show machine for a quarter. As I turn the crank, a couple—or at least a flickering image of a couple—makes out on a couch, then a freakish figure in a white gown interrupts them and drives them away.

. . . . .

Hungover, my mind humming, no, buzz sawing with caffeine and THC, I feel as out of it as I have in a while. The drugs are no match for the kickback from the alcohol the night before. All things considered, I'm considerably off.

I check out after a sluggish but large breakfast and get cash from an ATM at a nearby bookstore. A display in one of the windows hypes an upcoming book signing by Jose Canseco, admitted steroid user and fallen Oakland A's star.

Then I leave. I make my way south from Oakland to San Jose, the letters *SDR* frothing in my addled brain. Silicon, dread, and real estate might be more apt down in these parts.

The mental buzz saw is in high gear. I greedily quaff my coffee to the point of pain. The caffeine mixes with the THC (and perhaps the pain) in my cerebral cortex; a swirl of endorphins, and my mind hums its way from one non sequitur to the next...

There are sex drugs, drug drugs, and rock-and-roll drugs. Aphrodisiacs, pharmaceuticals, and recreational substances.

Dread. I dread a potential car crash. I imagine my Saturn cartwheeling through the air.

I might need to pull over.

I wonder if I am any better than local performance-enhancement poster boy Barry Bonds, if my words come better with the buzz saw revving high on coffee and high-grade marijuana. Does that make me a cheat, a fraud?

More dread. I dread not finding a parking space in San Francisco later today.

I drive in silence.

. . . . .

At noon I arrive at the Winchester Mystery House, once in the middle of a vast swath of wide-open farmland and now in the middle of a posh retail district.

Then I am on an hour-long tour with ten-year guide Wayne, who leads my group through the "very beautiful but very bizarre 160-room mansion" built by rifle heiress Sarah Winchester from 1884 until her death in 1922.

Then Wayne unleashes a maniacally jovial laugh.

After her infant child and husband's deaths, Sarah donned a black dress and went to a psychic in Boston who told her to go west to build a house and never stop building—"or else you will die!" "She wanted to confuse the spirits of the people killed by Winchester rifles," Wayne explains. "She built the house only for dead people, not for the living." He also explains that she was obsessed with the number thirteen: there are thirteen bathrooms, thirteen petals on the flowers in the stained glass, thirteen coat hooks, thirteen steps on staircases, and so on.

Dread central: the Winchester Mystery House

"A daisy has twelve petals, but a perfect one has thirteen," says Wayne. "This was the time of medicine shows and elixirs," he adds. "I'm a Catholic. That's why we have confession. She never got over the deaths of her husband and her child. My grandfather married his wife for her face and her body. That's all he cared about. But he treated her like gold."

And so on.

The tour ends after a full mile walk through 110 of the mansion's 160 rooms.

· · · · ·

After listening to the BBC report on modern Russia on my drive to the birthplaces of Apple and Google, it's past time for some rock and roll. I find a classic-rock station. Dylan.

The Doors. Jefferson Airplane. Hendrix. The buzz saw begins to rev once again, the music sparking the last fumes of coffee and *Cannabis indica* in my cerebrum.

I finagle through rush-hour traffic and actually score a perfect parking spot at the perfect time, only four blocks from SDR's apartment in Haight-Ashbury. My parking dread wasn't worth the effort.

I get coffee and connect to the Internet. A child—not a baby, but a six-year-old girl— wails outside as her punk-rock sideburned father ignores her and drinks his coffee. It gets on everyone's nerves—the barista, the customers, me.

She wails louder and louder and louder, and the only cure is rock and roll. I put on my iPod. Tom Waits. Beastie Boys. Cars. Queens of the Stone Age. Ween. Residents. Dirtbombs. My irritation melts away.

A few minutes later I'm at the corner of Haight and Ashbury.

"Hey, hey, mama, said the way you move," croaks a cross-legged bum with an acoustic guitar. "Gonna make you sweat, gonna make you groove…" His voice trails off.

I stop in at the Booksmith on Haight. I'm pleased to find they have a copy of *Ramble: A Field Guide to the USA* by yours truly on the shelf next to California Tiki and Basque guidebooks. I find a couple of Frommer's titles with my byline as well. I momentarily preen but do not attract the attention of the shapely brunette browsing nearby.

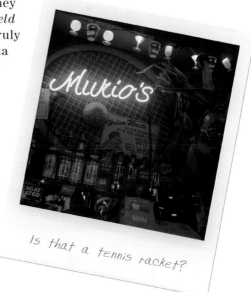

Is that a tennis racket?

Next up is a twenty-four-ounce can of Pabst Blue Ribbon at Murio's Trophy Room down the street and a call to Redick from the pay phone at the oddly out-of-place McDonald's a block away. On the way, a bum is pointing to something in his hand to two kids by his side. "There, you can see her snatch," he says.

I leave a voice mail and return the way I came. The bum and two kids are up and at 'em. The kids are clearly sky-high on LSD and who knows what else. "How's it goin', bub?" one asks me, leering.

"He snitched on Ziggy, he snitched on Larry," another bum tells yet another on my walk back to the bar.

Alcohol seems to affect me on the cellular level. At Murio's, the guys next to me tell me about the documentary *The Bridge*, about suicides off of the Golden Gate Bridge. "It's really good," says one, "but watch something happy afterward."

· · · · ·

Rock and roll is very important to me.

My rock-and-roll idols are Elvis and Ween and Ingvald Grunder, guitarist for Weird Al Qaida. If you've never heard of Weird Al Qaida, it's probably because I'm the lead singer.

Drugs—especially if you include caffeine and THC—are also important to me.

Sex is inescapable.

"Polly" by Nirvana comes on the jukebox. There are females at whom I briefly leer across the bar. Do sex and drugs and rock and roll really go together that well? And who coined the phrase?

"Shadrach, Meshach, Abendigo," rap the Beastie Boys, then Hendrix comes on. "Music, sweet music, I wish I could caress...Manic depression is a frustrating mess!"

Sometimes alcohol slows the buzz saw down and other times it catalyzes an inferno.

· · · · ·

A few hours later, at the Kezar, we meet SDR's friends Huck and Ernie and talk about Whispering Hill and Fort Mason and the Fisting Bushes in Golden Gate Park and various acts of public sex we have witnessed or engaged in.

"You're not writing this down, are you?" Ernie asks me.

"Some of it."

The conversation continues and tends to focus on sex. We talk about Russian chicks and Asian chicks at a nearby health club and American apparel and hookers.

Talking about sex is much less involved than having it.

Some conversational debris:

"There'll be that many more chicks for you to bang."

"I feel sorry for kids today. That stuff that seemed freaky fifteen years ago is pretty tame now."

"You need something just the perfect height to bend a chick over."

"How about this table?"

Of course, we also talk about drugs.

"Hippie Hill sucks now. They just want you to buy their drugs or not even look at you."

Rock and roll plays on the jukebox.

·····

Before bed, I tell Scott what I've been writing. "This one is a little more abstract."

"Our relationship has always been about abstraction," he replies.

He's right, of course. We played together in an ad hoc punk band in college, The Vocal Stylings of Doug Hammerschmidt & the Minstrels of Pain con Queso, an intoxicated underrehearsed mess that was nothing if not abstract. Our "songs" included "I'm on the Ice," about a curling underdog who sells his soul to the devil, and "Whatever Happened to the Bass Player for the Flock of Seagulls?"

I toss and turn on the air mattress most of the night.

·····

The gray morning in the Haight bears little resemblance to the night before. Schoolkids and

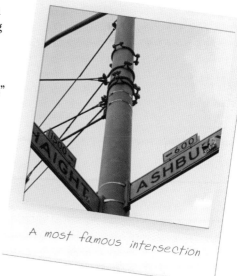

A most famous intersection

commuters are more visible than the tripping teenagers and grizzled bums. A pair of abandoned high-heeled shoes sits on the pavement, perhaps a trace of the sex and drugs and rock and roll from the night before.

After finding a more permanent parking spot—no problem at all—I take a shower and embark on a big walking loop. Outside, at 10:45 AM, there are signs of life in the Haight. Two cops interrogate a bum, and a girl in a Motörhead jacket enters a doorway in front of me.

I walk downtown, passing ever-imaginable kink, addiction, and musical taste in the process.

In Chinatown, a sign offers fortune cookies for $1.25 a bag—or $3.95 for X-rated ones.

When I'm in City Lights, the rain starts. After getting my fill of the famed bookstore, I wait out the rain over a beer in Vesuvio, then head past the tantalizing possibility of peeping at naked women at the Lusty Lady around the corner. But I'm not horny enough for a peep show (although going to a peep show inevitably makes one just horny enough for a peep show) and trudge uphill, get high, trudge farther uphill to the phallic Coit Tower and incredible views. Then I meander down to Fisherman's Wharf, where the Musée Mécanique features antique animated coin-ops about opium dens and execution (the coin-op wizard recommends patience)—then back to the Haight, which is just warming up for Friday night.

A study in lost shoes, 1

I meet SDR at Murio's again, and he tells me of the predecessor to Spitzer's call-girl ring, which included Shanghai sex spas where analingus was part of the standard package.

We retreat to his apartment before barhopping on Friday night.

But sadly, Scott is beset by the twitches. His muscles spasm at random: biceps, fingers, pectorals, buttocks, legs. It could be stress, dread, or perhaps repressed rage. Like a trouper, SDR fights through it. We eat Thai at the Citrus Club—the bowls of soup are approximately large enough to submerge one human head—then quaff meticulously overprepared, ridiculously overpriced gourmet cocktails at Alembic. I try to get Scott to listen to Weird Al Qaida's "Random Noise Randy," but he refuses my iPod's earbuds several times.

Temple of the Beats

"Maybe I could write a guest paragraph?" he suggests as the booze starts to take hold.

We have a last few beers at Club Deluxe while a jazz band beeps and bops.

"You should see her ass—it's ridiculous," says Scott, ripping apart a napkin to mock up a posterior that disregards gravity.

His twitches never subside.

· · · · ·

The next day, we get a late start—not rock-star late, but we didn't exactly party like rock stars either. SDR Googles his condition over noontime coffee.

I again try to play him "Random Noise Randy" off my laptop, and he again rebuffs me.

"It's fasciculation, that's what it is." According to the Wikipedia entry, involuntary twitches are usually benign and the result of sustained stress, although diseased motor neurons are another possibility.

We discuss going to the evening Gladiator Challenge at nearby Kezar Pavilion or a show at a club.

SDR plays an online war game. Not very rock and roll at all.

In the afternoon, we drive down to Colma and hunt down Emperor Norton's grave, which we find after a long search. After a stop in Pacifica for a view of the wrathful ocean, we return to the city for a remarkably late lunch at a Chinese restaurant, Eight Immortals.

Waiting for our combination dinner, Scott's expression suddenly changes. "I'm getting an eye twitch," he says, and sure enough, his eye twitches.

My friend Dave—and former bandmate in the franchise rock phenomenon known as The Barrys—calls. We are going to party in the Mission later, and he convinces me to stick around for his St. Patrick's Day party in three short days. He has a friend in town who wants to hit the bars, and his roommates drink liberally to boot. Redick is meeting his new girlfriend and some other girls. The Gladiator Challenge is thankfully out of the picture.

Things are getting more rock and roll by the minute.

One million yen and change

As far as drugs, I'm on two bottles of pale ale, four tabs of ibuprofen, and a half gram of high-grade weed.

And Scott finally listens to Weird Al Qaida. He likes it—especially the weird shit—but his toe starts involuntarily twitch-tapping to the music, which I can't peg as either a good or bad sign.

We meet Dave at the 500 Club in the Mission and move to another bar, the Elbo Room, for soul night. The dance floor is packed. After offering a professional diagnosis that Scott's fasciculation is benign, Dave ends up grinding with a female. SDR and his new girlfriend dance close. I twiddle my thumbs.

But Dave's grinding relationship is short-lived. We eat tacos and drink homemade plum wine (mellow, with a gasoline finish) with his roommates.

His friend Mike enthusiastically comments on his exploits on the dance floor. "That was as close as a penis and vagina can get without actual intercourse."

The dusty plum wine bottle is empty at 4 AM. I crash in Dave's room. We sleep in the same bed. Nothing happens.

· · · · ·

The next morning, Dave gives me a minitour of his neighborhood: egg-and-cheese bagels, dead things at Paxton Gate, and 826 Valencia, the city's only independent pirate shop.

Then I head back up the hill to Scott's. The sex and drugs and rock and roll dampened the stress and dread and repressed rage, but not the fasciculation.

Scott and his girlfriend and I head to Golden Gate Park for an afternoon amble.

It's an amazing swirl of greenery and humanity, a bum mumbling something about Deep Purple, a lesbian couple agility-training their dog, magnolia trees, a bum mumbling something about macaroni and cheese, a rotund Tolkienesque grayhair napping on a park bench, and a drum circle on Hippie Hill, surrounded by a horde engaged in pretty much everything from hacky-sacking to smoking pot to juggling to painting.

"That's a new variant: the transvestite hippie," Scott notes.

We plop down and smoke a joint rolled in transparent organic cellophane and eat bananas and gourmet potato chips.

Looking around, there are so many other new variants it's hard to identify them all. There's a meth-freak hippie. And is that a punk jock? Is that a homeless guy or a gangbanger hippie?

"Have you ever heard of furries?" Scott asks. I answer in the affirmative, and we briefly discuss the fetish for engaging in carnal acts while wearing an animal costume.

Scott and his girlfriend cuddle and nap. I wander the green and gander at the drummers, the guitarists, the hippie chicks and their sundresses twirling in the middle of the circle, the weirdos. A constant stream of drummers trickles into the circle. A guy, presumably on drugs of some kind, using a laptop as an iPod and singing an unintelligible song, wanders past us to commune with some dogs in a wooded area before returning to the fray.

Hippie Hill

Then a group including a woman in a cape, a dragon man, Tigger, and two Winnie the Poohs wanders through. I rouse Scott. "Freaks in costumes!"

Scott looks over. "Furries!"

The alleged furries do not linger at the drum circle. Perhaps there are Furry Bushes hidden in the park's bowels.

· · · · ·

A few hours later, Scott and I take a train downtown to meet his friend and former co-worker Sandy, who's in town from Chicago for fast-food focus groups.

"You need an Asian girlfriend in this city," Sandy says as we greet him in Union Square.

"How long have you been here?" I ask.

"Three hours."

"Give it some time."

"I have an Asian wife at home."

Sandy is impressed with SDR's immediate connection with a woman so soon after his move to the new city. "Redick's on fire," he says as we have a drink at the Top of the Mark bar overlooking the city.

"It's a great city to be a single guy in," Scott says later over more drinks at Tosca.

"I've had a hard-on all day," Sandy agrees, and notices me taking notes. "I'm happily married. Write that down."

Across the street, at Vesuvio, Scott wonders aloud, "Do you think that waitress has a little Asian in her?"

"I think all girls here have a little Asian in them," says Sandy. "As a midwesterner, you're exotic here, Redick."

"Gina told me not to get a new cell phone," Scott replies. "She said, 'It's kind of hot having a 773 area code.'"

Waiting for Dave to arrive via taxi, we wrangle our way into the legendary Condor—the first topless club in the city, then the first bottomless, now topless again—for one more drink. Girls of every description writhe on stage and around the pole.

The conversation shifts to drugs and their widespread availability in the city, from legal *Salvia divinorum* and booze to illegal crack and heroin. "Chris Rock said he'd never seen crack smoked as openly as it was in the Tenderloin," SDR says.

Sandy says the office back in Chicago already misses Scott. "You know, Scott has a huge following."

"I thought you were going to say a huge something else."

Dave arrives. Not one to frequent these heavily touristed streets, he says this is the second time he's been to a strip club. The first was apparently the Golden Banana in Boston.

Sandy is getting properly buzzed before a meeting with fast-food execs whose plane landed an hour and a half late. "Let's stay here for one more," he says, his deadpan expression almost masking a devilish grin. "I *am* a happily married man. Write that down."

A particularly charming Asian stripper doffs her top. "You could be at the Grand Canyon or a beautiful waterfall or anywhere in the world," I say to Scott, "but you'd still be looking at the chicks' asses there more than the waterfall."

Sandy catches a taxi to his meeting; Dave, SDR, and I get dinner at an Italian restaurant. Then SDR goes home and it's just me and Dave. We have one more drink at Tosca:

the house specialty of steamed milk, chocolate, and brandy served during Prohibition as coffee in disguise.

We take a taxi to the punk dive the Hemlock Tavern in the Tenderloin before calling it a night. An ER nurse, Dave tells me of a recent study where they tested the water in sewer systems for drugs. "Antidepressants and prescription drugs were stable all week long. Addictive drugs like heroin and crack were also stable. Recreational drugs like Ecstasy spiked on the weekends. Antidepressants were heaviest in terms of parts per million; meth was second."

The clock nearing 2 AM, we share a taxi that drops Dave off in the Mission before taking me up the hill to the Haight.

There is another pair of abandoned shoes on the sidewalk. Drugs were almost certainly involved, sex a possibility, and no matter what, shoelessness is pretty goddamned rock and roll.

· · · · ·

The next day I work and run errands and walk around in the Haight, grudgingly buying a pay-as-you-go cell phone so I can work from SDR's apartment before going to Dave's St. Patrick's Day party that night. SDR is working late this evening and—perhaps done in by the weekend—is not going to make it out tonight.

Dave e-mails me: Apparently the Catholic Church in Ireland shifted the St. Patrick's Day feast to March 15, 2008—two days past—instead of the traditional March 17 because of scheduling conflicts during Holy Week. I e-mail him back: Perhaps we need to rename the party the Papal Fallibility Sit-In.

A study in lost shoes, 11

I smoke some pot, drink some coffee, and wander around the Haight, first stopping for a snapshot of Charlie Manson's old place, then the Dead's old place, and then the Shoe Garden in Alamo Square. Old, lost shoes have found new life here as planters for an assortment of flora. Not nearly as rock and roll as being left on the sidewalk, but not nearly as depressing either—it's actually somewhat uplifting. And for all the beauty on my walk, the sight that captivated me the most was a redhead's bare-back midriff, with just a hint of ass cleavage, in a third-story picture window.

Lost shoes reborn

On the way back, I stop by the address I have for Janis Joplin's old place, but there is no building there.

I insert my iPod's earbuds and keep walking. Bauhaus. The Misfits. Cheap Trick. Motherfuckin' Audio Dream Sister and "Marijuana Swamp Child," perhaps the best unknown, drugged-out slab of a song ever.

Sometimes rock and roll delivers a better buzz than any drug.

I hit Haight Street at 5 PM and turn the corner east. The Queens of the Stone Age blast their cover of Romeo Void's "Never Say Never" into my inner ear. Ten seconds later a girl in her St. Patrick's Day green takes a hit of pungent marijuana in front of a head shop.

Wilco plays. I spy an Irish band playing on the sidewalk in front of a festive Irish bar—it is St. Patrick's Day in San Francisco, Catholic Church be damned—and go in to order a Harp. The first drink of the day is invariably the strongest.

I can feel the endorphins flow from my brain into my fingertips and back again.

I ask the green-clad bartender about the Catholic Church's move. My only green is my knit cap.

"That was only the parade," she assures me. "It's still St. Patrick's Day."

"But the pope is never wrong."

. . . . .

I drink red wine and smoke pot and shower and have two ibuprofens and drink a beer. I carefully pack all my belongings to head down to the party in the Mission. Green knit cap. Check. Digital camera. Check. Notebook. Check. Pen. Check. Torpedo of weed. Check. Lighter. Check. iPod. Check. Red pirate die from 826 Valencia. Check. Bouncy ball shaped like a baby's head that cries when you bounce it. Check. Film canister with a hit of acid and a mushroom cap. (Just in case.) Check. Bunny mask. (Ditto.) Check.

Jerry's former abode

Downhill through the Castro, I wear the bunny mask like a backward baseball cap. Not much action, just one somewhat flamboyant tall guy in a sparkly green hat.

My first conversation at the party is with Mike and is outlandishly funny and dirty, but it ends abruptly when I reveal the baby-head ball that cries when you bounce it on the ground. I bounce it on the ground. It cries.

"What the hell are you doing with that, bro?" He appears to lose respect for me.

Next I meet Natalie, who thinks the baby head would be a good form of birth control.

"Male or female?" I ask.

"Definitely male."

I laugh at the thought of a naked guy going to his roommate to borrow his baby-head ball because he is about to score. One bounce should be enough to turn her off and get her clothes back on.

As Dave is an emergency room nurse, many of the partiers work with him at San Francisco General Hospital. Many of them are among the city's best—and they've seen a lot of things, often horrible things—but they also clearly like to have a lot of fun.

We get drunker and drunker. The conversation gets weirder and weirder:

"On the way over, the cab driver gave me some coke."

"When you're high, you should be high. When it gets to be the norm, it's a problem."

"Senility, diapers, and regret."

At midnight, the cops drop by because of a complaint. Dave's roommate apparently uses a Jedi mind trick, telling them the party is secular. They leave and never return.

By 12:30 AM, Dave writes a lengthy decree about papal fallibility on the kitchen blackboard; I break out the bunny mask.

By 1:45 AM, Dave opens the second-to-last bottle of plum wine. I chase my glass with several Irish coffees, an interesting but ultimately awful pairing.

By 3:30 AM, the neighbors tell Dave to fuck himself.

Somewhere in here, Dave and I split the mushroom cap. It barely registers in my polluted thought stream, but where it does register it fits in nicely.

By 4:00 AM, a drunken guitar-and-saxophone jam begins in the living room. To pour gas on the situation, Dave breaks out his amp in order to amplify the drunken guitarist's rock and roll.

Dazed and confused, I leer at some of the last female party guests, smoke more pot, lean against the kitchen counter, which is entirely covered with empty and half-empty cans and bottles, plus a few half-eaten brownies.

Carnage in the kitchen, my brain a wild swirl of endorphins and imagery seen or imagined, the mind's buzz saw barely chugging, stalling then speeding up, curvy female body parts in tight cotton and denim, another drink, more drugs, the bleat of the sax, the ornery electric riff.

Sometime around 5 AM, the party officially ends. I'm thinking about walking back to the Haight because of some pretty high-decibel snoring on the adjacent futon, but Dave convinces me otherwise. My iPod saves me. I fall asleep to my friend California Littlefield's epic "Rocket Boy."

I somehow lose the tab of LSD and the red six-sided pirate die somewhere in the wreckage, but otherwise hang on to my myriad belongings.

"I had no idea you were living such a decadent lifestyle," I tell Dave after a morning conversation even too perverse to print here.

"Thanks."

Where to go...

The Maiden Pub
Village Center, Big Sur
831-667-2355

Esalen Institute Night Baths
5500 Hwy. 1, Big Sur
831-667-3000 or 831-667-3005
www.esalen.org

Big Sur River Inn
Hwy. 1 at Pheneger Creek, Big Sur
800-548-3610
www.bigsurriverinn.com

Waterfront Plaza Hotel
10 Washington St. in Jack London
Square, Oakland
510-836-3800
www.waterfrontplaza.com

Yoshi's San Francisco
1330 Fillmore St., San Francisco
415-655-5600

Heinold's First and
Last Chance Bar
48 Webster St., Oakland
510-839-6761

Winchester Mystery House
525 S. Winchester Blvd., San Jose
408-247-2101
www.winchestermysteryhouse.com

The Booksmith
1644 Haight St., San Francisco
415-863-8688
www.booksmith.com

Murio's Trophy Room
1811 Haight St., San Francisco
415-752-2971

Kezar Bar and Grill
900 Cole St., San Francisco
415-681-7678

City Lights Bookstore
261 Columbus Ave., San Francisco
415-362-8193
www.citylights.com

Vesuvio
255 Columbus Ave. at Jack Kerouac
Alley, San Francisco
415-362-3370
www.vesuvio.com

Musée Mechanique
Pier 45, Shed A, at the end of Taylor
St., Fisherman's Wharf,
San Francisco
415-346-2000
www.museemecanique.org

Citrus Club
1790 Haight St., San Francisco
415-387-6366

Alembic
1725 Haight St., San Francisco
415-666-0822
www.alembicbar.com

Club Deluxe
1511 Haight St., San Francisco
415-552-6949

Eight Immortals
1433 Taraval St., San Francisco
415-731-5515

500 Club
500 Guerrero St., San Francisco
415-861-2500

Elbo Room
647 Valencia St., San Francisco
415-552-7788
www.elbo.com

Paxton Gate
824 Valencia St., San Francisco
415-824-1872
www.paxtongate.com

826 Valencia
826 Valencia St., San Francisco
415-642-5905
www.826valencia.org

Golden Gate Park
In northwest San Francisco,
surrounded by Stanyan St.,
Fulton St., the beach,
and Lincoln Way
www.sfgov.org

Top of the Mark
999 California St., San
Francisco
415-616-6916
www.topofthemark.com

Tosca
242 Columbus Ave., San
Francisco
415-986-9651

The Condor
300 Columbus Ave., San
Francisco
415-781-8222

Hemlock Tavern
1131 Polk St., San Francisco
415-923-0923
www.hemlocktavern.com

A BEER DRINKER IN WINE COUNTRY

3 DAYS, 200 MILES, ZERO BEERS

I'm a beer drinker at heart.

I'm not ashamed to admit I've drunk dozens of Pabst Blue Ribbons in the past month. I like watery beer. I also like thick, dark beer. And amber ale and creamy wheat beer and beer infused with hot peppers. I like beer.

Nothing against wine; I like wine and am making a concerted effort to like it more. What I don't like is the seeming disconnect between my loud, rock-and-roll, hiking, lowbrow-art lifestyle and the wine-drinking lifestyle. I'm traveling to Napa Valley to try and close that gap.

I'm now part of a drinking minority. According to a 2007 Gallup poll, Americans said their favorite alcoholic beverage was wine, not beer: 40 percent of those polled picked wine as their poison, barely edging beer's 34 percent. This is the first time wine outdid beer since the Gallup people started asking about drinking preferences in 1992, when beer (47 percent) decimated wine (27 percent).

It follows that my Napa journey is all about tweaking my drinking toward Pinot Noir and away from PBR. I don't

want to lose the unkempt beer guy in my soul to some wine
snob who's waiting in the wings, but nonetheless I am
making a pact: I am leaving my beer-guzzling ways at home
and imbibing only wine while on my Napa Valley vacation.

That's right: no suds for three whole days.

· · · · ·

I arrive at the Wine Country Inn, just north of the posh
little town of St. Helena in Napa Valley. After meeting the
resident tailless cat, I check in and set out with my guide,
Kat Jarvis, an old college friend and wine guru.

"I was a wine judge in Monterey this weekend," Kat says
with a smile. "People were doing wine shots out of my belly
button." Maybe this wine thing is all right after all.

At our first stop, Napa Cellars in Oakville, Kat gives me
a quick primer in wine tasting: spit, don't swallow. I spray
my shirt, my notepad, and everything else with a fine mist
of 2003 Napa Valley Zinfandel. The wine is good, but my
spitting technique definitely needs a little work.

After a stop for another tasting, at Sequoia Grove, we
have tacos from a *carniceria* in Calistoga, at the north
end of Napa Valley. Small and
spicy, they are a pre-appetizer
to appetizers and dinner at
Brannan's Grill, just up the
road in the center of town.

At the restaurant, we
crack a bottle of 2002
Bennett Lane Maximus, a
blend of Syrah, Cabernet
Sauvignon, and Merlot
that Kat dubs a "frat guy's
wine." It's a description I
can live with, and it goes
great with my pork
porterhouse and
fingerling potatoes.

After dinner, I stick
to my pact and order

A small chunk of California's vineyards

wine at Susie's, a dive across the street. "This is more of a beer bar" comes the bartender's retort. I hold fast and get a glass of white that tastes like apple juice and vinegar compared to what I just quaffed across the street.

What the hell am I doing?

Then a patron, a middle-aged woman in a bandanna, starts howling—loudly. Kat and I play a game of pool. After the howler gooses me with her cue and a guy with a PBR shirt tries to hustle me, spitting wine into a bucket earlier strikes me as quite sensible. We decide to call it a night, and I leave my glass half full at the bar.

Shoot. I forgot my toothbrush.

I begrudgingly apply toothpaste to my finger, try to work off the slight purple tint my teeth have taken on, and go to sleep. Thankfully, the front desk has "a funky little purple toothbrush" for me in the morning.

Our first tasting of the day is at Bremer Family Winery, an off-the-beaten-path winery dating back to the 1880s. Today, Bremer produces 4,000 cases of wine a year and does not distribute; its wines are available only at the winery. In a tasting

room that feels more lawyer's office than wine bar, Otto Sheridan pours us each a Zinfandel.

Otto says he got a degree in philosophy and that he went into the wine business for philosophical reasons. "I felt it was something I could believe in: taking something from the ground and turning it into art."

He pours Kat and I tastes of 2001 Bremer Family Claret. "This is what I affectionately call the ringer," says Otto, noting that it has four out of the five Bordeaux grapes.

Then we head back west toward Calistoga, for Bennett Lane Winery, the first such operation to sponsor a NASCAR team.

The author posing in a parked racecar

After a career in advertising, Randy Lynch opened Bennett Lane with his wife, Lisa, in September 2003. They'd bought a house in Napa Valley with twelve acres two years earlier. "Four acres were still producing, and nobody wanted to buy the grapes," Lynch tells me. "One thing led to another, and we bought a winery. I'm glad we did."

Alongside casks of aging Cabernet Sauvignon in Bennett Lane is a surprising sight: a NASCAR race car emblazoned with the winery's logo amidst bunches of grapes. Lynch, a racing crew chief in the late 1960s, has been part owner of a racing team for several years. Bennett Lane became the first winery to sponsor a NASCAR car when Lynch put his two interests together in 2004.

"We're changing beer guzzlers to wine sippers, one race at a time," says Lynch. "Historically, NASCAR has an image of Winston cigarettes and Budweiser beer. Now there are 75 to 80 million NASCAR fans. Their palates have matured; they've grown up. Now I go to the pits and guys ask, 'Did you bring us some wine?'"

Bennett Lane's Stephanie Longton teaches me about tannins and how they just about beg to be cut by food—preferably high-fat food like beef, chocolate, or cheese. Sounds good to me. Randy praises red wine for lowering his cholesterol. Even better.

Kat says she couldn't fit into a button-down shirt that morning. "That's what happens when you go to wine country," laughs Stephanie. Uh-oh.

After the tour, we relax for a few minutes in the picnic area next to the winery, enjoying the views of Mount St. Helena, a pine- and moss-covered hulk poking into the clouds, rising more than 4,200 feet above the valley floor. It's a hiker's paradise, I'm told, and it looks it too, but that adventure will unfortunately have to wait for another trip.

We drive back south into St. Helena, swerving off for one last tasting before lunch. Much bigger and better-known, Beringer Vineyards is a stunning winery to look at, but its tasting room feels more like a gift shop than a wine bar. I appreciate the wines we taste, but think something might have been lost in mass production.

Red, white, or both?

After Beringer, we go to Taylor's Refresher in St. Helena, one of the few Zagat-rated fast-food joints anywhere. I have a Texas burger, a big, tasty mess dripping with guacamole and jalapeños, and a glass of Pinot Noir. Somehow I don't feel one bit pretentious as I alternate between the two. It tastes too good to feel pretentious.

Then we venture farther south to the Vintner's Collective in Napa, the valley's population center. This attractive space is the tasting room away from home for about twenty small wineries in Napa Valley. "All these little spots are tasting rooms," says the attendant, motioning to labeled square-foot areas on the bar. He points to the one in front of me. "This is Vinoce's tasting room."

He pours us wines from Ancien, D Cubed, Richard Perry, Judd, and Spelletich Cellars, finishing the session off with a "big hitter": the 2003 Melka Cabernet Sauvignon.

I take a hearty drink and don't spit. The wine is bold, almost hot and spicy. I swallow. It tastes especially good going down.

On the way back north from downtown Napa, we stop at Hagafen Cellars for a tasting. I ask winemaker-owner Ernie Weir for a few tasting tips.

"It's horrible how Merlot got maligned," he responds. "It got overused by a lot of wineries. It turned out wimpy, and a lot of fine winemakers had to fight against that."

I think of Paul Giamatti's Miles character in *Sideways* and his famous rant: "If anybody orders Merlot, I'm leaving! I am not drinking any fucking Merlot!" So did Ernie, who describes the retort on a roadside sign posted in Napa Valley: "Obviously, Miles never tried Napa Valley Merlot."

Our final tasting of the day is at Darioush, home to one of the valley's most opulent tasting rooms. Its distinction, according to the attendant, is "It's the only Persian-themed winery in the valley." Inside the pillared entrance is a wall made of water and another painted orange, ambient background music plays, and a number of flickering flat-screen TVs are on. Darioush feels a bit over the top, sure but comfortable, and the wines taste pretty good.

Kat explains how the creamy flavor of the Chardonnay is the product of malolactic fermentation and how the Merlot has round tannins, and why that is a good thing. I get a pour of the winery's 2002 Signature Cabernet Sauvignon. I take too big of a gulp and spit out only some, wondering about the finer points of spitting etiquette.

After returning to the Wine Country Inn, Kat and I go our separate ways. Mine involves a hike in Bothe-Napa Valley State Park, just a few miles north of the inn. While the trailhead is just a stone's throw from the highway, the traffic noise quickly melts away. On my two-mile hike through a mossy forest, I scare a whitetail deer, take photos of century-old gravestones, and key my initials into a eucalyptus alongside "Juan"

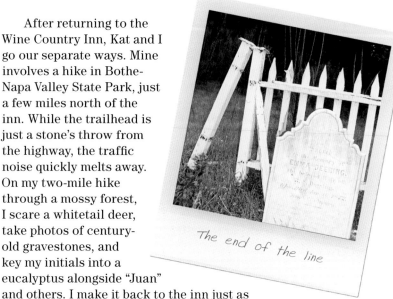

The end of the line

and others. I make it back to the inn just as the sun dips below the horizon.

I decide not to wear my MC5 wristband to dinner at Cindy's Backstreet Kitchen in St. Helena. Kat and I start with a half-bottle of 2004 Robert Sinsky Pinot Blanc and flatbread with local cheese and truffle oil that Kat says she's "dreamed about." I order the Mighty Meatloaf, slathered in barbecue sauce and served with mashers, with kicks of horseradish and garlic, respectively. Kat gets quail.

We open a bottle of 2002 Bennett Lane Maximus we'd picked up earlier in the day. The big, bold red goes quite nicely with the meatloaf, perhaps even better than the Pinot went with the Texas burger.

Dessert is a delectably gooey slice of s'mores-inspired Campfire Pie. We leave the restaurant a little after 10 PM, commiserating over our inability to party like we could in college. It hits me that that was where good wine came into play: a potentially healthy belt of booze that goes better with a meal than with a long night.

We check out of the Wine Country Inn at 9:30 AM on Wednesday and browse the shops in Calistoga. Kat considers but ultimately dismisses an aquarium-themed lamp for her fiancé. I consider and ultimately buy a souvenir T-shirt for $24. En route to our final tasting stop, Frank Family Vineyards, I take a picture of a local eccentric on an artfully decorated bike.

Kat tells me how Rich Frank, former Disney president, bought a Napa Valley estate that still produced grapes. This led him to bid low with his partner, longtime Napa stalwart Koerner Rombauer, and nab the third-oldest operating winery in the valley, the former home of Kornell Champagne Cellars, in 1992. In the time since, Frank Family Vineyards has earned the reputation of being the ultimate insider's winery, the off-the-beaten-path gem that attracts those who are in the know.

I enter the tasting room, a ramshackle space that has absolutely nothing in common with what I'd seen at Darioush. No pillars, no flat screens, no ambient trip-hop; just cases of wine, a trophy case with ribbons and medals, and photos plastered on the slightly slanted walls. I meet Zephyr, the winery's resident cat. I'm told of the cat's allegedly part-bobcat lineage and its ability to sleep through just about anything.

As a nod to former owner Hanns Kornell, a visit to the Frank Family tasting room starts in the front room with the winery's effervescent offerings. Napa Valley was once known for its Champagnes, I'm told, but they fell out of favor in the 1970s after the area garnered a world-class reputation for its Zinfandels and Chardonnays.

Next stop is the memorabilia-bedecked Marilyn Monroe room, where Frank Family's still wines are poured. Kat ushers me into an office in between the two tasting

The cat with no tail

bars for our appointment with Dennis Zablosky, the tasting room manager, a former pro baseball player with a big gut and an even bigger personality. I'm immediately struck by his gift of gab and sense of humor.

"We show people a good time here," Dennis says. "We're probably one of the last old-fashioned wineries in Napa. Nobody used to charge for tastings, and everybody had a good time."

Indeed, of the numerous wineries we've visited, Frank Family is the first that has no tasting fee.

I tell Dennis I'm a beer drinker. He tells me Napa Valley is full of beer drinkers. "When we crush," he says, "we can't keep the fridges full of cold beer."

He then starts us off with a pour of 2004 Frank Family Napa Valley Chardonnay, pointing out the "cream soda finish." I concur; it's terrific. Then he pooh-poohs white wine in general, saying, "I think all wines would be reds if they could."

Next up is the 2004 Reserve Chardonnay. I notice Dennis has a half-full glass of red in front of him. I ask him about spitting versus swallowing.

"I'm a drinker, not a spitter," he says. "I never spit. I can't get the wine unless I swallow."

I follow up and ask for advice on broadening my palate. "By drinking a lot of different wines," he answers. "Don't fall in love with one or two wineries. I think some people overanalyze what they read on here," he continues, motioning to the tasting guide, "and say, 'I don't taste that, I must not have a good palate.'" Not true, Zablosky tells me. "You are an expert. You just have to realize if you like it or not."

He pours us Zinfandel, then Cabernet Sauvignon, then a reserve port. I hunt for various tastes and smells. In some ways, it seems like I'm trying to learn a new language.

On my way out, Pat Cline, a Frank Family salesman, chats me up for a few minutes, telling me how the business has been built on word of mouth and Dennis's charm. "For people to enjoy wine, they have to be comfortable," he says. "Coming here is kind of like going to grandpa's house and tasting world-class wines." He goes on to say that a busy summer Saturday here is akin to a "fraternity-house jail-break," then rescinds that description in favor of something much tamer.

Kat takes me on a quick tour of the winery, highlighting the old-school Champagne-making operation. Then it's time to go. I pick up a bottle of Cabernet Sauvignon, bid Kat fare-well, and drive back to the Oakland Airport, contemplating whether my palate has expanded or not.

I don't arrive at any particular conclusion. I like wine more than I did before the trip, for sure, but I'm still a beer drinker at heart. Old habits die hard.

One of the first things I do when I get home is crack open one of the last cans of PBR in my fridge, right after unpacking my 2001 Frank Family Cabernet Sauvignon and my 2004 Napa Cellars Sauvignon Blanc. I look forward to enjoying them on a special occasion, and with a good meal.

Ahh. Cold beer. So refreshing.

Where to go...

Wine Country Inn
1152 Lodi Ln., St. Helena
888-465-4608
www.winecountryinn.com

Napa Cellars
7481 St. Helena Hwy., Oakville
707-944-2565
www.napacellars.com

Sequoia Grove Vineyards
8338 St. Helena Hwy., Napa
800-851-7841
www.sequoiagrove.com

Brannan's Grill
1374 Lincoln Ave., Calistoga
707-942-2233
www.leftcoastrestaurants.com

Susie's Bar
1365 Lincoln Ave., Calistoga
707-942-6710

Bremer Family Winery
975 Deer Park Rd., St. Helena
707-963-5411
www.bremerfamilywinery.com

Bennett Lane Winery
3340 Hwy. 128, Calistoga
877-MAX-NAPA or 707-942-6684
www.bennettlane.com

Beringer Vineyards
2000 Main St., St. Helena
707-967-4412
www.beringer.com

Taylor's Refresher
933 Main St., St. Helena
707-963-3486
www.taylorsrefresher.com

Vintner's Collective
1245 Main St., Napa
707-255-7150
www.vintnerscollective.com

Hagafen Cellars
4160 Silverado Tr., Napa
888-HAGAFEN
www.hagafen.com

Darioush
4240 Silverado Tr., Napa
707-257-2345
www.darioush.com

Bothe-Napa Valley State Park
Five miles north of
St. Helena on Hwy. 29
707-942-4575
www.parks.ca.gov

Cindy's Backstreet Kitchen
1327 Railroad Ave., St. Helena
707-963-1200
www.cindysbackstreetkitchen.com

Frank Family Vineyards
1091 Larkmead Ln., Calistoga
800-574-9463
www.frankfamilyvineyards.com

CHAPTER 7

CENTRAL CALIFORNIA: THE COAST AND THE VALLEY

INTRODUCTION

With its breadbasket and its wild and woolly midsection, respectively, California's Central Valley and Central Coast hark back to a simpler way of life. Inland, that simpler way is based on the seasons, namely the planting and harvesting ones, and the price of commodities on the global market. On the coast, that way of life has more to do with the rhythms of the tides, the rhythms of sardines and shellfish, and, in some cases, the rhythms of partying all night and sleeping all day.

The suburbs don't sprawl quite like they do in Southern California or the Bay Area in these parts. On the coast, the Monterey area is one of the few urban hubs, with San Luis Obispo the population center farther south. But by and large, the Central Coast is rugged and sparsely peopled, just like a little chunk of Wyoming with a Pacific view.

In the Central Valley, surrounded by miles and miles of fertile farmland, Sacramento, Fresno, and Bakersfield are the big cities. They can feel as if they're stuck in something of a time warp, especially in contrast with the megahyper

STATS & FACTS

- Despite popular opinion, Weed, California, was named not for marijuana but for Abner Weed, the owner of a lumber mill. Sweet name, though.

- Fresno County is the top-producing agricultural county in the United States. Its annual production, just shy of $5 billion in recent years, would rank in the top ten agricultural states by itself.

- Big Sur, the rocky, wild, and of course big coast south of Monterey, might just be the world's first Spanglish term. "Grande South" just doesn't have the same ring.

- Despite popular opinion, Cool, California, was named not for the catchall adjective for all things good but for Aaron Cool, an itinerant preacher. Sweet name, though.

- Parkfield, midway between Bakersfield and San Luis Obispo, is known as "The Earthquake Capital of the World." The town (population thirty-seven, not too surprisingly) gets hit by a big tremor once every twenty-five years because of its location atop the San Andreas Fault.

cities on the coast—and that might just be a good thing. They are also preposterously hot come summertime.

Not to say the weather is bad in the middle of the state. In some ways, it's perfect, with mild winters, lush springs, and comfortable falls more than making up for the summer heat. And that's what pretty much any plant will tell you, if only plants could talk. The urban areas are nestled amidst fields and orchards, where the resident chlorophyll-based life-forms seem to love the weather pretty much all the time, or at least until we yank them from the ground for something to eat.

BIG THINGS AND OTHER ROAD ART

Bubblegum Alley
700 block of Higuera St., San Luis Obispo

One of the downright grossest works of public art on the planet, Bubblegum Alley is exactly what it sounds like: an alley plastered over with gum chewed by thousands of mouths. Since the 1960s, passersby have molded their own used Bazooka, Juicy Fruit, and Big Red onto a grimy collage of sticky bubblegum. Now entirely swathed in a layer of gum several sticks and a few balls thick, the alley's walls play host to truly nauseating abstract murals that would have even sickened Jackson Pollock. Best (or possibly worst) of all, Bubblegum Alley is interactive. Nearby storefronts keep their gumball machines stocked with plenty of ammo.

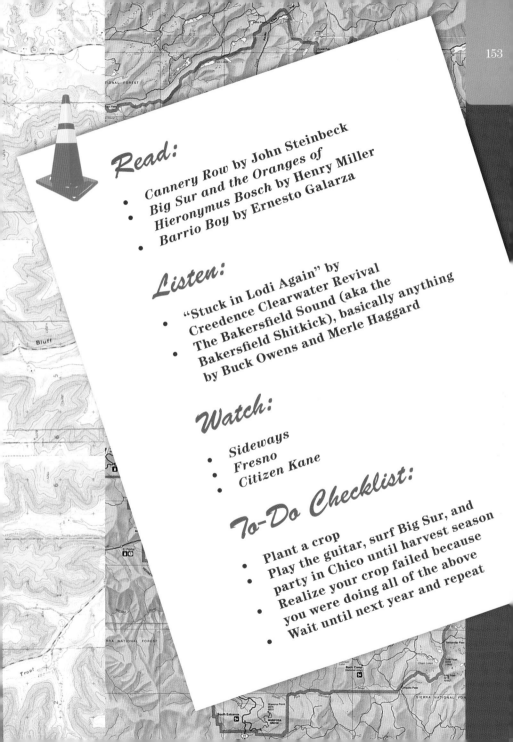

Read:

- Cannery Row by John Steinbeck
- Big Sur and the Oranges of Hieronymus Bosch by Henry Miller
- Barrio Boy by Ernesto Galarza

Listen:

- "Stuck in Lodi Again" by Creedence Clearwater Revival
- The Bakersfield Sound (aka the Bakersfield Shitkick), basically anything by Buck Owens and Merle Haggard

Watch:

- Sideways
- Fresno
- Citizen Kane

To-Do Checklist:

- Plant a crop
- Play the guitar, surf Big Sur, and party in Chico until harvest season
- Realize your crop failed because you were doing all of the above
- Wait until next year and repeat

Giant Clams
Pismo Beach

These are some pretty honkin' bivalves. Modeled after local Pismo clams—which in turn are some of the world's biggest, sometimes topping seven inches in diameter—you'll find enormous clam sculptures scattered on the sidewalks of Pismo Beach, including one right next to the chamber of commerce on Price Street. The clam statues are sometimes hard to identify as shellfish, since they're painted and repainted over and over again for holidays. In March, they bear shamrocks; come December, they're reindeer. Pismo Beach's industrial clamming days have passed, but you can still get a permit and dig for your dinner south of the pier.

Nitt Witt Ridge
881 Hillcrest Dr., Cambria
(reservations are required for a guided tour)
805-927-2690

The perfect counterpoint to the Hearst Castle in San Simeon, Nitt Witt Ridge is somewhere between a folk-art environment, a scrap heap, and a house. Much more financially limited than William Randolph Hearst, creator and resident Art Beal was an artist and something of a hermit who bought the sloping lot in the late 1920s and spent the next half-century fashioning his castle all by himself. Beal's materials include beer cans, pine, abalone shells, junked woodstoves, and, allegedly, leftovers from Hearst Castle. Beal passed away in 1992, and his ashes were spread about the property. New owners have since battled the elements in an ongoing attempt at a restoration, but the annual maintenance budget is probably something around what the Hearst Castle gift shop generates in an hour.

Reiff's Gas Station House

52 Jefferson St., Woodland
530-666-1758
www.reiffsgasstation.com

If you look at it from the northwest, Mark Reiff's house looks like a 1950s gas station. From its southeast side, the home looks like a magnet for disaster, impaled by both a Cessna airplane (through the roof) and a vintage Chevy (through the sod, the white picket fence, and the wall). And from yet another angle, the place looks like a movie theater. And that's just scratching the surface. Call Reiff ahead of time for a guided tour. He also throws an annual street party every June on his otherwise normal residential street.

R.I.P.

Senator Capitol Kitty, 1991–2004
**California State Capitol,
10th St. and Capitol Mall, Sacramento**

Alternately known as Senator Kitty and Capitol Kitty, this feral feline was a very lucky black cat that lived on the capitol grounds for thirteen years before a clerk noticed she was sick and had a vet put her to sleep. While she resisted pethood, Senator Capitol Kitty lived a remarkably full life: debating local politicians, staring down protesters, and eating handouts from legislative staffers to the point of portliness. Insert fat cat and politician joke here.

Henry Miller, 1891–1980
Ashes scattered off the Big Sur coast

The lustful bard who helped push sex into the mainstream—but not before countless bans and bonfires featuring his books—Henry Miller was a Big Sur resident for much of his adult life, settling on the coast when returning from Paris in 1940. While he was allowed back into the United States, his words by and large were not, because his famed *Tropic of Cancer* and *Tropic of Capricorn* were banned until the Supreme Court ruled in 1964 that they

were literature, not obscenity—a milestone in the sexual revolution. Miller's style, while certainly horny, left a lasting mark on the Beat writers, who dug his autobiographical style, humor, blunt honesty, and far-out viewpoint.

Alvin Edgar "Buck" Owens, 1929–2006
Greenlawn Cemetery
3700 River Blvd., Bakersfield

The inventor of the "Bakersfield sound," a wearer of some of the sweetest rhinestone-bedecked nudie suits ever, and the best thing about *Hee Haw*, country music legend Buck Owens is one of those artists who grows on you and grows on you and grows on you. During the heyday of Buck Owens and the Buckaroos, they were musical rebels, bucking (pun intended) the trend of smooth country pop in favor of a honky-tonk-meets-mariachi style that's been much imitated, but never duplicated.

John Steinbeck, 1902–1968
Garden of Memories Memorial Park
768 Abbott St., Salinas

Another of the country's true literary legends, John Steinbeck's books focus on Central California's poor, downtrodden, and eccentric, and many of his *Grapes of Wrath* and *Tortilla Flat* characters were based on locals he knew from the vicinity of his hometown of Salinas, most famously marine biologist Ed Ricketts who became Doc in *Cannery Row* and *Sweet Thursday*. Beyond his

renowned fiction, Steinbeck also penned classics of the biological variety (*The Sea of Cortez*) and dog-friendly travel writing (*Travels with Charley*). Though he lived much of his life in Manhattan, Steinbeck is buried in the city where he was born, where downtown is centered on the impressive National Steinbeck Center.

James Dean, 1931–1955

Memorials on Hwy. 46 in Cholame and twenty-seven miles east, where he made his last stop, plus the junction of Hwy. 46 and Hwy. 41, officially known as the James Dean Memorial Junction

Live fast, die young, and leave a good-looking corpse. Well, two out of three isn't bad.

James Dean's star was white hot after *East of Eden*, landing him the part of Jim Stark in *Rebel Without a Cause*. But Dean never lived to see his defining role onscreen. He was killed when he smashed his Porsche into a Ford making an ill-advised left turn on September 30, 1955. *Rebel* opened a week later. Half a century later, nobody has captured youthful angst quite like Dean did.

His star still burns bright in this wide-open dusty corner of California, where fans from all over the world pay their respects to the actor whose image represents the peak of American cool forevermore. The memorials include an abstract aluminum sculpture in Cholame proper and a roadside portrait just west of Lost Hills. The road has been re-routed since Dean's death, so the fatal stretch of blacktop is now on private property.

Ishi, Circa 1860–1916
Memorial mural at Robinson St. and Huntoon St., Oroville

The Yahi people were thought to be long gone, the victims of disease and genocide and a rapidly changing West. Ishi's tribe was massacred when he was a child and he spent the next forty years in hiding with his mother and other survivors—until he was the only one left. Orovillians discovered Ishi holed up in a corral in 1911, and he soon became a tenant of the anthropology building at the University of California at San Francisco. There, researchers learned that he was the last speaker of what was long thought to be a dead language, and an excellent archer. Ishi is said to have lived the last five years of his life in contentment at the university until the last of the Yahi died of tuberculosis in 1916.

VICE

Chico

Laced with green parkland, drunken coeds, and the scent of burning cannabis, Chico is the prototype for a balls-out college party town. Free-flowing booze and loud music are never more than a block or two away. It's not uncommon for faculty to get busted for growing or selling weed. The central plaza hosts free concerts every Saturday night, not just violins and folkies but loud guitars and psychedelic light shows attended in equal numbers by Chico State undergrads, local eccentrics, hippie kids, and bums. (Many folks fit into several of these categories.) You can find a happy hour most any hour of the day if you consult the free weeklies or just stumble aimlessly from bar to bar. Specials of $1 pints of Sierra Nevada—the mega-microbrewery aptly located in town (1075 E. 20th St., 530-345-2739, www.sierranevada.com)— are not uncommon. And campus is immediately adjacent to downtown. With bars like the cavernous Madison Bear Garden

(315 W. 2nd St., 530-891-1639, www.madisonbeargarden.com) nearly on campus, students can easily stop in for a quick happy-hour special between classes. Or else they can get lost in Bidwell Park, one of the country's largest parks, which is complete with swimming holes and underwater caves.

STAR MAPS

- The infamous scene where a crop duster takes a dive at Cary Grant's character in *North by Northwest* was shot on the Garces Highway, west of Delano.

- The Trash Film Orgy (www.trashfilmorgy.com) takes place on Saturdays in the summer months at midnight in Sacramento, where bad-movie goers dress up in garish outfits, drink too much, and generally make fun of the cheesy movie onscreen.

- World-famous pharmaceutical connoisseur Rush Limbaugh got his start on the Sacramento airwaves.

- Washed-up action star Arnold Schwarzenegger, who now serves as California's governor, is often seen dining at the Esquire Grill at 1213 K Street in downtown Sacramento.

HUH?

Lantrip's House of Ashtrays
3420 Orange Ave., Oroville
(call after 11 pm for an appointment)
530-538-9624 or 530-990-1158

Dean Lantrip wasn't smoking when he started collecting ashtrays, but somehow the hobby drove him back to the habit.

Now he's got upward of 7,000 ashtrays, and counting. Lantrip began collecting in 1996 and eventually his wife, June, forced him to move his collection out of the house. That's when he opened the world's first ashtray museum, right next door to his home. He is meticulously organized: there are shelves dedicated to humorous ashtrays and souvenir ashtrays and ashtrays shaped like houses, tires, pigs, dogs, and frogs— wait, those are real dead frogs—not to mention pottery craft ashtrays, plastic ashtrays, smokeless ashtrays, and ashtrays from casinos, restaurants, and tourist attractions.

But perhaps the most compelling ashtray categorization Lantrip has come up with is that of ashtrays made by organizations that will never produce ashtrays in their name again, including ones bearing the names of hospitals, Little League teams, Disneyland, Aetna Insurance, and the 1984 Olympics.

In terms of sheer numbers, Lantrip's collection outshines his 1,000-piece candlestick collection—which apparently is why the ashtrays got kicked out of the house—and the 2,000 tools (including numerous mystery tools) at Bolt's Antique Tool Museum, across town at 1650 Broderick Street in Oroville (530-533-3096, www.boltsantiquetools.com).

Toad Hollow
**At the US Post Office at 2020 5th St.
and Pole Line Rd., Davis**

In the 1990s, eco-conscious Davis leaders worried that a new overpass would benefit human commuters but negatively impact their amphibious counterparts. Believing the overpass would block a popular migration route for frogs and toads, Davis politicos pushed through a plan to build a network of tunnels the frogs could use to get from the post office parking lot and other places to a nearby protected wetland. Unfortunately, not one amphibian ever figured out that the tunnels were intended for their use, so it's proven to be a fairly inexpensive government boondoggle, highlighted by Toad Hollow outside the Davis Post Office, complete with a toad hotel, a toad outhouse, and a toad tavern. Like the tunnels, there is no proof that toads or frogs have ever used any of these amenities.

Point Lobos Mysteries
Point Lobos State Reserve, just south of Carmel

There are many legends about the rugged and beautiful out-cropping known as Point Lobos. First, there are the ancient cypress trees, allegedly planted by Tibetan monks on a California vacation around AD 900. More recently, during the Spanish mission era, local Indians supposedly would go out on foggy days to cheer up the fog spirit, so a priest decided to exorcise one of the pagans. The priest allegedly went nuts and leapt to his death in the rocky surf. Then there are the stories of sea spirits, great winged demons, inky little humanoids, ghosts, and "The Terror," which allegedly grips hikers and sends them the other way. (I felt no such urge on my hike here.) Perhaps the best mystery of all—and there is no *alleged* in this one—is the mystery of the Point Lobos sea otters. Presumed extinct in 1841, sea otters were animal non grata on the West Coast for almost an entire century until 1938, when a local spotted a horde of the whiskered mustelids frolicking off the shore. Where they frolicked for the intervening century is the big mystery here.

GRUB

La Super-Rica Taqueria
622 N. Milpas St., Santa Barbara
805-963-4940

The late Julia Child's favorite Mexican eatery, La Super-Rica, opens at 11 AM and has a line out the door by 11:05. Not much

to look at, the hole-in-the-wall offers patio seating (sheltered in winter), a great view, and knock-out tacos. While the kitchen is not all about tacos—vegetarian tamales and other creative specials change on a daily basis—I myself had the three-taco La Super-Rica Especiale (#16), doused in three kinds of house salsa, and ate with purpose, lustfully even, then became a little sad six minutes later when my tacos were all gone.

Artichokes
Castroville

For 'choke fiends, Castroville is sin city. Every May, the Artichoke Queen is crowned at the Artichoke Festival—local heroine Norma Jean Baker, before she dyed her hair and became Marilyn Monroe, was famously the first one in 1948—next to the showcased artichoke art, artichoke soup, pickled artichoke, and costumed artichoke characters. The

most decadent delicacy is likely deep-fried artichoke heart, notably available at the Giant Artichoke (11261 Merritt St., Castroville, 831-633-3501), a great market and restaurant so named because it has a giant artichoke integrated into its architecture. There are very few things that simultaneously excite one's taste buds and one's cardiologist to such a great extent.

Abalone

The cream of the crustacean crop, abalone is one of the Central Coast's most heralded—and most expensive—delicacies. The reason for its high price is its slow growth rate: under the best conditions, red abalone bulks up at a rate of about four grams a year, and market size starts at a quarter pound—meaning it takes years for an abalone farmer to  go from seed to market. The stuff is delicious enough to make vegetarians turn a blind eye to the animal-plant borderline, thus wild abalone fishing limits three at a time or twenty-four in a year.

In Monterey, ask the folks at the Monterey Abalone Company (Municipal Wharf No. 2, 831-646-0350, www.montereyabalone.com) for fresh abalone or their recommendation for a prepared meal (expect to spend around $30 for an entrée). Most any upscale restaurant on Cannery Row or Fisherman's Wharf serves abalone.

Sardines

Once upon a time, Pacific sardines were the target of the country's largest fishing industry, and Monterey's Cannery Row was ground zero. Traveling in massive schools and reproducing like slimy earless rabbits, they were fished and

fished and overfished, and the ocean's fickle mood shifted, making for a better environment for anchovies—and sardines virtually disappeared overnight in the 1940s. But sardines have made a big comeback in the time since, and they're again available on Cannery Row—if you can stomach their very salty, very fishy flavor. In Monterey, try the Sardine Factory (701 Wave St., 831-373-3775, www.sardinefactory.com) or most any seafood restaurant or market in town.

Belly Flops
1 Jelly Belly Ln., Fairfield
800-522-3267
www.jellybelly.com

Not all jelly beans that roll off the conveyor belts at the Jelly Belly factory are worthy of the Jelly Belly logo. Some are too small, some are too big, and some are Siamese or Triamese Jelly Bellies (i.e., several beans accidentally fused together into one candy). These beans get caught by the sophisticated filters in place at the plant and dumped into huge bins of rejects, which are in turn packaged as Belly Flops. Available at the Fairfield factory store, these irregular jelly beans are a bargain in comparison to the beans that earned the brand. I got six pounds for $16, less than half the going rate for regular Jelly Bellies. At the factory store, twenty-four-pound cases cost even less per pound, at $48.

SLEEPS

Madonna Inn
100 Madonna Rd., San Luis Obispo
800-543-9666
www.madonnainn.com

The grand dame of kitschy hotels, San Luis Obispo's Madonna Inn offers guests an outlet to indulge their darkest fantasies, whether it's caveman-style sex, or gypsy-style sex, or pioneer-style sex, or just plain old sex in a really tacky room. Each of the 109 rooms here is unique and hard to forget, unless you drink yourself into a stupor. And, based on the dizzyingly polychromatic wallpaper, such a move is not recommended.

If you don't have time for either caveman-style sex or drinking yourself into a stupor, just stop in for a visit to the men's restroom, regardless of your sex or gender: the copper urinal is the only one I've ever seen with a waterwheel.

Delta King and *Captain Dutch's* Sailboats
1000 Front St., Old Sacramento
800-825-5464
www.deltaking.com

If you want to sleep on a boat in California's midsection, I've got two recommendations on opposite sides of the water-slumber spectrum.

Sacramento's *Delta King* is a riverboat that ran passengers between San Francisco and Sacramento during Prohibition for partying and gambling. The US entry into World War II marked a new era for the riverboat as a naval vessel in San Francisco Bay, but the end of the war marked yet another era for the storied boat: it deteriorated and ultimately sunk to the bottom of the bay for eighteen months until it was dredged out, towed to its former port in Old Sacramento, and restored as a hotel/restaurant/theater. Rooms run about $200.

But if you want a bigger body of water and a smaller boat, *Captain Dutch* of Monterey Bay Sailing offers a much more intimate setting in its sailboats: a stayover on a double berth in one of its boats runs $100. And unlike the *Delta King*, you can take your boat out on a cruise or sailing lesson with Dutch the next day.

Treebones Resort
71895 Hwy. 1, Big Sur
877-424-4787
www.treebonesresort.com

In Big Sur, modern construction seems like an unnecessary barrier between you and nature. Treebones strips this un-natural separation from the outdoors to the bare minimum. Its yurts and campsites allow travelers to get away from it all—and in this context, "all" is not an exaggeration. The resort has no cell phone coverage or electrical outlets, and you can't drive to the yurts or campsites.

MISC.

Esalen Institute Night Baths

The middle of nowhere, fifteen miles south
of the community of Big Sur
5500 Hwy. 1, Big Sur
831-667-3000 or 831-667-3005
www.esalen.org

Normally a very private alt-education campus and think tank, the Esalen Institute invites the public to use its renowned hot baths every night, but you've got to pay a $20 fee, stay up late—the slot is 1 AM to 3 AM, seven nights a week—and check your modesty at the gate. The coed baths are clothing optional, but very few customers opt to wear it. (The lack of lighting, however, is sure to hide most flaws in your naked appearance.) But this is the perfect place for a soak: the waves crashing against the crags below, the penetrating silence, the undiluted night sky—it's just you, the ocean, and the Milky Way.

National Yo-Yo Museum

320 Broadway (in the back of the
Bird in Hand shop), Chico
www.nationalyoyo.org

Nicknamed the "Cooperstown of Yo-Yos," Chico is the center of the yo-yo universe. Not only is the city home to the US National Yo-Yo Contest the first weekend of every October, but it also is home to the National Yo-Yo Museum, packed with yo-yos of every description, ranging from 1920s relics to modern-day yo-yos that detach from their string for special tricks. Of special note is Big Yo: at 256 pounds it's the world's largest working yo-yo and requires a crane to work it, although it ended up floating in San Francisco Bay after its rope failed on its initial test run. But yo-yos, big or small, are nothing without the person on the other end of the string. Augie Fash, 2004 National Yo-Yo Champion, works at the Bird in Hand shop and the museum, helping yo-yo shoppers and offering free lessons on Sundays. It's beyond impressive to watch him work his yo-magic, national title notwithstanding. If you stop in, ask him to perform the Pangalactic Gargle Blaster—you won't believe your eyes.

GROW TRIP

4 DAYS, ABOUT 500 MILES

Driving south out of Chico to the Sacramento Valley, I see a sign on the side of the highway. "Dan Logue" it reads. "State Assembly. Secure Our Borders!"

Behind the sign there is field after orchard after field all the way to the horizon. Same goes for the other side of the road.

And I know the great majority of the people working them crossed at least one border to get here.

. . . . .

I meet my cousin Jen for lunch the next day in Old Town Sacramento, once an ornery riverboat and railroad hub, now a somewhat sleepy tourist area. She's a plant biologist and works as a statistician for the US Department of Agriculture in Sacramento. Her job involves forecasting grape and walnut crops, surveying California farms to profile the state's enormous agriculture industry, and measuring the occasional nut in the field to see how everything is going.

By and large, according to the hefty California Agricultural Resource Directory 2007 she hands me over burgers at Fanny Ann's Saloon, it's going good.

California agriculture has contributed more than $30 billion to the state's economy in recent years. This makes it the top-producing agricultural state by far, roughly doubling up second-place Texas and third-place Iowa. (Note to and/or from Iowan editor: Iowa still beats it on a per-capita basis.)

"As an industry, it dwarfs Hollywood," I note. "I think movies bring in like $10 billion a year."

Jen flips through the directory and shows me a county-by-county table. All the top-producing counties are in the heart of the state: Fresno, Tulare, Monterey, Kern, Merced, Stanislaus. She points out that California's top commodity is milk; grapes are second.

I tell her that I heard marijuana was technically California's top crop and that taxes on medical weed contributed $100 million to state coffers in 2007. Jen says that the USDA doesn't keep any statistics on that, but it would certainly push the top-producing county list to the northwest part of the state.

She gives me some agricultural trivia of her own. "You know Ore-Ida frozen potatoes?"

"Sure."

"It's Oregon and Idaho—that's where the name comes from." She is also quick to mention that California's potato crop is decidedly smaller than those two potato giants.

. . . . .

After lunch I make my way north from downtown Sacramento to Woodland and the Tractor & Truck Museum at the Heidrick Ag History Center.

The tractors and assorted other machines are massive. There's a wheat combine that can process enough grain for 73,000 loaves of bread in a single hour, huge orange and green machines with sharp red and blue blades and gears. Mechanical monsters with monstrous engines.

A small exhibit hall provides some context. One interpretive display informs me that 90 percent of the 4 million people in the United States in the early nineteenth century worked on a farm. Now it's less than 1 percent of 300 million—and dropping. "Ten of eleven men needed for farming in the 1880s are free to do other types of work today," a plastic plaque informs.

"The typical 1890s family farm was diversified and self-sufficient, producing a wide variety of crops that relied heavily on horsepower," reads another display. "Work horses pulled farm machinery, provided manure for fertilizer, and transported crops to market."

A sunny and romantic image of farming bubbles into my consciousness, a simpler life that's quiet and pleasant.

The next plaque rains on that mental picture, describing complex businesses and specialized production. "Today's farmer purchases *everything* necessary for his success, including the best seeds, powerful specialized machinery, crop fertilizers, livestock feed, pesticides and herbicides, fuel for their tractors and transportation, and food for their families."

Whatever happened to the romantic notion of self-sufficiency, living off of the land? Has it been replaced entirely by diesel fumes and chemicals and increasingly more beastly machines?

Technology, it seems, has not made life simpler for the farmer. On average, it seems to have made things much more complicated.

· · · · ·

After watching Jen's seven-year-old son, Boris, play in his Little League game, I have dinner with my Aunt Jean, who's been gracious enough to let me crash in her spare bed for the night. It's chicken casserole, my late Auntie Kay's recipe.

"All those Lutheran ladies in Sierra Madre would get together and have potlucks," Jean says. "Everything had a can of Campbell's soup in it."

Even the dessert?

Later, I'm driving back to Davis from nearby Winters and think of the disconnect in our modern American food chain. What once was an agrarian society where everyone ate eggs from their chickens, milk from their cows, crops and the occasional animal from their fields has somehow graduated into a society where the closest we get to that is dumping a can of Campbell's soup into the casserole dish.

Not that the casserole wasn't delicious, and not that I have any desire to work on a farm, but I'm usually fine to not know where my food is coming from. I'm happy for someone else to do everything for me: plant the seeds, water them, tend the plants, harvest the fruit, ship it, slice it, dice it, cook it, and serve it to me while I watch the game and drink beer.

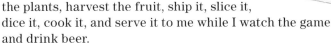

A capitol dome and an orange tree

And I rarely ask where any of it came from, or if it's got chemicals in it, or meat in it, or both chemicals and meat in it. I do love food, but not to the extent that I'm willing to plant a garden.

Which pretty much makes no sense at all.

· · · · ·

I get up the next day and have a bagel and coffee (both of unknown origin) with Aunt Jean before leaving Davis. I drive west toward San Francisco but stop well short of the Pacific. I exit I-80 in Fairfield for the Jelly Belly factory tour.

A huge inflatable anthropomorphic jelly bean greets me. "Lemon," reads his back, like a name on a football jersey. One of my favorites.

Inside, the tour begins. Like the production floor below, it is mostly automated, with a guide leading us from view

of the factory floor to view of the factory floor, and video monitors doing most of the heavy lifting. One such monitor informs my group that jelly beans, descendants of the Islamic delicacy known as Turkish delight, were invented in 1861 and marketed to Union soldiers. They were beans because apparently Union soldiers ate a lot of beans and ate a lot of jelly. In the 1930s, the American marketing machine co-opted them and marketed them as an Easter candy, supposedly because of their resemblance to colorful eggs, the symbol of new life that Jesus Christ's proxy the Easter Bunny started delivering to children every spring around this point in time.

However, it wasn't until 1976 that the Jelly Belly, the first gourmet jelly bean, was born. And soon, washed-up movie actor turned California governor Ronald Reagan was trying to kick the pipe (tobacco) in the late 1970s and turned to jelly beans to satiate his cravings. Ronnie could not say no to the shiny balls of colorful sugar, and he even wrote a note to the Jelly Belly people that included this line: "It has gotten to the point where we can hardly lead or make a decision without passing around a jar of Jelly Bellies." More than three tons of Jelly Bellies were delivered to his 1980 inauguration.

We see mosaic Jelly Belly portraits of Ronnie, Elvis, Pope John Paul II, and Spider-Man hanging above the floor below, which is packed with robotic arms and conveyer belts and huge bins of brightly colored beans.

But what remains a bit of a mystery is exactly why these little neon pellets taste so good. "It begins with an idea," the video's narrator informs us. "They start with the flavor they are intending to duplicate."

Then it gets a bit hazier. Apparently the nuts and bolts of flavor chemistry—the mixing and matching of all sorts of compounds and oils and esters to make a chemical-and-sugar legume that tastes like a pineapple while containing exactly zero pineapples—are either too boring or too horrifying for the masses.

However, I'm pleasantly surprised that Jelly Bellies require one to three weeks to make and that the logo on every bean is made from the same pigment that's used to whiten marshmallows.

The tour guide tells us to look at a waving robotic arm. Instead, I briefly make eye contact with a sad-eyed worker on the floor who seems so small next to the robots and a mountain of yet-to-be-filled cardboard boxes. Only one other worker is in sight; humanity a rarity in the modern candy factory.

Bins o' Bellies

The end of the tour is marked by a Jelly Belly mosaic of Governor Schwarzenegger—I'll never get used to typing that—and a free one-ounce bag of Jelly Bellies. I also get jalapeño and pomegranate beans from the sample bar and buy three huge bags of imperfect Belly Flops for $16.

Then I'm back on the highway, nearly getting chewed up in the tires of a huge semi undoubtedly hauling agricultural products, but make it to Lodi, where I don't get stuck but instead get on California Highway 99 south toward Stockton, where I also don't get stuck.

Somewhere along the way I fish my free bag of Jelly Bellies out of my pocket and start eating them one by one. Distracted by the hyperflavors of the beans, I miss a fruit stand on the left. I realize I also have a box of Girl Scout cookies I randomly requisitioned from Jen in Davis. I'm tempted to eat them, just because they're there, but resist after briefly wrestling with the cellophane. I have no idea where any of the ingredients in any of this stuff came from.

Gospel, hip-hop, mariachi, and country on the radio, the flavors I like best are the citrus ones. I do not like coconut or piña colada. Cola and cream soda: pretty good. Blueberry is okay. I have no idea what the second-to-last one in the bag is supposed to taste like. I think the last one is kiwi.

I skirt the western edge of Modesto and head onto the back roads in search of a fruit stand. I miss another one on the left and ultimately tear into the cookies.

A huge pile of almonds. What kind of tree is that? Two bovines getting it on, then slumbering bovines and rusting machinery, then out of nowhere, a sparkling new suburb pocked with For Sale signs.

Little Caesars. Burger King. An egg ranch with an Oranges for Sale sign. I definitely don't want to buy oranges from an egg ranch.

I veer right and brake hard on the gravel at a fruit stand on the outskirts of Merced. He has strawberries and green onions. I go for the strawberries.

"How much for one?" I point to the pints, laid out in rows of three.

"Five dollars," answers the stand's proprietor.

I give him a five and he puts not one but all three pints in a plastic bag. A huge bounty of fresh fruit.

"You grow 'em here?" I ask.

He nods yes and goes back to shucking the scallions.

I take a look and, sure enough, there is a big field of juicy strawberries behind the shack. I finally know exactly where my food is from.

And the strawberries are the best I've ever had, dripping with juice and flavor, fresh as fresh can be, far beyond what any jelly bean could possibly aspire to.

I'm getting back on 99 and see a hitchhiker on the ramp and stop to pick him up. He's a young guy named Steven, a bookstore employee in Portland heading home to visit his family in Missouri. He's a big reader and Vonnegut fan, so we have plenty to talk about on the ride to Fresno.

After a random and circuitous tour of the greater Fresno-Clovis area, I drop Steven off at a gas station on the south side of town with a half pint of strawberries and a dog-eared copy of *Fear and Loathing in Las Vegas*. I tell him to give me a ring if he has nowhere to sleep and I'll let him crash on the floor.

Next stop is the local chamber of commerce to inquire where I might find a meal made primarily if not exclusively of local ingredients. They have little in the way of advice.

"Isn't this the top agricultural county in the country?" I ask.

One of them smiles. "The beauty of Fresno is we grow it here, we pack it here, we ship it all over the world, and it comes back to Fresno," he says. I assume he is joking.

Or maybe he isn't. The clerk at the University Inn is completely ambivalent about eating locally produced food. "That trend hasn't hit here yet."

I mention the unbelievably good strawberries from Merced, and it strikes a taste bud. "Now you've got me craving strawberries," she says. So I run out and get her one.

She agrees that it is pretty good.

Perplexed about dinner, I explore my options in a local magazine's dining guide and decide that the only listed vegetarian place is my best bet for locally grown stuff. But again I am proven wrong.

"Not too many" is the waiter's off-the-cuff estimate of how many ingredients are grown in Fresno County.

"But it's the biggest agricultural county in the country!" I protest.

"We get our ingredients from Sysco," he replies. "We'd like to get local produce, but it's too expensive."

The place is almost empty.

I end up ordering the gourmet fried rice from the menu—which is far from meatless—and to add insult to injury, they have no beer.

But I am fucking hungry and when I get fucking hungry, I don't really care where my food originated or whether it's organic or the ratio of chemicals to meat. Without food, I get manic, jittery, irrational, and indecisive, perfect for a mammoth hunt, provided a less hungry and more decisive caveman is leading the charge. I'd probably eat a dead buffalo's rotting nether regions if it was my last option— especially if I had a bottle of hot sauce.

But my plate comes out quickly, with green beans, carrots, and tofu amidst perfectly greasy fried rice. I slather it with hot sauce.

It's pretty good, like Aunt Jean's interpretation of Auntie Kay's chicken casserole, and also just like Aunt Jean's casserole, I have zero idea where any of the ingredients came from.

Soon there is only one bite left. I feel much better.

I have a General Sherman IPA next door at the Sequoia Brewing Company and overhear a sarcastic exchange about the soup of the day, turkey chowder.

"He just whipped it up? It isn't Sysco?"

"No, we raised the turkeys out on our ranch in the country," the bartender jokes back. "They're all natural."

In actuality, the ingredients came from who knows where via Sysco, but the soup was not premade, delivered frozen in a big waxy cardboard carton.

Apparently, the county seat of America's biggest agricultural county is pretty damn disconnected from its own bounteous harvest.

After taking note of an advertisement for Grandma's All Natural, a market with "locally grown produce," in the laminated, wire-bound menu and making plans to go there in the morning, I retreat to the University Inn around 9:30 PM.

A little after 10 PM, Steven calls and tells me he didn't get a ride. I tell him he can crash on the floor and take a shower—he mentioned he hadn't gotten one in several days—and go to pick him up where I'd left him five hours earlier. On the ride back, I tell him how hard it was to find a locally grown dinner.

"You should write about that," he tells me. "That's ridiculous."

"I'm way ahead of you," I reply.

Soon he's zonked out on the floor and I'm dozing off on the bed.

· · · · ·

We wake around 7 AM and prepare to hit the road. I tell Steven I can take him down to Visalia, but I need to hit Grandma's All Natural first. We get there at 9; unfortunately, it doesn't open until 10.

So we kill an hour driving around Fresno before returning to Grandma's place. Grandma is nowhere in sight. Neither is any produce, just gardening gadgets and greenery and a burly bearded hippie behind the counter.

"Do you guys still have locally grown produce?" I ask.

Negative, says the mountain of a hippie. "We used to sell it, but we shut it down. Nobody really wanted it around here."

Local produce?

We divert to a little outdoor market down the street and ask an old vendor if he has anything that was grown in Fresno County.

"I don't know."

The bananas have Del Monte tags.

I ask a young vendor the same question, and he points to a box of oranges. I grab two, and he lets us have them for free. By the time I drop Steven off near a hitchhikeable on-ramp on 99, only the rinds remain.

"Have a good trip," he says.

"Good luck," I respond.

Then the Saturn takes me to downtown Visalia—a lady in a PT Cruiser flips me off en route, and I reply with my own middle finger high in the sky—and meet Beth, the local tourism bureau's sales manager, at her office.

She takes me out to lunch and then to the citrus orchards east of town. First it's a stop at Lindcove Ranch, which specializes in pomegranates and citrus crops, including the country's only successful etrog citron orchard.

What is etrog citron?

"It's not a significant part of the citrus industry," says ranch patriarch John Kirkpatrick. "It comes from Israel."

"Some people believe it comes from the Garden of Eden," adds his son Greg.

I learn etrog citron is an important part of Sukkot, the Orthodox Jewish holiday that roughly translates as "Festival of Joy" and that the Kirkpatricks have serendipitously specialized in it since the early 1980s. I also learn their primary market is New York and that the fruit is the most labor-intensive, and thus the most expensive, in the world. Perfect specimens can command upward of $1,000 for a single piece of fruit. And they aren't to be eaten.

"It's a centerpiece and a symbol of beauty and perfection," Greg says. "When we grade it, we do it with a magnifying glass."

Very interesting—the diamond of the citrus industry.

John tells me he's a third-generation citrus grower, making Greg a fourth-generation guy. "It's got a hold of us.

Greg wants to do it, but a lot of our kids don't. It's not happy times—the age of the average farmer goes up every year.

"You live until you die," he adds.

John leaves us in Greg's capable hands for a tour of the orchards. I get some lemons and some tangelos off their trees before we hit the etrog citron orchard. Four Mexican workers diligently tie each branch of the trees to a wooden enclosure to maximize their exposure to sunlight. A few small fruits are bursting from the flowers, but Greg locates a huge leftover from last season, bigger than a softball and wrinkled yellow. He cuts it in half, and inside it looks more like a squash than a lemon—no juicy fruit—but the flesh tastes creamy and mildly sweet, with a mellow citrus tang.

"This would be great in a salad," Beth says.

"Only if you can get it for less than $1,000 a pop," I interject.

Next we head right across the dirt road to the Lindcove Research and Extension Center, part of the University of California system and solely dedicated to citrus-related research. On the way, Beth tells me she grew up in the farmland surrounding Visalia. "We had pigs and cattle and pretty much every other animal."

"Do you miss that lifestyle?"

"Not at all," she answers.

At the citrus research center, Superintendent Kurt gives us the grand tour and tells us how scientists recently irradiated the budwood of mandarin orange trees to produce seedless mutant varieties called tangos. I ask him what citrus he likes best. His answer: "The standard navel orange."

The endless groves of Lindcove

He tells me about the facility's tastings in mid-December, when the public can come and sample the more than 100 varieties of citrus grown in the state.

We stop on the hillside, the orchards unfolding below. I inhale. Nothing in the world smells quite as nice as the waft of a spring citrus bloom. Kurt and Beth discuss a proposed suburban development in a nearby valley and side against it.

Back in the office—where "Have you seen this bug?" posters call attention to the unintended malevolence of the diaprepes root weevil and the Asian citrus psyllid—Beth and I bid Kurt good day and drive back into the city from the country. The city's not too big, not as big as the country, and that's a good thing.

· · · · ·

At dinner at the historic Depot eatery in downtown Visalia, locally grown ingredients are relatively easy to come by, especially compared to the dire situation in Fresno. (Tulare County is the second-largest ag county in the state and the nation, although it has beaten Fresno County in some recent years.)

Beth and her husband, Grant, and I feast on octopi, artichokes, prawns in jalapeño cream, and French dip sandwiches. The maitre d', Mando, tells us the place—once a railroad depot for forty years after it opened in 1916— is haunted, but that he also doesn't believe in ghosts, no matter how many times they harass him or the customers.

Soon my stomach is nearing capacity. I know where some of the stuff in it grew, sure, but only a fraction. But it was quite good, the best meal on the trip bar none, with the possible exception of yesterday's strawberries.

My initial plan was to hit the downtown Visalia bars after dinner, but I dispose of that plan because I have a 6:30 AM coffee date with Bob, field man with the California Citrus Growers Association, and 6:30 is way before my rise time.

Apparently oranges and lemons need far less sleep than I.

· · · · ·

The morning comes remarkably quickly. I wipe the crust from my eyes and throw on some clothes and put a tangelo in my pocket for good measure.

Outside, the sun is just coming up, birds are chirping, and there is a whiff of manure in the air. I cross the courtyard and meet Bob, with whom my cousin Jen works, estimating citrus crops.

I pour my first of several cups of coffee and discuss the state of California's citrus industry.

I learn that 98 percent of navel oranges come from the surrounding San Joaquin Valley. "This year we have the biggest crop ever," says Bob. "About 94 million cartons." The prior crop was only about half that, thanks to a devastating winter freeze.

But the banner crop is not good news. "What's happening is we're planting more and more acres. We almost have too many acres. You can only move so much crop. We need to find a way to market a certain amount of this fruit for a better price," he adds. "The whole industry loses money. But with a manageable crop, things look good."

We talk about size-picking, where pickers take oranges of a certain size and leave the little ones for later, which makes for bigger oranges. Why is this not an industry standard?

"It costs more," answers Bob.

"So the farmers are gambling?"

"A lot of it is weather," he replies. "But it is a gamble, like anything else. It gets tougher and tougher every year. Some farmers think you just buy some land and irrigate—it doesn't happen that way."

I ask Bob about labor issues in the face of escalating anti-immigrant rhetoric in Washington, DC.

"The crackdown hasn't happened yet," he tells me. "But that's who picks the fruit: the Mexican people. How many are illegal? A quarter? A third? I don't know. But this is what they've done all their life."

The labor market is getting squeezed, crackdown or not. "People say they're taking our jobs, but that's not true," Bob adds. "You're not going to pick oranges. It's a hard life. You're going up and down a ladder with a sixty-pound sack of oranges on your back." And pickers' kids don't want to follow their parents' footsteps, careerwise. "They want better jobs."

On our way out of the coffee shop, I ask Bob if suburbs threaten to engulf the orchards like they did in Orange County. "We're not worried about that," he answers. The citrus orchards apparently grow faster than the suburbs do in these parts.

But I see plenty of houses for sale and shiny new exurbs amidst the orange groves and vineyards en route to Porterville. In town, I see a schoolyard of Hispanic kids having lots of fun. Just south of town, I'm almost sure I see a gibbon or a lemur eating oranges on the edge of an orange grove on a country road.

Dr. Kenneth Fox's Salute to the Farmer

I stop. I have no choice because an unexpected monkey sighting may or not be involved.

Whatever it is scurries away before I get a good look. Maybe it was a cat.

So I slowly walk past orderly row after orderly row of orange trees, shooting a sideways glance down each earthen aisle. All of them are dotted with loose oranges, but no cat, no monkey.

So I get back in the car, start it back up, and zigzag my way to Bakersfield via Richgrove and Famoso. Amidst all the orchards and vineyards, I see only a handful of people working, maybe one human per 1,000 acres.

Arriving in Bakersfield around lunchtime—and accidentally steering into one of the most decayed ghettos I've seen in a long time—I stop for a stroll around downtown and happen across a bust of Abraham Lincoln. I take a picture of his iconic mug, wondering what he'd think of the current labor situation in the California fields and the immigration debate in Washington, DC.

Then I make my way to an old favorite, Wool Growers, established in 1954 and the best of several Basque restaurants in town. I'd visited here a decade before, doing inspections for the Mobil Travel Guide, and one of the owners, Danny Maitia, gave me a T-shirt that I wore until the armpits were open-air.

The place is packed, but I'm immediately seated at a long table. A pitcher of ice water and a glass are waiting for me.

A couple of cold swallows later, the waitress takes my order—oxtail stew—and comes back a minute later with a loaf of homemade bread and a salad of lettuce, tomato, red onion, and green pepper drizzled in oil and vinegar. The colors are vivid. The tomatoes are perfectly ripe and juicy.

Then the oxtail stew arrives, accompanied by a sizeable platter of fries. I start laughing. This is an amazing feast—for all of $8. The meat falls off the bone like good barbecue, the savory stew loaded with intense flavor and bright orange carrots.

One of the proprietors, Danny's sister Jenny, is making sure things are all under control. I catch her attention and ask about local ingredients on my plates.

She tells me that most everything is indeed local: the lettuce, potatoes, carrots, and onions are all from the Bakersfield area. "You might pay a little more for your ingredients, but it supports the local economy."

When I ask about the Maitia family philosophy, Jenny smiles warmly. "You have to put a little love into your business."

I tell her how Danny gave me a T-shirt that I wore down to rags a decade before. She

The one and only

explains that he had to stop working because of a brain tumor. "He's doing good," she adds. I'm touched when she brings me a replacement T-shirt on the house.

Then the feast resumes. I should never take another meal for granted. In fact, for the first time in my life, I think I understand why people pray before meals, and the reason I never understood before is the same reason why I took food for granted in the first place. And it has much more to do with the hard work of others than anything supernatural.

I take my time working the meat off the oxtail and munching on my fries, and ultimately feel guilty that I can't finish it all.

As I pay my check, the clerk asks me how everything was today.

"Terrific," I answer. "Best meal of the trip."

Where to go...

Fanny Ann's Saloon
1023 2nd St., Old Sacramento
916-441-0505
www.fannyanns.com

Heidrick Ag History Center
1962 Hays Ln., Woodland
530-666-9700
www.aghistory.com

Jelly Belly Factory
1 Jelly Belly Ln., Fairfield
800-522-3267
www.jellybelly.com

Merced Fruit Stand
Somewhere west of Merced on
Hwy. 140

University Inn
2655 E. Shaw Ave., Fresno
559-294-0224
www.universityinnfresno.com

Sequoia Brewing Company
777 E. Olive, Fresno
559-264-5521
www.sequoiabrewing.com

Lindcove Ranch
Exeter
209-732-3422

**Lindcove Research and
Extension Center**
22963 Carson Ave., Exeter
559-592-2408
groups.ucanr.org/lindcove

The Depot
207 E. Oak Ave., Visalia
559-732-8611
www.thedepotvisalia.com

Wool Growers
620 E. 19th St.,
Bakersfield
661-327-9584
www.woolgrowers.net

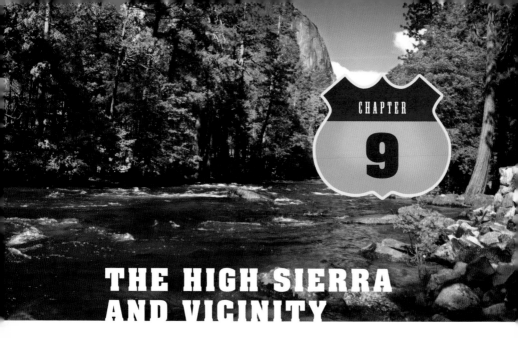

THE HIGH SIERRA AND VICINITY

INTRODUCTION

The spiky granite Mohawk running down California's spine, the Sierra Nevada is one of the world's great mountain ranges. The landscape up top is like an entirely different planet than the desert below. Fittingly, many of the locals are like aliens, or else conquering spacemen from other planets, only on skis.

Surrounded by the historic gold country where B&Bs now far outnumber mines, the jagged scenery is no mere backdrop. The mountains define the work less, play more culture, the moody weather, and just about everything else. What they don't necessarily define, however, is the personal backdrops of the locals, who range from antigovernment hermits to dot-com millionaires to strung-out metalheads.

Across these different groups, outdoor recreation is the dominant religion, with recreational drug use and outdoor drug use not far behind. That is not to say the populace is perpetually outside or perpetually stoned. These people need to sleep, too.

STATS & FACTS

- Truckee was known for its ice industry in the early twentieth century. The river was dammed, and workers cut blocks of ice that were shipped as far as New Orleans.

- The tree known as General Sherman in Sequoia National Park is allegedly the world's largest single organism, weighing in at an estimated 2,800,000 pounds. California has a dozen fourteeners—aka 14,000-foot peaks—second only to Colorado (fifty-three) in the lower forty-eight and far ahead of third-place Washington (two). Ten of the Golden State's twelve superlative mountains are in the Sierra Nevada.

- Volcano, now one step from a ghost town, was the site of California's first private school, theater troupe, and astronomical observatory.

- Regularly occurring earthquakes in the High Sierra cause sudden growth spurts of up to a near-instantaneous foot and a half.

- In 1986, Rosie the Ribeter set the record for longest frog jump at the annual Calaveras County Jumping Frog Jubilee near Angels Camp: twenty-one feet, five and a half inches. You get five grand if your frog beats it.

But it's easy to see why these mountains attract them. The crazy beauty of the area beckons year-round. You've got the superlative waterfalls and formations of Yosemite National Park, the highest peak in the lower forty-eight in Mount Whitney in Sequoia National Park, the idyllic blue waters of Lake Tahoe, and, come winter, a white frosting of snow and a phalanx of ski resorts atop this mountainous cake.

It's amazing how easy it is to find yourself absolutely lost in the woods in the afternoon out here after leaving the city in the morning. It would probably also help if you smoked less dope and brought a map.

BIG THINGS AND OTHER ROAD ART

(Big roadside kitsch doesn't fare too well in the face of much bigger roadside mountains, but I'll give it a shot nonetheless.)

Dr. Kenneth Fox's Giant Statues
Scattered around Auburn

Local dentist Kenneth Fox has a deft hand not only with teeth but with concrete. He's populated his town of Auburn with gigantic statues of historical stereotypes (Native Americans, Chinese railroad workers, and miners) as well as an enormous Amazonian archer that is forty-two feet tall and weighs more than 100 tons—and is topless.

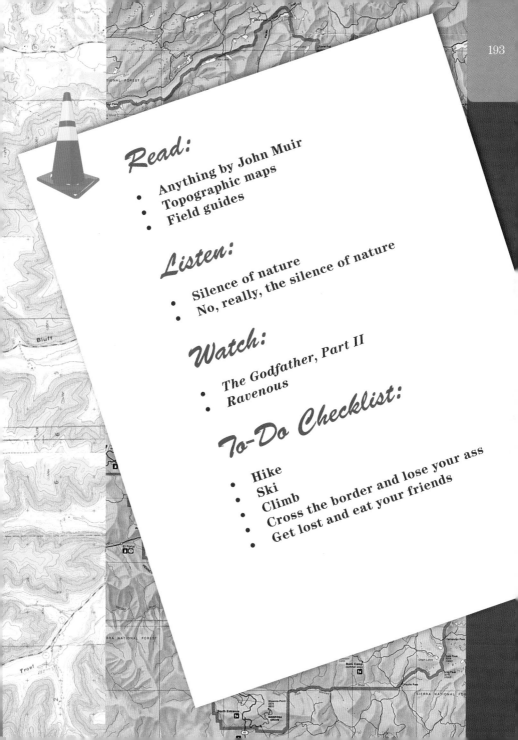

Read:

- Anything by John Muir
- Topographic maps
- Field guides

Listen:

- Silence of nature
- No, really, the silence of nature

Watch:

- The Godfather, Part II
- Ravenous

To-Do Checklist:

- Hike
- Ski
- Climb
- Cross the border and lose your ass
- Get lost and eat your friends

Vikingsholm

Emerald Bay, Lake Tahoe (Tours available in summer only)
www.vikingsholm.org

A Christian Scientist from Illinois who helped finance
Charles Lindbergh's first transatlantic flight, Lora Knight is
perhaps best known for her castle of a summer home on the
shore of Lake Tahoe. During the summer of 1929, 200 very
skilled workers built the hidden castle based on medieval
Scandinavian castles and churches, complete with a snarling
dragon and a sod roof. Knight, who was not of Scandinavian
descent, thought that Emerald Bay resembled a Norwegian
fjord. Best of all, the castle is not mixed in with the strip
malls and motels lining the main routes around the lake—it's
accessible only by hiking two miles of trail.

R.I.P.

Donner Party, born in the late eighteenth and early to mid-nineteenth centuries, died the winter of 1846–1847
Donner Memorial State Park, Truckee

The sadly misguided Donner Party left the East for California in 1846 and followed some seriously bad advice in a guidebook.

Lansford Hastings's *An Emigrants' Guide to Oregon and California* recommended a route that went south of the Great Salt Lake instead of the traditional northern route, claiming it saved 350 miles. A mountain man warned that the party should stay on the main road, but the Donner patriarchs took the guidebook's advice nonetheless.

The route was not easier and proved an exhausting waste of time, making the party the last California-bound group east of the Sierra Nevada when an early winter rolled in. And it kept on rolling, to the tune of twenty-two feet of snow—the worst winter of the century. The ill-equipped Donner Party ended up in a camp just east of where the city of Truckee is now. Back then, there was nothing except a few leftover shacks.

At first they ate the starved oxen. Then they ate nothing. Then some of them died. Sadly, hunger drove the survivors to the desperate act of cannibalism.

And then people started acting weird, evil even, most notably one Lewis Keseberg, who chose to keep eating one of his dead comrades even after the snow melted to reveal frozen oxen carcasses. He never lived that down.

Survivor Virginia Reed later advised the readers of her memoir to "never take no cutoffs and hurry home as fast as you can."

The moral of the story: don't trust guidebooks.

STAR MAPS

- Charlie Chaplin's *Gold Rush* was filmed in Soda Springs, and cast and crew stayed at the River Street Inn in Truckee.

- With Mount Whitney's peak looming above, the Alabama Hills, a craggy landscape in the Owens Valley in the eastern Sierra Nevada, provided a suitably western location for such Westerns as TV's *The Lone Ranger* and the silver screen's *How the West Was Won* as well as the non-Westerns *Tremors* and *Gladiator.*

- Trekkies take note: William Shatner owns a vacation home in Three Rivers.

VICE

Iron Door Saloon
18761 Main St., Groveland
209-962-8904
www.iron-door-saloon.com

The oldest bar in all of California and looking the part, the Iron Door was built out of granite in the 1850s and got started in the booze biz in 1896. The ceiling is covered with dollars, the walls are clad in random bullet holes and photographs of John Muir and a tribute to Black Bart, and there are also the massive iron doors from which the bar takes its name. As the story goes, the near-impervious entrance gates were manufactured in England and installed here for fire safety: if Groveland caught fire, the plan was to seal the place shut and wait the inferno out.

Tourist Club

10010 Donner Pass Rd., Truckee
530-587-7775

If you want to get down and dirty and drunk, and mingle with the locals, this is the timeworn and beerworn place to go. The T-Club was formerly the Truckee post office, but replaced mail with booze in 1954. It has great happy hours and outlandishly cheap specials—take Tuesday nights: drinks are merely fifty cents at 9 PM, then the price ticks up fifty cents every half hour until last call or the bar overflows with puke.

Cottonwood

10142 Rue Hilltop, Truckee
530-587-5711
www.cottonwoodrestaurant.com

What began as the nation's first mechanized ski resort is now home to a lively eatery and watering hole perched above downtown Truckee. Born in 1928 as a warming hut made out of abandoned railroad ties, the Hilltop soon installed rope tows and eventually a Poma lift—powered by an old car—that hauled skiers up the hill until 1969. It sat vacant for almost twenty years until it reopened in 1988 as the Cottonwood, an upscale restaurant and Friday night hot spot featuring acoustic music and a bustling bar.

HUH?

Pink Snow
Scattered around the High Sierra in summertime

Better than yellow snow but still not recommended for human consumption, the pink snow phenomenon has nothing to do with fairy dust or California drug culture. It is in fact alive with microscopic algae known to biologists as *Chlamydomonas nivalis,* often mixed up with the pollen from whitebark pine. The pink—also called watermelon—snow owes its color to a pigment not unlike that found in either flamingos or tomatoes. Just be thankful the Sierra's summer snow is not infested with snow worms, or worse yet snow fleas.

Rocking Stone
Spring St. and Keiser Ave., Truckee

Either a natural miracle or an ancient altar, Truckee's Rocking Stone was discovered by early white settlers who were mystified by this seemingly random boulder firmly sitting above what is now downtown Truckee but more than willing to sway at the touch of a finger. While it remains a mystery exactly how it became so perfectly perched, the two most popular hypotheses are glacier or ancient tribe, which could possibly have moved it to form a temple. As one of only twenty-five such stones in the world, the unique boulder became an oddball tourist attraction after its discovery, is sheltered by a small tower, and even hosted the Olympic

torch for a night in 1960. But sadly, the stone rocks no more. It was shored up with cement to protect it from (a) vandalism, and (b) becoming a rolling seventeen-ton stone careening into, say, a bar, boutique, or barbershop in unwitting downtown Truckee.

Tessie
Allegedly somewhere below the blue surface of Lake Tahoe

Perhaps fact but probably fiction, California's own Loch Ness Monster is known as Tahoe Tessie. Paiute legend described a sixty-foot sea creature, and sightings still occur regularly today. Naysayers argue that such reports of USOs (unidentified swimming objects) are merely the result of light diffusing through waves on the lake or perhaps humongous sturgeon. Nonetheless, there are rumors Jacques Cousteau explored the lake's depths and said, "The world is not yet ready for what is down there," in turn setting off rumors of a Tessie or herd of Tessies or a mob graveyard perfectly preserved by the icy depths, but my research indicates otherwise. There is no evidence Cousteau ever explored the lake, let alone made such a foreboding statement.

GRUB

Loomis Eggplant Festival
Loomis
916-652-7252
www.loomischamber.com

This annual event in early October celebrates regional agricultural heritage through a beautiful purple crop that sadly does not grow in the area. (Apparently all of the appropriate locally grown fruit crops were already taken by other festivals when the town incorporated in 1984.) Nonetheless, if you like eggplants, this is fucking Mardi Gras. Eggplant cuisine runs the gamut from the traditional eggplant Parmesan and eggplant pizza to more unusual fare like eggplant waffles, eggplant tacos, and, of course, eggplant ice cream and eggplant syrup. There's also eggplant merch and eggplant racing (aka the Egganapolis 500).

Whoa Nellie Deli

Tioga Gas Mart, Hwy. 120 and I-395, Lee Vining
760-647-1088

Gas station food rarely generates much of a Pavlovian response in my salivary glands, but this is the exception. I can think of only a few places in the West I'd rather eat, and none of them sells gas, although the H&H Coffee Shop and Car Wash in El Paso, Texas, is a close second. But Chef Matt Toomey—who summers here but winters in nearby ski burg Mammoth Lakes—is a master of filling a plate with flavor, color, and sheer mass. Some of the finer delicacies include the likes of St. Louis–style barbecued ribs with huckleberry sauce, mango margaritas, lobster taquitos, and pork tenderloin with apricot–wild berry glacé—not to mention the "insane soup of the day." The plates are perfect post-hiking fare, full of greens and fruit and side dishes, and the counter service and Formica tables mean you won't be out of place, even if you haven't showered since Tuesday.

Squeeze In

10060 Donner Pass Rd., Truckee
530-587-9814
www.squeezein.com

Sure, there are other places with a bunch of shit hanging on the walls, and there are other places that let patrons graffiti whatever they want on the walls, but the Squeeze In is the only restaurant I've seen where you can hang a framed photo of yourself—or pretty much anything, within reason—on the wall. Oh, and the place also makes some of the best breakfasts in the Sierra, including sixty different omelets.

SLEEPS

Yosemite Bug
6979 Hwy. 140, Midpines
866-826-7108
www.yosemitebug.com

While it isn't even in Yosemite National Park, the Yosemite Bug is one of the smartest, funkiest, and all-around best lodging establishments in the state. I even like staying at the Yosemite Bug more than I like staying in Yosemite Valley— I prefer my majestic natural beauty without the Disneyland-style crowds.

The Bug is the perfect antidote to the overbuilt valley in that it feels like everything perfectly fits. From the swimming hole to the web of walkways connecting the facilities, the Bug subtly perches on what basically amounts to a forested mountainside. This arrangement makes for an invigorating walk from the restaurant/gathering place/lobby to the parking lot above, but it also makes for a development that's organic to the landscape.

Rooms range from hostel bunks to themed private rooms, including a psychedelic one.

The Bug Café is an award winner and a local favorite. Its grub is pretty satisfying for the money (example: a chili-rubbed chicken breast with a side of buttered garbanzos and carrots for around $8), and the beer is cheap, too; amazing, considering the lack of booze-peddling competition in these parts.

And at the base of the hill, there's that swimming hole, fed by its own miniature waterfall, looking just like paradise on a hot summer day.

Other Sierra Picks

Beyond the Bug, my other Yosemite picks are the isolated, idyllic Sunset Inn (33569 Harden Flat Rd., Groveland,

888-962-4360, www.sunsetinn-yosemitecabins.com); the historic Evergreen Lodge (33160 Evergreen Rd., 800-935-6343, www.evergreenlodge.com), recently renovated and updated into a great cabin resort; and my tent and sleeping bag in the Yosemite backcountry.

In the Sequoia/Kings Canyon area, I love the Lake Elowin Resort (Dineley Dr., Three Rivers, 559-561-3460, www.lake-elowin.com), a funky, extremely laid-back cabin resort centered on the dinky lake of the same name, with a swimming hole on the Kaweah River to boot.

Truckee

When it comes to skiing Tahoe, I'll take Truckee over any of the lakeside resort towns. The former rough-and-tumble ice-cutting and mining town is now a rough-and-tumble skiing and partying town with a wild, historic core. The main drag is festooned with rowdy bars and plenty of local color, plus you're still within easy striking distance of the slopes. Plus, it's more affordable than the overbuilt, overpriced lakeshore. My pick: the River Street Inn (10009 E. River St., 530-550-9290, www.riverstreetinntruckee.com), a onetime ice-cutter bunkhouse turned slick-but-unpretentious B&B.

MISC.

Mono Lake
East of Lee Vining
www.monolake.org

In *Roughing It*, Mark Twain described this alkaline, hyper-saline lake just east of Yosemite National Park as the "lonely tenant of the loneliest spot on Earth," and little has changed in the century and a half since. It's still as salty and beloved by flies as ever, and there are still two major islands in its waters. But Twain would be struck by an ominous difference: the tendrils of tufa—unusual rocks that slowly formed over thousands of millennia due to the lake's unusually high levels of calcium—that were exposed in the 1940s as Los Angeles siphoned off some of the lake for its drinking water. The lake received legal protection in 1994 and the water level has steadily risen since, but it still remains about thirty feet below its historic highs. Thus the gnarly rock tentacles remain. At least the nesting birds seem to like them.

The Wildlands

Yosemite National Park
Seventy miles north of Fresno
209-372-0200
www.nps.gov/yose

Sequoia and Kings Canyon National Parks
Forty-six miles east of Visalia
559-565-3341
www.nps.gov/sequ

Ansel Adams and John Muir Wilderness
Located between Yosemite and Sequoia/Kings Canyon
559-297-0532
www.fs.fed.us/r5/sierra

I love Yosemite National Park, but it's just not meant to be explored by car. The roads in the valley become a congested mess come summertime, and there are too many campgrounds, too

many hotels, and just too many damn people. I go to the woods to get away from it all. That's why I prefer to explore Yosemite by boot. Same goes for the adjacent Sequoia and Kings Canyon national parks to the south, tethered to Yosemite by the 211-mile John Muir Trail. Then there's a great swath of remarkable—and remarkably empty—backcountry between the parks in the Ansel Adams and John Muir Wildernesses. Between all five of these federal properties, there are some 2.4 million acres, more than 2,000 miles of hiking trails, and more than a lifetime's worth of places to explore.

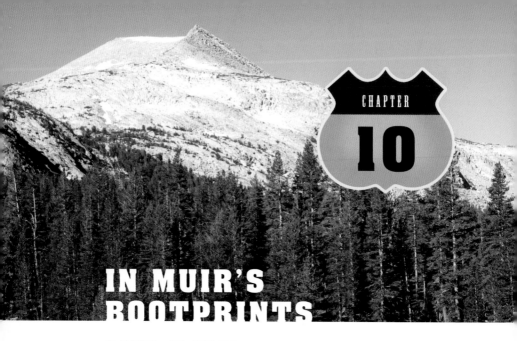

IN MUIR'S BOOTPRINTS

3 DAYS, 30 MILES, 6,000 FEET IN ELEVATION GAIN

> "The clearest way to the universe is
> through a forest wilderness."
>
> —John Muir (aka Father of the National Parks),
> conservationist and writer

Ditto.

I discovered Muir's writings—and his killer beard—
on a trip to Yosemite National Park some years ago and
was instantly grabbed by his vivid descriptions of nature in
action. For me, too, a good hike in the woods is a favorite
psychological getaway.

But Muir would surely be horrified by modern Yosemite,
with its traffic jams and rampant commercialism, just as
certain as he'd sue many who trash his good name. Prime
example: The Muir Lodge in Midpines rips off passersby with
billboards offering $29 rooms, only to pull the rug out by

saying the $29 rooms are gone but pricier ones are available. If you push for the lower rate—as I did in 1998—you'll get a spider-infested hellhole with a toilet that overflows when flushed. Then you go pay another $30 for the better room.

In the name of the real Muir—well, the Muir I personally imagine to be real—I'm going looking for the universe in a forest wilderness.

The centerpiece of my trip to Yosemite: a three-day backpacking trip in the southeastern section of the park and the adjacent Ansel Adams Wilderness Area. I've got an ambitious plan, a thirty-six-mile, one-way trek down the John Muir Trail, a 211-mile route through the High Sierra first funded by the California legislature in 1915, a year after Muir's death. My only problem is getting back—hitchhiking?— to my car once I get out of the woods, a problem I've been contemplating as I drive around Northern California.

As a gateway to my trip to Yosemite, I stop at the John Muir National Historic Site in Martinez, his former estate northeast of San Francisco. I'm embarking on my hike the morning after next.

In the visitor center, I ask the ranger on duty about Muir's grave; the site's official website instructed visitors to ask for directions here.

She humorlessly tells me it is National Park Service policy not to disclose that information because of a parking shortage.

I badger, but she won't budge. I opt to tour Muir's home before investigating other grave-seeking options, wandering to Muir's writing room—aka his "scribble den"—then up to the oppressively hot bell tower, where I of course ring the bell.

Whose house? Muir's house.

In the attic below, a display explains Muir's warning of the "eternal battle" to protect the country's national parks. Nearly a century after his death, the war wages on.

After leaving through the turnstile, I fill my tank at the gas station across the street and ask inside about Muir's grave. The fourth person gives me decent directions. I find it and take a snapshot, then do a contemplative loop around a nearby statue memorializing the man.

A few minutes later, I find myself stuck in an East Bay traffic jam. Sometimes getting away from it all can be so difficult.

I finally get to Evergreen Lodge at 9:30 PM and find it the ideal locale for my trip to the universe to begin. After two beers with GM Joe Juskiewicz, I make it to my room for the night. I catch a spindly bug that sneaks inside. Holding it between my thumb and forefinger, I consider squishing it. Instead, I take note of its elegant anatomy and let it go outside, shutting the screen door behind it.

Joe gives me the grand tour the next morning, starting with a trip up the road to Hetch Hetchy Reservoir and a look at the dam that flooded a pristine valley to collect drinking water for San Francisco, the dam John Muir fiercely opposed and was even said to have died of a broken heart over after the dam was approved. Joe says he'd like to see them drain the reservoir and make the dam a bridge to allow for continued trail access.

I get some advice from the lodge's recreation director. He suggests a thirty-three-mile loop that ends just five miles down Tioga Road from where it

Hated Hetch Hetchy Dam

begins. It does have a doozy of
a pass on day two, I note,
and file it away in my mind
as another option.

Then I take off, spend-
ing much of the afternoon
in splendid, overdeveloped
Yosemite Valley, waiting
in line at the supermarket,
walking around the administra-
tion building, and signing my
father up with the Yosemite
Association as a Father's Day gift.
The incredible views fade into the
backdrop of everyday life.

Islands in the stream

On my way up to Tuolumne
Meadows—the prime base camp for
Yosemite's high country—I pick up a
hitchhiking backpacker named Rick. I
could well end up hitching myself if I elect to hike the John
Muir Trail to Red's Meadow, a plan I'm reconsidering.

Rick is a recent college grad, studying for his MCAT, on
vacation from his job as an ER tech in Atlanta. He says he's
been hiking the Yosemite backcountry for the better part
of the month, with a week or so to go. He's seen a ton of
the park, hiking all over the high country above Tuolumne
Meadows.

I tell him I might be hitching in a day or two and could
use the good karma.

He says he hopes it pays off. He also highly recommends the chocolate cake at the Whoa Nellie Deli at the
Tioga Gas Mart in Lee Vining.

After dropping Rick off at White Wolf Lodge, I check in
down the road at the Tuolumne Meadows Lodge, where $80
gets you a slightly stained canvas tent cabin with three marginally comfortable beds, a fireplace, and concrete floors.
After taking inventory and putting out my slightly damp tent
to dry—I'd camped out during a downpour near Crater Lake

for some unknown reason a few nights before—I hike down the Muir Trail for a few minutes and, after passing a string quartet beautifully playing in a clearing, civilization quickly fades away.

Then I return to the relatively urban lodge complex for a quick last survey of my gear before meeting my friend Kenny for dinner at the lodge.

Dinner is everything my tent isn't: a fine shrimp scampi with a spicy kick. Northern California sure does know its food.

After dinner, Kenny introduces me to the trio working the front desk who've worked at the lodge for more than fifty summers combined—and counting.

Kenny tells one of them my plans to hike thirty-five miles down the Muir Trail to Red's Meadow. I tell him I plan to scale it back, maybe hike up the pass a bit, and then retrace my steps and loop around Vogelsang—a considerably less ambitious plan.

"I don't really want to kill myself," I tell him.

Bradley smiles. *"Enjoy* your hike."

Good advice.

I sleep well without lighting my woodstove.

· · · · ·

After coffee in the lodge, I make my last-second preparations and move my car to the trailhead, just a half mile away. Per park regulations, I stow my excess food and scented toiletries in a roadside bear box. How to remember which box? I jam it in the one with the Restore Hetch Hetchy! bumper sticker.

At about 8:30 AM, I'm finally hiking, gloriously leaving the real world behind as I make my way up Lyell Canyon, a long green finger cut by the Lyell Fork of the Tuolumne River that leads the way to 11,056-foot Donohue Pass.

I take a break after five miles and recount two deer, five marmots, and eighteen people—not yet exactly away from it all. But it's an absolutely beautiful day, not a cloud in the sunny sky, a perfect green forest and a perfect blue river coursing over perfectly worn granite.

"You were right, Muir," I say aloud. "Un-fucking believable."

Imaginary Muir doesn't respond.

It's so nice out here, I think I'll push it. I settle on the recommended loop that takes me halfway to Red's Meadow on the John Muir Trail before it detours east and then north over the 12,260-foot Koip Peak Pass and east back to Tuolumne Meadows.

The trail starts to climb Donohue Pass and it gets cooler, a nice breeze wafting down from the mountaintops.

"Why'd you live in Martinez where it's so fricking hot?" I ask Imaginary Muir.

Again, he doesn't answer.

The trail slopes ever more uphill. I in response sweat. Every so often, I grab a handful of snow and mold it to crown my navy blue baseball cap, theorizing three effects: (1) The white snow reflects light much better than the dark cap; (2) The cold snow provides immediate relief to my sweltering brain; and (3) The melting snow evaporates, thus further cooling my head via heat transfer. More often than not, it falls off or melts into my eyes.

I pass several more people as I climb. I slow down. My pack weighs heavier on my shoulders.

"Damn you, Muir!" I curse between breaths, only partly in jest. I take it back when I sit at an idyllic alpine lake, set in front of a stunning mountain vista.

On the final few steps up and over Donohue Pass, I look at the trail, ornately engineered from chunks of granite. No matter how hard it is to hike a trail, it's much, much harder to build one.

I take a break at the pass and have one of my backcountry staples: a peanut butter burrito. Simple to make and perfectly full of fat and protein and sugar and salt, this dish consists of a tortilla liberally frosted in peanut butter and rolled into a cylinder. They are of prime importance in my backpacking diet because I think peanut butter has the most bang for its weight: there are 5,000 calories in one twenty-eight-ounce jar.

As I eat, a marmot loafs on a nearby rock. He may be semitrained to hang around in hopes of a Funyun or something. He gets nothing.

And there at the top of a remote pass, I find a shredded green children's balloon on a pristine length of white lace. I pick it up and put it in my pocket.

One thing is certain: I need to go farther into the woods. Crossing into the Ansel Adams Wilderness Area, I descend into the valley below with its lightly forested granite crisscrossed by crystal-clear streams.

Encountering patches of heavy mosquitoes, I make a mental note: Muir wrote lovingly of the light in the Sierras, and the water, and the trees, but never of the mosquitoes. I don't even think he mentioned them.

I try to look at them as the beauty of nature incarnate, but it doesn't hold. I must kill a thousand of them—1,001 if you count the one I swallow and cough back up.

Besides the mosquitoes, another hiker's ill strikes: blisters on my two smallest toes on my left foot. They don't hurt too badly.

Down at about 10,000 feet, I find a previously occupied campsite near a babbling brook under a spectacular collection of peaks. It's 6 PM—almost ten hours since I left my car. Time to stop.

The sky is perfectly blue, the sunlight perfectly golden. And then there are the mosquitoes.

A small bird in a tree overhead begins to squawk noisily.

Maybe he's talking to Imaginary Muir.

The brook babbles.

The bird squawks again.

Maybe he's talking to me.

He should shut up and come down for some of these tasty mosquitoes.

Loafing marmot

I ignore the shrill rant and head to the creek to refill my seventy-ounce Camelback bladder and forty-eight-ounce Nalgene using a hand-powered water purifier. It's a tedious process. I should use lighter, hassle-free iodine pills, but they turn the water brown. I know it's purely image, but I'll take the drudgery of pumping in exchange for clear water.

As the sun nears the mountainous horizon, the air and the light are brilliantly clear as well. I make dinner: one peanut butter burrito and two instant soup cups.

As I slurp one of the latter, a small deer invades my campsite and cocks its ears looking at me—another lazy animal looking for a handout.

"Hey, Bambi! Nothing for you!"

All told, I hiked about fourteen miles today, with a 2,500-foot elevation gain followed by a 1,000-foot drop. "Not bad, eh, Muir?"

No response.

I realize I have left my bear canister open. Designed to keep food and other smelly goods from the voracious and indiscriminate maws of bears, the hard plastic canister—provided by the National Park Service for $5 and a swipe of my credit card—opens and shuts with two screws that are best turned with a quarter. I hop out of my bag, into my Crocs (my in-camp backpacking footwear), and out of my tent, turn the screws tightly shut, and return to my bag, zipping the tent behind me, leaving behind a few curious mosquitoes.

Tucked in, my thought rewinds to the sage advice I'd gotten the night before—"*Enjoy* your hike"—which I've definitely followed, at least so far.

I read myself to sleep, but the night is cold and windy and my rest fitful. In the morning, the same little deer returns and eyeballs my breakfast of coffee, a granola bar, and, you guessed it, a peanut butter burrito. As I eat, a steady stream of hikers heads the opposite direction over Donohue Pass. Time to get going.

I pack my sleeping bag, pump my empty Nalgene full of water, break down my tent, reload my pack, and change

into my hiking duds. It always surprises me how much energy a backpacker must expend before even taking step one on the trail.

And after that first step, I'm soon met by pain. One of my blisters bursts and must be attended to. I stop and remove my boot and sock, swath the injured toe in moleskin (adhesive padding, for the uninitiated), and regear. It works like a charm. The pain is pretty much gone.

It makes me think that there should be a moleskinlike product for backpackers' shoulders and perhaps their hips. I make a mental note of it and file it alongside an idea from the day before (a one-piece combination tent/sleeping bag/ air mattress).

I see a marmot on my way down to Waugh Lake, a mirror of water reflecting the snow-crowned peaks above. The lake is in every way perfect until I hike to the end and find a mottled-gray concrete dam.

Waugh Lake

Next is Gem Lake, which sits just above 9,000 feet. I'm 1,000 feet below where I camped, which I've got to make up before I even start up the prime obstacle between me and the way back to my car: 12,260-foot Koip Peak Pass. As I head up the heavily forested prelude—Gem Pass—I get a tiny bit worried about the future.

But my worry subsides as the trees thin and the views—stretching all the way south to Mount Whitney—take over. I can see for literally hundreds of miles, the Sierra Nevada rising and falling in front of me to the end of the Earth.

I follow a trail around the canyon wall and onto a lush plateau and a view of the towering wall of rock behind it. Although I can't make out the trail, somewhere it goes up and over the seemingly sheer mountain slope.

On the plateau is the crystalline series of Alger Lakes. I take one last lakeside break and refill my water before tackling the pass.

This is seriously wild country up here. I haven't seen a human since I broke camp. On the plateau, there are gnats on the shoreline, fish teeming in the water, a scene of bloody feathers on the trail.

Nalgene full, I put my pack back on and calmly continue on the level terrain. The mountains loom higher and higher as I approach. I lose the trail and am soon wandering up a grassy bluff speckled with glacial granite.

Finally, a set of daunting switchbacks come into focus, almost invisible amidst the shards of rock that make up the surrounding surface.

Then I'm on the mountain, toiling my way skyward, step by step by step.

Huffing and puffing, I'm forced to take a break and remind myself every so often, "I'm *enjoying* my hike."

On one of my breathers, I shout, "Can you hear me, Muir?" The echo is the only response.

The higher I go, the better my view of the Sierra Nevada. I *enjoy* the amazing landscape in front of me on each and every one of my breaks, but it's hard to appreciate it while on the move.

I lose count of how many switchbacks I've trudged up at nine. There are certainly many more than that, but my steadily increasing respiration is temporarily commanding my brain's share of my blood.

It's no cakewalk, but I make it through a couple of snowy patches and up to the rocky saddle separating the route up from the route down. About 3,200 feet above Gem Lake, there is an entirely new view in front of me, one of rocky canyons and waterfalls and—in the distance—Mono Lake.

And the route down looks even more intense than the route up, a dizzyingly steep and tight squiggle of switchbacks dropping 1,000 feet over the course of less than a mile of trail.

Boot portrait atop Koip Peak Pass

I make myself another peanut butter burrito. I'm really getting sick of these things. I also eat my last three apricots. One more day out here and I'll be eating peanut butter with a spoon. But I still have some soups and ramen in store for dinner, plus a can of chunked pineapple I've been saving for a special occasion.

Then I begin my descent. It's not as bad as I thought it would be—the tight switchbacks are actually quite level in places—but it takes forever. Again and again, I think I see the final switchback on the slope below, but there are five more, ten more, a seemingly endless squiggle down through the rocks, which clang metallically when they bounce off my boots.

My blisters, long since burst and bandaged, begin to hurt again. The alpine meadow, blissfully level, beckons below. Long downhill stretches are actually more treacherous than long uphill ones, ankles and feet suffering in place of the lungs and heart.

After an interminable amount of time, I finally make it to the mouth of the meadow, which opens onto a sharp slope, the eastern front of the Sierra Nevada. I navigate a labyrinth of waterfalls and make it to a trail that leads to a grassy, pond-laden meadow still dotted with snow.

My day is done. Not only am I dead tired, but the Yosemite boundary is just ahead, and park regulations ban camping in that area. I pick a less-than-ideal spot in the open, 100 yards from a snow-rimmed pond and 11,000 feet above sea level.

I quickly set up my tent and change into my nighttime clothes. Expecting a very cold and very windy night, I make sure my tent stakes are pounded snugly into the rocky earth. The sun is setting. I covered thirteen miles—over a 3,200-foot rise—in thirteen hours. Almost out of sunlight, I pump a bottle from the pond and make two cups of soup and one more peanut butter burrito. I need sustenance in any form to regenerate into a normal human being come morning.

A frog croaks, pauses, croaks again. It amazes me that frogs can survive in this still-icy meadow more than two miles above the ocean. There are certainly plenty of bugs for them to eat.

The sun is gone. I decide to have my can of pineapple as a deserved dessert and call it a night. I pry back the tab and then start to pull, but the tab separates from the can. I think of my can opener in my backpack, but it is quickly getting cold and I am tired. I stash the pineapple with the rest of my remaining rations in the bear canister, screw it shut, and retreat to my tent an hour after pitching it, at 9 PM.

My burst blisters look pretty bad, soggy and stretched sacs of skin, and they don't smell much better.

But I definitely *enjoyed* my hike today and am glad I challenged myself with Koip Peak Pass. Tired and content, I drift into dreamland.

Waking to urinate in the middle of the night, I brace for the worst, pulling my cap snugly over my ears and slipping into my Crocs before extricating myself from my tent.

I'm shocked. It's not cold at all, nor is it windy. It's remarkably pleasant for the middle of the night at this altitude. It's strangely warm.

Peeing, I look into the sky and see everything: planets, stars, the Milky Way, the universe. It's staring right back at me.

The night sky and my consciousness briefly connect; everything is at once infinitely vast and microscopically small and I'm irrevocably at the center of it. I took a walk in the woods and somehow arrived at the doorstep of the universe.

"Muir?"

A moment passes. The frog croaks. I take it as a yes and climb back in the tent.

· · · · ·

I rise at the crack of dawn in hopes of making a quick return to civilization. My boots smell like puke, but I put them on over my now-dried blisters anyway. After a quick coffee and a granola bar, I tear down camp in record time, but don't leave until I fish out my can opener for my pineapple reward. I start hiking, immediately reentering Yosemite at sunrise.

Worth the pain

It's a beautiful hike through a forested valley, with numerous deer along the trail. It strikes me that I haven't seen another human being in more than twenty-four hours, just the trail and me. Perfect.

But soon enough I'm back in the real world, an arrival preceded by the sound of traffic on Tioga Road. The trail paralleling the road, which I thought would lead me to my car, peters out almost immediately. I'm forced to walk on the side of the road.

I stick out my thumb, modestly at first, then with more conviction. I'm summarily ignored by the first fifty cars or so—a group that includes a couple of beat-up vans and a park ranger—until a guy in a passing hatchback pulls into a turnoff ahead and waits for me to catch up. It's my karmic reward for picking up Rick three days earlier.

My ride's name is Nick, who, like Rick, is a young guy who once worked for the park concessionaire. Now he works at the Whoa Nellie Deli in Lee Vining, which, like Rick, he highly recommends.

Nick drops me off. I grab my backpack from his trunk and shake his hand and he's gone. The Hetch Hetchy sticker has been painted over on the bear locker, but my stuff remains.

I'm thoroughly dirty and know I can buy a shower at the nearby lodge for $4. After an interminable organization process—I realize my Crocs must still be in Nick's trunk, probably to his dismay when he finds them—I march toward the lodge and see the sign: Hikers can shower from noon to 4 PM. Damn it. It's only 10 AM. There's only one place I can go: the Whoa Nellie Deli in Lee Vining.

I pour water on my head and change shirts and make a general spectacle of myself in the lodge parking lot. An official-looking vehicle with government plates circles by.

But I make it to Lee Vining without incident—aside from a final aftershock of being truly back in the real world. I shake it off and make my way to the front of the line at the deli. I'm blown away by the selection, but spare no expense and settle on the lobster taquitos and a large drink, pink lemonade.

The taquitos are truly mind-blowing, topped with salsa verde, served in a vivid presentation with huge heaps of fruit and salad and slaw. It's one of the best meals I've had in a long time and the perfect antidote to the peanut butter

burrito. I finish the last scraps of salad, slurp down some pink lemonade, and linger, looking forward to a shower and a beer in a few hours at the Yosemite Bug.

As good as the universe is, civilization has its merits.

Where to go...

John Muir National Historic Site
4202 Alhambra Ave., Martinez
925-228-8860
www.nps.gov/jomu

John Muir's Grave
East end of Strenzel Ln.,
Martinez

Evergreen Lodge
Evergreen Rd.,
just outside the east
Yosemite entrance
209-379-2606
www.evergreenlodge.com

Yosemite National Park
209-372-0200
www.nps.gov/yose

Tuolumne Meadows Lodge
Tuolumne Meadows,
Yosemite National Park
Tioga Rd., near the park's eastern
entrance on Hwy. 120
801-559-4884 (reservations)
www.yosemitepark.com

Ansel Adams Wilderness Area
559-297-0706
www.fs.fed.us/r5/sierra

Whoa Nellie Deli
Tioga Gas Mart, Hwy. 120 and I-395,
Lee Vining
760-647-1088

Yosemite Bug
6979 Hwy. 140, Midpines
866-826-7108
www.yosemitebug.com

THE CALIFORNIA DESERT

INTRODUCTION

The hot, dry Mojave Desert and the hotter, drier Colorado Desert represent a huge swath of more or less uninhabitable real estate in southeast California. Thanks to real-estate scams and air conditioning and sheer antisocial will, however, people do live out here, desert rats lost in the sun and the sand and the cacti and the junked appliances.

The harsh and rugged environment attracts artists, misfits, and outlaws in equal numbers, and at least as many outlaw misfit artists as anything else—and then you have Palm Springs. Here you have a fairly even mix of gays and retirees and golfers, if you don't allow for the statistical overlap.

Such little oases of sprinkled green grass and drag queens at piano pars and rusting trucks and mountains of trash alongside double-wides are the exception to the rule, of course. This is scorched Earth, salty with the remnants of a once-vast sea, and beautiful only in its utter and complete bleakness. In that regard, however, it's hypnotically beautiful.

This is a place where one of the great natural treasures is called Death Valley, and if that's not alarming enough, the second-lowest valley on the continent is just a Joshua tree forest and a couple of rocky swells away. No national park like its northern cousin, this valley is instead filled with the accidentally reborn hypersalty waters of the Salton Sea, born thanks to an engineering error a century ago and polluted by agricultural runoff in the time since. And just somehow it's one of the most productive fisheries anywhere.

The toughest, most hard-core specimens call the California desert home. Chuckwallas and coyotes and desert pupfish and all sorts of life, humans included, remind you that Los Angeles is artifice sandwiched between two vast seas, one with water and one without, and this sea of dry land is more alive than it first appears. Which is not alive at all.

STATS & FACTS

- The Mojave Desert is 25,000 square miles—larger than the five smallest states combined.

- Long since retired from his career acting in Tarzan movies alongside Johnny Weissmuller, Cheeta the chimpanzee lives at an ape retirement home in Palm Springs. At press time, he is the world's oldest living chimp. He was born in 1932.

- Bob Hope was appointed honorary mayor of Palm Springs in the 1950s.

- Mojave Air and Space Port is the only private airport in the United States with an official commercial spaceflight license.

So Death Valley is something of a misnomer, as long as you have water and you don't drink the poisonous water that is the only water anywhere for miles and miles and miles, as far as the eye can see, shimmering under the totalitarian sun...salty, toxic, poisonous oh-so-sweet water! So it's not a total misnomer either.

But it's easy to see the attraction for all of the desert rats, the artists, the misfits, the retired gay golfers, and the guy with ten smashed TVs and a plastic jungle gym in his chain-linked half-acre. A different energy, a certain neuro-psycho-magical-electromagnetic current pulses around here, and if you tune into it, there's no place else you'd want to be. At least until it's summer again.

BIG THINGS AND OTHER ROAD ART

World's Largest Thermometer
I-15, exit 246, Baker

The heat in the California desert can be downright demoralizing. I guess it's always been that way: places get names like Death Valley for a reason.

The lowest spot in the Western Hemisphere—bottoming out at 282 feet below sea level—Death Valley saw its sizzle hit a North American record of 134 degrees Fahrenheit back on July 10, 1913.

About three-quarters of a century later, Willis Herron, one of the proprietors of the Bun Boy Restaurant in the parched little town of Baker, brainstormed for a way to kick-start the local economy and came up with a sixty-foot thermometer. Somebody mentioned that it should be 134 feet, in honor of that horrific day back in 1913. Herron was happy to oblige and refused to listen to his family's pleas for a beach house as he sunk $700,000 into the monster thermometer, lit with almost 5,000 bulbs on three sides to reflect the current temperature.

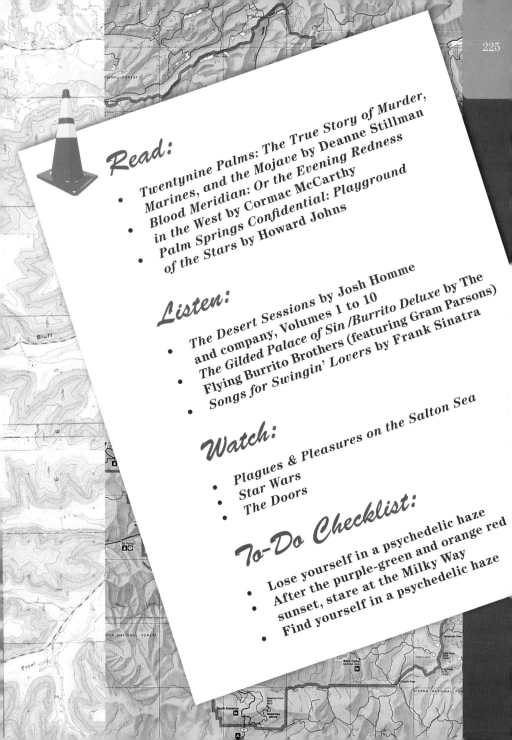

Read:

- Twentynine Palms: The True Story of Murder, Marines, and the Mojave by Deanne Stillman
- Blood Meridian: Or the Evening Redness in the West by Cormac McCarthy
- Palm Springs Confidential: Playground of the Stars by Howard Johns

Listen:

- The Desert Sessions by Josh Homme and company, Volumes 1 to 10
- The Gilded Palace of Sin /Burrito Deluxe by The Flying Burrito Brothers (featuring Gram Parsons)
- Songs for Swingin' Lovers by Frank Sinatra

Watch:

- Plagues & Pleasures on the Salton Sea
- Star Wars
- The Doors

To-Do Checklist:

- Lose yourself in a psychedelic haze
- After the purple-green and orange red sunset, stare at the Milky Way
- Find yourself in a psychedelic haze

Easily the world's largest thermometer—and only seventeen feet shorter than the Statue of Liberty—Baker's claim to fame did indeed give the town's tourist trade a nice boost when it went up in 1991. It remains the best man-made photo op in the California desert.

Noah Purifoy Outdoor Desert Art Museum
63015-63030 Blair Ln., Joshua Tree (Visits by appointment only)
www.noahpurifoy.com

Noah Purifoy's canvas was the desert, and his medium humanity's debris, detritus, and junk. The late Purifoy personified the outsider artist, working on the fringes of the scene on the fringes of civilization, creating sculptural statements both whimsical and political from toilets and bicycles and vacuum cleaners, the end result being a hybrid of collage, found art, and installation art. After growing up in Alabama and coming of artistic age in Watts in the crucible of the 1960s, Purifoy moved to the desert in 1989 and filled this two-and-a-half-acre piece of land with a Rube Goldberg–like maze of junk recycled as thought (or maybe thought recycled as junk). And while the climate out here can be forgiving, it's not totally forgiving. Purifoy passed away in 2004, and the extreme summers make preservation an uphill battle. As Noah probably would have wanted, his alternately haunting and hilarious work is slowly becoming one with the surrounding desert, but a remarkable site as it does just that.

Felicity: The Center of the World
Just west of the California-Arizona border
760-572-0100
www.felicityusa.com

Sure, the exact location of the center of the world is subjective, at least if you believe it's on the Earth's surface. And just how subjective—and random— Felicity's center-of-the-world status is will likely surprise you. It seems a man named JAI wrote a children's book named *COE the Good Dragon at*

the Center of the World, and in the book the center of the world was in a pyramid in the desert, as was suggested by said author's wife, Felicity. So JAI took it upon himself to build a real pyramid in a town of his own creation, named for his wife. JAI, of course, was mayor of Felicity.

The precise center of the world is located on a plaque inside the pyramid, which appropriately is located in Center of the World Plaza. Felicity also is home to a spiral staircase that was an original fixture on the Eiffel Tower and a three-dimensional bronze rendering of the arm of God from Michelangelo's mural on the ceiling of the Sistine Chapel, pointing to a church on a nearby hill.

Besides naming his town after his wife, JAI also commissioned a French firm to come up with Felicity perfume. So, besides the whole center-of-the-world thing, she's also got that going for her.

Salvation Mountain
Slab City, east of Niland
www.salvationmountain-site.com

In 1984, Leonard Knight's old Chevy dump truck broke down near the Salton Sea on a former military base now populated by snowbirds and squatters and known as Slab City. "I was going to stay one week," he explains. "Twenty-four years and 180,000 gallons of paint later, I'm still here." Knight's one-man folk-art masterstroke is a mountain that looks like a Christian-themed cake frosted in Day-Glo frosting. But Salvation Mountain is made almost entirely of homemade adobe and objects he found in the desert, such as trees, tires, and car doors—and plenty of donated paint. A Vermont native and Korean War vet, the septuagenarian Knight continues to add to his immense art project week by week, despite the fact that he sleeps in a hammock and has no electricity or running water. "It's going supergood," he says. "It's been here over twenty years and survived earthquakes and rainstorms and it's still here. I'm sold on adobe."

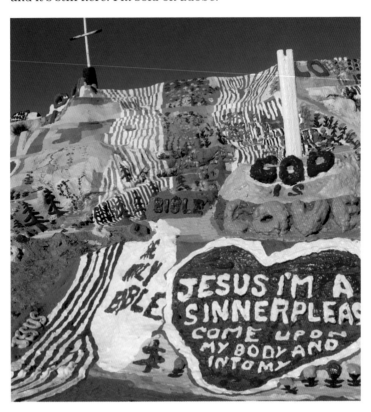

R.I.P.

Gram Parsons, 1946–1973
Cap Rock, Joshua Tree National Park

After just barely scratching his own musical surface, the alt-country godfather met his early demise from an overdose of whiskey and heroin in room 8 at the Joshua Tree Inn, just a couple of months before his twenty-seventh birthday. Then two of Parsons's friends decided he wouldn't have wanted to be buried in New Orleans, so they got drunk and snatched his coffin at the airport and hightailed it to Cap Rock in what is now Joshua Tree National Park. There they conducted an impromptu primitive cremation, dousing the wooden box with gas and setting it on fire. A massive fireball whooshed his ashes into the desert sky, and Parson's spontaneous funeral was over.

Frank Sinatra, 1915–1998
Desert Memorial Park
31705 Da Vall Rd., Cathedral City

A Palm Springs local from the 1950s until his death, Ol' Blue Eyes wasn't just a great singer or a good actor or a tough guy with a couple of goons at his beck and call—he was all of the above. Sinatra not only personified the no-bullshit entertainer, he personified the no-bullshit human. The stories and rumors run rampant, from Vegas to JFK to the Mafia to the chicks, but above all Sinatra was the baseline for American cool. And perhaps because he was more stable than Elvis but a partier on the order of Morrison, Sinatra will never lose his cool.

VICE

Ski Inn
9596 Ave. A, Bombay Beach
760-354-1285

Bombay Beach may well be the most fucked-up town in California. And it has an appropriate leader: Mayor Wacko, who spends some of his time riding around in a golf cart picking up cans with a mechanical grabber and the rest of his time hanging out at the Ski Inn, this ramshackle trailer-town's only watering hole. And appropriately, the Ski Inn is a totally fucked-up place, loaded (and I mean really loaded) with drunks and eccentrics, its ceiling plastered with oily dollar bills and faltering drywall, its ambience equal parts local color and dry rot. But the beer is really cheap and the pickled eggs aren't half bad.

Pappy and Harriet's Pioneertown Palace
53688 Pioneertown Rd., Pioneertown
760-365-5956
www.pappyandharriets.com

Hippies Use Side Door reads the joke of a sign on the woody exterior of this offbeat desert honky-tonk, but inside you'll find not only hippies but bikers and eccentrics and folkies and hipsters and just about everybody else. The atmosphere is fun, funky, and rough-and-tumble, the music is great, the barbecue addictive, and the beer cold. A favorite of Gram Parsons and countless musicians since, this is just the spot in the desert to catch a buzz and a show, and then stumble to your room at the Pioneertown Motel across the way.

Melvyn's
At the Ingleside Inn
200 W. Ramon Rd., Palm Springs

Anyplace that still touts its 1980s kudos from *Lifestyles of the Rich and Famous* on its brochure must be a little off. Especially when that place has a bar covered in tilework my mom would have envied in 1985, but not 1995, and definitely not today. But this was a former haunt of Frank Sinatra and still has a little ka-ching shazam ba-da-bing or whatnot, so it must be doing something right, $5.50 bottled beer notwithstanding. I love people-watching, and this is just the spot to watch either the bar or the dance floor or the mirror, adorned with pictures of proprietor Melvyn Baber glad-handing with Arnold Schwarzenegger and Maria Shriver, John Travolta, and Cher.

Jimmy Swaggart Prostitute Plaque
Clark's Travel Center, Historic Route 99, Indio
760-342-4776
www.clarkstravelcenter.com

The second time Jimmy Swaggart was caught red-handed with a hooker—the time he told his congregation, "The Lord told me it's flat none of your business," not the time he tearfully confessed and prayed for forgiveness—he picked his date up at this historic gas station. The proprietors commemorated the infamous 1991 event with a nice plaque.

ON THIS DATE, OCT 11, 1991, REVEREND JIMMY SWAGGART PICKED UP A "DATE" AT CLARK'S TRAVEL CENTER

STAR MAPS

The wash below Artist's Palette, a mountainside of pink, blue, orange, and red in Death Valley, is known as "R2's Arroyo," so nicknamed because of its cameo during the little droid's getaway in *Star Wars*. They also filmed the Sandcrawler scene, where Luke at first buys a droid with "a bad motivator" before getting R2-D2, near Zabriskie Point. The first glimpse of Mos Eisley, what Obi-Wan describes to Luke as "a wretched hive of scum and villainy," is from Dante's View, south of Badwater.

The first spaceport to see the launch of a privately funded spaceflight, Mojave Airport and Spaceport has had many more star turns than your average airport. Its credits include *Die Hard 2*, *Speed*, *Dragnet*, *Hot Shots*, and *Waterworld*.

Cheeta, the legendary chimpanzee actor of *Tarzan* fame, is retired and living out his golden years in a Palm Springs ape retirement center. At seventy-six, he's the world's oldest chimp (at press time). Now that he's not acting, Cheeta's hobbies include painting and playing the piano, but his handlers forced him to give up boozing and smoking more than a decade ago.

The otherworldly formations known as the Trona Pinnacles are one of the most popular sci-fi locations in cinema history, providing a backdrop for *Star Trek* movies, *Lost in Space*, and the awful *Planet of the Apes* remake.

HUH?

Integratron
2477 Belfield Blvd., Landers
760-364-3126
www.integratron.com

The father of the Integratron, George Van Tassel, was a visionary scientist, a true UFO believer, and world-class nutball.

Located in the California desert so as to take advantage of a magnetic vortex emitted by Giant Rock—touted by proud locals as the world's largest freestanding boulder—the Integratron was designed by Van Tassel as a rejuvenation chamber and a time machine. Sadly, it doesn't function properly in either regard. On the plus side, its sonic acoustics are really funky—management holds that the wooden parabola known as Integratron "delivers sound deep into cellular levels."

Check out the sound bath and soak for a half hour in the resonance of nine quartz-crystal singing bowls. The management touts the resulting "waves of peace, unbounded awareness, and relaxation of the mind and body."

Van Tassel didn't care much for the separation of church and science. He took architectural inspiration from the Bible, making the Integratron in the image of the tabernacles described in its pages. He also made much of the Integratron's geographic relationship with the Great Pyramid of Egypt. Like his plans to master time and death with the Integratron, both these correlations hold little water today.

Zzyzx

Located just inside the California-Nevada border, Zzyzx is an exit on I-15 that is overwhelmingly ignored by passing cars, and even if they do exit it's a bumpy nine miles down a dirt road until you get to the end of the road, which for all intents and purposes is the middle of unforgiving nowhere. The former site of the Zzyzx Mineral Springs and Spa and current site of the Desert Studies Center is also a haven, oddly enough, for an endangered desert chub. Curtis Howe Springer was the guy who came up with the name Zzyzx in 1944, claiming it was the last word in the English language, and he was the founder of the spa and ran it until his arrest for food and drug violations in 1974, at which point the government took hold of his property and shut down the spa. While the exact definition of Zzyzx remains uncertain, it is still the utterly final place name in terms of alphabetic order in the United States.

Singing Dunes
Kelso Dunes, Mojave National Preserve, eight miles south of the Kelso Depot

These 600-foot-tall castles of sand are not only some of the tallest in the state—and the country—but they are also some

of the most musical. More likely to break into song these days than Frank Sinatra, buried just seventy-five miles away in Cathedral City, the Kelso Dunes are not too melodious as they noisily lose a layer of sand. As I scaled the ever-shifting hills, my demand of "Sing, damn it!" never paid off.

However, the interpretive roadside marker compares the dunes' tune not to Sinatra or fellow former Palm Springer Elvis, but to the low hum of a decelerating aircraft. I don't know if I'd call that singing, but anybody who's seen a Barrys or Weird Al Qaida gig might say the same thing about me.

GRUB

The Mad Greek
72112 Baker Blvd, just off I-15, Baker
760-733-4354

The Greek kitsch can be overwhelming, a phalanx of artificial marble master-pieces and faux Mediterranean décor, but this is hands down the must-eat diner in the California desert, with mind-blowing strawberry shakes and some of the best grub in the West. A remarkably thorough menu offers Greek stalwarts alongside American standards alongside the full slate of breakfast offerings alongside those transcendent strawberry shakes, which are worth a stop by themselves.

Indio

The self-named "Date Capital of the World," Indio is a dusty and sleepy desert town with a stranglehold on the US date market: the surrounding area produces about 80 percent of the country's supply of the twisted little fruits. Home to a store and a significant retail oper-ation, the Shields Date Gardens (80-225 US I-111, 760-347-7768, www.shieldsdategarden.com) is the industry granddaddy and known for its educational plant porno, *Romance and Sex Life of the Date*. And if you're in the area in mid-February, the Riverside County Fair hosts the National Date Festival (www.datefest.org) annually.

SLEEPS

Joshua Tree

Funky yet upscale, Spin and Margie's Desert Hide-a-Way (near Joshua Tree, 760-366-9124, www.deserthideaway.com) has colorful cabins done up in high wacko-kitsch style. Joshua Tree Inn (61259 Twentynine Palms Hwy., Joshua Tree, 760-366-1188, www.joshuatreeinn.com) has been a longtime Hollywood favorite—Ackroyd and Belushi hung out here in their *SNL* daze—and the site of Gram Parsons's fateful overdose. More old-school than Parsons or Belushi, the Pioneertown Motel (5040 Curtis Rd, Pioneertown, 760-365-4879, www.pioneertownmotel.com) was Roy Rogers's home away from home. Its own oasis in the town of Twentynine Palms, with deluxe cabins and one of the best pools on the planet, the Twentynine Palms Inn (73950 Inn Ave., 29 Palms, 760-367-3505, www.29palmsinn.com) is another ideal place to crash.

Palm Springs

If retro's your bag (or at least somewhere in your bag), several of the midcentury motels and hotels in Palm Springs have been restored to their original grandeur—and beyond—and you'll be hard pressed to find more funky Art Deco places in a square mile than the downtown area. Standouts include the Del Marcos Hotel (225 W. Baristo Rd., 800-676-1214, www.delmarcoshotel.com), Orbit In (562 W. Arenas, 877-996-7248, www.orbitin.com), Caliente Tropics (411 E. Palm Canyon Dr., 800-658-6034, www.calientetropics.com), and the Rendezvous (1420 N. Indian Canyon Dr., 760-320-1178, www.palmspringsrendezvous.com)—I stayed in the "Pretty in Pink" room, just like Marilyn once did. Betty told me her ghost is frequently sighted across the pool—"If you're pure of heart."

Mojave

Funky and out of the way, Nipton (10735 Nipton Rd., 760-856-2335, www.nipton.com) is a former railroad town, former ghost town, and current B&B and cabin complex. The eco-cabins are a bit cheaper than the rooms in the old hotel. There is a cantina and a shop on-site.

Death Valley

Pickings are pretty slim in these parts. If you don't stay at one of the hotels or campgrounds in national park boundaries, try the Amargosa Opera House and Hotel (Death Valley Junction, 760-852-4441, www.amargosa-opera-house.com), a 1920s boomtown lodging turned movie theater turned mural masterwork/opera house/hotel by Marta Becket. The theater features an intricate portrait of an entire royal audience; room walls provide habitat for angels and peacocks and juggling acrobats.

MISC.

Death Valley National Park
The middle of nowhere
760-786-3200
www.nps.gov/deva

Perhaps the most extreme ecosystem on the planet, Death Valley is a misnomer: this ancient seabed is remarkably alive. A diverse array of birds, mammals, and reptiles—along with rare desert pupfish—call the park home. These creatures make do in an unforgiving environment that bottoms out at aptly named Badwater, 282 feet *below* sea level. The record high temperature in the park is 137 degrees Fahrenheit.

Uhebebe Crater is the otherworldly scar left by a relatively recent volcanic eruption, perhaps just a few hundred years ago. You can view this pockmark of the fire gods from the safety of the parking lot or hike the mile-long trail that loops around it. Better yet, scramble down the trail less taken to the bottom of the crater, a steep 500 feet below its rim.

Death Valley is ultimately so massive—3 million acres in all, bigger than Yellowstone—and so remote, that it's best to stay at one of the lodgings inside park boundaries: the regal and historic Furnace Creek Inn; the more family-oriented Furnace Creek Ranch; or the more budget-oriented Stovepipe Wells Village. For information and reservations, call 800-236-7916 or visit the websites www.furnacecreekresort.com and www.stovepipewells.com.

Joshua Tree National Park

Just south of Twentynine Palms
760-367-5500
www.nps.gov/jotr

Joshua Tree is the name of a town and a national park in California, not to mention a U2 album. The monikers are all a nod to the Joshua tree, the distinctive yuccalike plant named by Mormon pioneers after the biblical Joshua. Not surprisingly, they grow in greater numbers in Joshua Tree National Park than anywhere else on the planet and are surprisingly photogenic—for plants, anyway.

The park also marks a transition zone between two drastically different deserts: the Mojave and the Colorado. In the former, the Joshua tree dominates; the latter is known for cholla cactus and ocotillo. The line between the two, not a boundary, is a particularly vibrant ecosystem in itself, with the best of both worlds in terms of plant and animal life.

THE DESERT, MAN

5 DAYS, 500 MILES

A lizard flashes across the blacktop.

One second later and it would have been under my car when I passed. If it was an extremely unlucky lizard, it would have been under one of my tires at precisely the wrong moment.

But it safely makes it to the other side.

I'm glad I'm not an unlucky lizard.

· · · · ·

An hour later and I'm in Death Valley, enjoying a quickly warming Budweiser tall boy in the shade of a palm grove, next to a canal fed by a trickle from a white PVC pipe. The continuous flow of water from the pipe helps make Furnace Creek one of the few green motes in the vast valley.

I see a golf cart zipping along beyond another wall of palms 100 yards away. In the foreground is a colorful plastic playground. The golf cart darts between the playground and me.

Welcome to the desert. It's 109 degrees Fahrenheit in the shade.

This is where people go to define and redefine themselves. That's what Jesus did, I think. So did Jim Morrison, in this very desert.

A raven wanders from the shady canal, its beak dripping. He walks toward me until he's just twenty feet away. Another raven follows. Then they start to make out. They jump up on the adjacent picnic table and make out some more.

I'm not sure what it means. And my beer is getting quite warm.

The ravens stand there, beaks agape, one behind the other. I think they may be about to get it on. I watch and wait. Nothing happens.

Then they hop off the table back into the canal, quickly wandering out of sight.

· · · · ·

Badwater, 282 feet below sea level. I look to the rocky red crags above the Badwater Basin trying to pinpoint exactly where the ocean's surface would be, but there's no water, just dense and dry air, coursing with heat.

You can't get any lower

There is actually a little water here, the cruel joke being the various unpalatable (albeit nontoxic) salts that dominate the soil. While water pools on the valley floor here, it's no good to drink.

But there are various miniature beasties swimming in it, beasties I observe before wandering the well-worn path into the vast salt flat alone.

The heat bears down on me. The air is slightly hotter than my blood. Sweating profusely, I enter the dreamlike womb of the desert. But unlike in the womb, I have no liquid sustenance, only a camera. It's time to turn around.

Water equals life, reinforced.

I drive north to Artist's Drive and turn right onto one of the most unearthly six-mile stretches of pavement on Earth, stopping for snapshots above and below the multihued formation known as Artist's Palette. (Below is "R2's Arroyo" from *Star Wars*, where the gutsy little droid made a break for it to find Obi-Wan.)

The nearly psychedelic landscape beckons. I wander the crisscrossing network of trails, shooting snapshots in a woozy, heat-drunk haze. It feels good, different, new.

I gulp greedily at my water bottle. I remembered it this time, but forgot my sunglasses instead. Retinas poached, I make a mental note that it is check-in time at the Furnace Creek Ranch, the motel-like property—with a pool and the aforementioned golf course and air-conditioning—where I've got a room for the next two nights.

It's approaching 110 degrees Fahrenheit. The pool beckons. The landscape, savage and strange, has overpowered me.

I retreat from the desert to the artificial.

. . . . .

Checking in, I note a sign on the lobby wall: "This facility contains chemicals known by the State of California to cause cancer and birth defects."

Maybe I was better off in Badwater.

The lure of the pool remains strong, and my room is an entirely different facility, presumably free of carcinogens, so I get my room key, park my car, and unpack a few bags before changing into my trunks.

Fed by a natural hot spring, the pool is probably pushing 90 degrees, but it feels cool, a divine contrast to the oven nearly everywhere else.

Floating there, staring at the dancing spiderwebs of light on the pool's bottom, a new feeling overcomes me, not the woozy, weird danger of the untethered foray into the reality of the desert, no, the near opposite: the serene and placid bliss of water.

It's hard to find my center, however, amidst the chatter of German tourists and San Berdoo bikers and midwestern families, each squawking their own unique brands of conversation. Particularly disconcerting, a mother keeps yelling my name—"Eric!"—at her misbehaving son.

I trade the pool for the air-conditioned cocoon of my room, tired but quickly bored by the synthetically cooled opposite of the big bad desert outside. I leaf through the official Death Valley National Park newspaper and map I received upon entry, taking special note of the Racetrack, a remote basin where rocks mysteriously move on their own.

The last of an ancient sea

I need to know more.

"You don't need real high clearance," a park ranger tells me about the twenty-eight-mile unpaved road to the Racetrack, "but there are some real sharp rocks out there." He recounts a story from the week before about the park's superintendent getting stranded out there after losing two tires while taking a couple of congressmen on a tour.

I buy a book, *Strolling Stones: The Mystery of Death Valley's Racetrack*, instead of risking the Saturn's flimsy Firestones, then go on a hike in nearby Golden Canyon as sundown approaches.

The possibility of heatstroke be damned, I hike a mile up the canyon and scramble up to the base of the Red Cathedral, a wall of blood red rock spires that indeed resemble some sort of postapocalyptic house of worship. After a quick rest, my warm blood, abuzz with endorphins, feels increasingly good on the much cooler descent.

"What an amazing study in geology," says a sweating hiker passing me on his way up.

"And climate," I retort.

His laughter echoes off the canyon walls. I feel even better.

But my brain, devoid of some mineral I've presumably sweated out, aches slightly. Back in my room, I try to pacify it with a banana, crackers, and a peanut butter sandwich, then a twenty-four-ounce Tecate on the patio, then *Strolling Stones*.

Down that rock-fanged road, it seems there is a basin about three square miles in area where stones—sometimes weighing more than a half a ton—mysteriously move about, leaving tracks behind in the mud. Some say the phenomenon is a result of slick winter ice and wind. Others say it's mud and slimy cyanobacteria on the stones' undersides. Yet others claim the rocks move in concert with experiments at nearby Area 51 in Nevada.

Some of the strolling stones have jitterbugged thousands of feet over the years, but nobody has seen any of them move even an inch, so their velocity is a great big unknown, like a tree falling in the vacant woods.

It's not even 8 PM. I contemplate the pool, the bar, and then the bed. My mind sluggish and sore, I fall asleep watching TV very soon thereafter.

· · · · ·

Even rocks cast long shadows at dawn

My early night makes for an early morning. A coyote trots by as I leave Furnace Creek Ranch around 6:30 AM. As I drive north to the mouth of Titus Canyon for a hike before the heat returns, the panorama of Death Valley unfolds, unforgiving terrain streaked with red and bordered by hostile-looking peaks. A quote from a nineteenth-century visitor cycles into my consciousness: "Before us lays a splendid scene of grand desolation."

I'm at the trailhead by 7:30. Before departing up the canyon, I scare a little lizard into the restroom as I enter, and it cowers next to the pit toilet as I pee. I shoo it out because I wouldn't want it to be trapped in the outhouse, a fate only marginally better than those unfortunate lizards that select the absolute worst time to cross the road.

Do not do as the silhouette does

It's cool and exceedingly quiet in the shady canyon. The last drops of my dull headache finally evaporate as my heart rate increases. The beautifully bleak canyon trail climbs uphill, shades of red and blond and brown punctuated by occasional splashes of green and wildflowers. Only a few small birds make their presence known.

"I'm nobody," I mumble to myself absentmindedly. "I'm everybody."

After this offhand remark rises from my subconscious, I think to my somewhat contrived mission of defining and/or redefining myself in the desert. Human, check. Male, check. Writer. Hiker. Thinker. Animal lover.

I get to a shady outcropping and see several vultures lazily soaring above, cutting perfect circles into the clear blue sky. I left my watch in the car, but water is far more important than time here, and my water is half gone. Time to turn back.

On the way down, I make an attempt at self-redefinition. I want to be a better person. I don't want to be complicit in destroying the planet. I'm not sure exactly how to accomplish either off the top of my head. Nonetheless, once again, I feel really, really good.

My next stop is Scotty's Castle on the northern fringes of the park. The impressive Mediterranean-inspired mansion was named by Walter Scott, aka Death Valley Scotty, himself an intriguing study in California desert self-definition/redefinition. The $11 tour proves both entertaining and enlightening.

A former performer with Buffalo Bill's Wild West show, Scotty landed in Death Valley just after the turn of the twentieth century and recruited investors for a fictitious gold mine. One such investor, Albert Johnson, a Chicago insurance tycoon, bought into the project to the tune of several thousand dollars before realizing the legendary mine only existed in Scotty's fertile imagination.

Rather than forcing Scotty to pay him back (and redefine himself as a fraud or a felon in the process), Johnson found the man to be such a likeable and funny con artist that he enabled Scotty to build on his crazy self-definition. Johnson built the castle as a vacation home, but he had absolutely no problem with Scotty telling visitors that it was his castle, and that he built it with the riches from his gold mine, and that the mine was directly below the castle itself.

So it went that Scotty defined himself as a mining baron instead of a con man, perhaps because he helped sickly insurance magnate Johnson redefine himself as a western adventurer. A mining center then supporting several now-abandoned towns, Death Valley proved an ideal setting for both men's malleable identities.

After the tour and a short hike to Scotty's grave on the hill behind the castle,

Scotty's Gates

I drive a few miles to Uhebebe Crater. Geologists once held that this volcanic pockmark in the desert, a half mile across and 500 feet deep, was the result of an eruption about 2,000 years ago, but lately they've changed that estimate to merely 300 years ago, a relative blink of an eye in Earth time.

The hot wind howling, I hike the trail around the equally stunning and ghastly crater, and then I'm thinking about descending the steep trail to the bottom.

As I contemplate the energy involved in hiking back up the trail, two ravens land by my side. I guess I have to go down. The meditative, solitary moment turns out to be well worth the sweat.

· · · · ·

My hair bristled like a mad scientist by wind and perspiration, I return to my air-conditioned room at Furnace Creek Ranch with a fresh can of Tecate, thinking of little except the pool. And it feels good again. I have a beer at the bar, dark and cool but underwhelming, and opt not to be that guy sitting alone over there in favor of another early night. Back in my room, I call my father to arrange meeting him at noon the following day and watch the Nuggets lose a playoff game.

It's a few minutes before 8 PM.

I don't need to fake it as much as I need to be me all the time.

I drift off to sleep.

· · · · ·

I'm on the road to Joshua Tree at 6:30 the next morning. Before I make a stop, I leave the confines of the valley thinking, "Good-bye, Death Valley."

As legend has it, one of the first pioneers stranded in the valley said those very words after her eventual rescue, coining the moniker that the native Timbisha Shoshone people detest to this day.

The plan is to meet my father at noon at the Integratron, about 250 miles across the Mojave Desert from Death Valley. There are more than a few lizards crossing my path en route. About an hour in, I'm pretty sure I hit one.

Before I enter the Mojave National Preserve, I stop for a photo of the World's Largest Thermometer in Baker. After I leave, I stop for a snapshot of the shoe tree in Amboy.

But for the most part I maintain my heading toward Joshua Tree and arrive at the Integratron a half hour ahead of schedule.

The unfinished domed structure is the creation of George Van Tassel, a onetime aerospace engineer who traveled to the area in the early 1950s and felt he simply must be in the desert. While running a diner at Giant Rock, Van Tassel claimed he had a close encounter with some Venusians in 1953, which lead him to create "the world's first 'time machine'"—the Integratron—nearby.

Nancy Karl, who now owns the structure with her sister and sister-in-law, tells me to go on ahead. Their weekly public sound bath will start in about thirty minutes.

On the first floor of the Integratron, I find couches, a wide range of reading material, and a scale model of the Integratron. "The UFOs are real" reads a bumper sticker on the wall. "The Air Force doesn't exist."

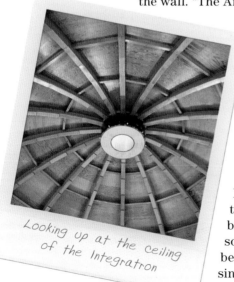

Looking up at the ceiling of the Integratron

Soon I hear my dad arrive, chatting with Nancy as he pays his fee for the sound bath. This sort of thing is definitely not a normal activity for him. He's no New Ager, and a bit of a skeptic to boot.

But he's a good sport about it. We take our place lying on our backs of the Integratron's upper floor with the half-dozen other sound bathers in attendance. Nancy soon appears and takes a seat behind a nonet of quartz-crystal singing bowls.

She first gives us a little background on the Integratron and "UFO contactee" Van Tassel, explaining how he built the wooden structure with nary a nail or screw, how its acoustical properties are unique, and how she maintains it ("a lot of caulk and paint"). Van Tassel had plans of installing electrical technology based on the work of Nikola Tesla, she explains, but he passed away before that dream came to fruition. Nancy also demonstrates its sonic properties by circling the room while speaking: her voice is loudest when she's at my mirror position on the opposite half of the circular floor.

Then she talks about the intense magnetic and electrical fields on the property, which grow even more intense in the Integratron itself. "It just amplifies whatever you bring into it," touts Nancy. "The Integratron juices up your potential."

Now it's finally time for the sound bath. I take a deep breath and look at the underside of the dome above me. The first tone rings out, startling in its resonance. It oscillates in volume and echoes around the room.

Another tone follows, then another and another. They dance, intertwining, disappearing, reappearing, shifting shapes, changing colors. I can see the sound. Or am I asleep?

I want to be more me.

After a good half hour of the bowls singing and sound-bathers bathing, Nancy starts playing a CD of relaxing music. A few minutes pass and the bathers begin to quietly get up, one by one, and descend to ground level.

"I'm sounded out," my dad whispers as he sits up.

"Me too," I answer.

Outside, we chat with Nancy and her sister at their combination souvenir stand/snack bar, featuring misters to keep patrons cool in the desert heat. They tell us how they bought the Integratron in 2000 after renting it from its previous owner for a dozen years. "Our agenda has always been preserve it, then restore it, and then share it."

I ask Nancy what she thinks of Van Tassel's theories on the power of the Integratron.

"It's certainly been proven to me," she says. "We've seen it maximize my potential. I've become a better person."

She tells us that musicians, writers, and artists often rent it out for private events. "Everybody can use it as they see fit. As long as it's positive, it's okay with me."

My dad pipes up. "I definitely felt something," he says. "I was very relaxed."

"Those sounds literally wash the nervous system," says Nancy. "You have no choice."

I still feel incredibly relaxed. Before I leave, I take Nancy's advice and return to the second floor of the Integratron, stand in the center, and talk aloud. I recite what she told me—"Your voice goes back into your body"—a number of times, and my voice indeed resonates right back into my body.

Next we drive down the bumpy dirt road to Giant Rock, where Van Tassel once operated his diner, the Come On Inn—his wife's pies were said to be outstanding—and later made contact with the Venusians. Today, there is nothing there except the world's largest freestanding boulder from which the spot earned its name. A massive chunk that fell off in 2000 sits next to it.

Fried Liver Wash

After retreating to the town of Joshua Tree, we have lunch at the bustling Crossroads Café and Tavern. I leave my car and hop in pop's Jeep for an excursion to Noah Purifoy's Outdoor Desert Art Museum, a ramshackle collection that toed the line between junk and art (i.e., assemblage art). Of course, it has been subject to the ravages of the desert climate since creator Noah Purifoy passed away in 2004, but his "art ranch" is still a relatively positive reshaping of the desert in an area where most of the houses feature a fenced yard of junk with no artistic merit.

Hello there, Joshua tree

After we leave, my dad talks about how the Joshua Tree area first emerged as a real-estate opportunity for beleaguered blue-collar types in LA when he was a kid in the 1950s. Deals for lots—"$29 down and $29 a month"—were advertised, and some individualists decided to relocate or retire here, redefining themselves in the process—in all likelihood, my dad notes, to their wives' chagrin.

We grab my car, and my dad follows me to Pioneertown, a onetime location for B-Westerns, complete with fake storefronts and two real businesses, the Pioneertown Motel and legendary BBQ joint/biker bar/music venue Pappy and Harriet's Pioneertown Palace.

We check in and drink a few beers from a six-pack my dad bought. It's a warm night, perfect for wandering the faux Main Street before enjoying dinner at Pappy and Harriet's.

The country-tinged band the Thriftstore Allstars is one of those rare acts my father and I agree on, and prove to be quite entertaining. Before it gets too late, we call it the end of a long day and wander to our rooms at the motel, mere stumbling distance away.

"This was one of the most interesting days I've had in decades," my dad says.

I'm quite glad to hear him approve of my bizarre yet intricately planned Sunday in the desert.

· · · · ·

We leave the motel early the next morning. My dad overrides my aversion to Denny's before we make our way into Joshua Tree National Park for a day of hiking and general exploration. First is a short loop hike in the heart of the Joshua tree forest—Hidden Valley—followed by a mile stroll at Barker Dam, the site of some of the only standing water in the park.

The sun shines. Birds chirp. A peaceful feeling permeates my being. I think back to the sound bath, wondering if I wasn't experiencing some lingering effects, and ask my dad if he feels anything.

"My back hasn't bothered me once since then," he says.

"How often does it normally bother you?"

"Constantly."

· · · · ·

Next we drive down the one-way road to Keys View, a hazy panorama of mountains and a number of other notable features to the south, including the visible San Andreas Fault and beyond it the blue waters of the Salton Sea. From there, we head south into an entirely different desert ecosystem for an afternoon hike amidst the cactus-speckled granite. We spot several lizards amidst the rocks, the biggest being the chuckwallas that breathe deep and inflate themselves in nooks and crevices to prevent predators from pulling them out.

The three-mile loop trail hits its highest point at Mastodon Peak, which I scamper up for a snapshot while my dad waits below. From here the Salton Sea glimmers more and more, less than twenty miles away.

From the summit, we finish the loop at the parking lot where we started and retrace our route to the north side of the park, stopping in at the visitor center in the town of Twentynine Palms for a chat with Joe Zarki, the park's chief of interpretation.

During a discussion of the park's ecological issues, my dad asks how fire affects the Joshua tree forest. Zarki tells us it's a point of debate, that historically fires occurred here only once every century or so. Lately it's been bone dry—less than an inch of rain has fallen in the past eighteen months—and the prospects of a prolonged drought loom. And nitrogen from Southern California's air pollution catalyzes the growth of exotic grasses in the park, which in turn prove ideal tinder for wildfires.

In tandem, these conditions have made for much more than one wildfire a century, Zarki says, and while Joshua trees—and piñons and junipers—might be able to survive the occasional fire, two successive fires in a short time frame are plenty capable of wiping out all three, along with a whole host of other native plant species.

"Very few desert plants are adapted to fire," he says. "With global warming, we could be looking at the end of the desert woodland ecosystem and the rise of a new grassland ecosystem."

"So instead of Joshua Tree National Park, it'll be Exotic Grassland National Park?" my dad cracks.

Zarki looks more alarmed than amused. "It's not a pretty picture for the future," he says.

Maybe it's best to not redefine yourself too radically.

After glancing at the Oasis of Mara behind the visitor center—which once was an actual oasis, but is now kept wet by plumbing—we retrieve my car from the town of Joshua Tree, fifteen

Salton Sea memories

miles away, and retreat to our room for the evening at Spin and Margie's Desert Hide-a-Way, a funky-but-chic place to stay a few miles away. We unwind for an hour or so, then go back to the Crossroads Café for dinner. Over a Reuben (my dad), a salad (me), and draft microbeer (both of us), we talk about Western movies, Mormon history, and televangelism. Another good day comes to an end.

· · · · ·

In the morning, my dad, garrulous and outgoing to his core, meets Paula from Wisconsin in the next room over and ends up giving her a ride to the airport in Palm Springs, as he's heading back to his apartment in Orange County and has time to spare. Me, I've got my final day of my California desert journey mapped out: a day exploring the shoreline of the notorious Salton Sea.

After bidding my father good-bye, I follow the same route we took to Mastodon Peak the day before and exit the park before 9 AM, crossing I-10 before taking one of the loneliest roads in the state through eerie desert badlands.

Thoughts run through my head. I want to be more like Dad in some ways. Who cares what Jesus would do, what would I do? I've already redefined myself. It's a continual process.

Likewise, the Salton Sea has constantly been defining

and redefining itself, for eons, and continues to redefine itself now. A 376-square-mile body of saltwater in an ancient seabed 235 feet below sea level, the Salton Sea is California's largest lake, but known first and foremost as an ecological disaster, mostly because it was more or less dry—in between regular floods from the Colorado River, just sixty or so miles to the east—before a burst dike created the modern sea in 1905. In the years since, polluted agricultural runoff compensated for the evaporation, algae blooms killed millions of fish, and botulism ravaged the local pelican population. The New River, said to be the country's most polluted, flows into the sea, carrying with it raw sewage from Mexico.

Against this backdrop of ecological chaos is a failed real-estate vision. In the 1950s, infrastructure for several resort areas was built up, but the increasing pollution kept homebuyers from materializing, and much of what was built was ultimately abandoned.

The result is a few seaside towns that are dominated by empty lots and dotted with rotting trailers, abandoned motels, and other unsightly abodes. In Salton City, the community hub for the few thousand people who call the area home, there are some signs of life amidst the vast vista of undeveloped real estate, its emptiness accented by street signs like "Sea Elf" and "Shore Gem" and the maze of electrical wires ready to power the houses that were never built.

I drive out to a crumbling concrete jetty and walk to its tip. The scent of rotting fish omnipresent but not overwhelming, I look across the shimmering waters and up at the mountains and find the view oddly beautiful.

To my surprise, the Salton Sea real-estate market is showing signs of life. Most of the lots near the jetty bear "For Sale" signs, but one is marked "Sold," for $150,000. I see fresh new suburban-looking homes here and there, one bearing a price tag of $229,000. It's a testament to the nutty, overheated Southern California market that you need a quarter of a million dollars to buy a four-bedroom, three-bath house with a view of the polluted sea and the stench of dead fish.

I stop at the small-but-thriving town center in Salton City, complete with a new strip mall featuring a branch of Countrywide Home Loans. In the town's only market, the line for the only cash register is a dozen customers long, snaking into the produce aisle. I wait patiently, surveying the off-kilter group and eavesdropping on the conversation of the two local middle-aged women in front of me.

"I didn't even recognize one person there," one of them says.

"And the parking lot was totally full!" the other exclaims.

These apparent longtime Salton citizens sound as if they're on the fence about the recent boom, regardless of the fact there's still hardly anybody here.

After ten minutes, I pay for my Gatorade, copy of the local *Salton Seafarer* newspaper, and a map of the area. Gulping my thirst away, I leaf through the paper, taking special note of the stories about a volunteer dead-fish cleanup and the possibility of Tesla-designed turbines powering the world with the sea's saltwater, before unfolding the map. I decide I have time to reverse course and check out the even more sparsely developed eastern shore before calling it a trip.

Salted fish anyone?

There is very little here, just a railroad, a state park with its assorted shoreline campgrounds, and great mountain views. Farther south is the Sonny Bono Salton Sea National Wildlife Refuge, an important stopover for migratory birds (including the endangered peregrine falcon). While the sea is touted as the world's most productive fishery, I only see one boat on the water all day.

Farther south still, a storm rolls in and bombards the water with lightning. The rare thunderstorm glances the road while demonstrating its equivalent potentials for starting and putting out fires. I think of the mountains of Joshua Tree slowly changing from desert forest to exotic grassland, and of this basin's shifts from sea to desert to sea again, from failed real-estate vision to the quasi boom now underway.

Above it all, the stark reality of the fish die-offs and the polluted runoff is unsettling. All things considered, I'm not too high on the local real estate.

Once again, a thought coalesces in my mind: maybe it's best not to try too hard to be something you're not.

Where to go...

Death Valley National Park
760-786-3200
www.nps.gov/deva

Furnace Creek Inn & Ranch
Death Valley
800-236-7916
www.furnacecreekresort.com

World's Largest Thermometer
Baker, I-15, exit 246

Mojave National Preserve
Barstow
760-252-6100
www.nps.gov/moja

The Integratron
2477 Belfield Blvd., Landers
760-364-3126
www.integratron.com

Crossroads Café and Tavern
61715 29 Palms Hwy., Joshua Tree
760-366-5414
www.crossroadscafeandtavern.com

Noah Purifoy's Outdoor Desert Art Museum
63015-63030 Blair Ln.,
Joshua Tree
www.noahpurifoy.com

Pioneertown
www.pioneertown.com

Pioneertown Motel
5040 Curtis Rd.,
Pioneertown
760-365-4879
www.pioneertownmotel.com

Pappy and Harriet's Pioneertown Palace
53688 Pioneertown Rd.,
Pioneertown
760-365-5956
www.pappyandharriets.com

Joshua Tree National Park
760-367-5500
www.nps.gov/jotr

**Spin and Margie's Desert
Hide-a-Way**
Near Joshua Tree
760-366-9124
www.deserthideaway.com

Salton Sea
www.saltonsea.ca.gov/thesea.htm

RAMBLE MANIFESTO

From the second I wake, the pull is strong. My soul once again demands motion. I've slept in the same bed every night for nine weeks or so, about sixty sleeps in all. It's time to go.

At some point in recent memory, I was just as ready for home as I am now ready for the road. Before this homebound stint, I'd been on the road for the better part of two months, driving from the West Texas badlands to the Rockies to Venice Beach, California. Cut to the present: I've only ventured more than fifty miles from home a couple of times in the sixty days since.

All of that stability adds up. I've been sitting too still for too long. The coffee isn't helping quell my nomadic impulses, to be sure; instead it fuels the restlessness building in the pit of my gut. Day after day, the feeling has gotten stronger and stronger and by now I've convinced myself the only cure is the road. Regardless of my diagnostic accuracy, I go through the rituals of preparation. I pack a bag of clothes, a smaller bag of toiletries, a backpack, a camera bag, and assorted other bags of various sizes.

I get up early. I load my car. I fill my travel mug with coffee. I double-check everything. I say good-bye to the dog and leave a key under the mat.

Then I go.

After a passing thought regarding the position of the coffeemaker's power switch, I recline into my new role. Roles, actually: driver, traveler, nomad. A man going on a journey, a stranger coming to town.

That first morning, that's the road trip big bang, where it all begins. What happened before departure is no longer relevant. Home and bills and jobs and everything else in the rearview mirror can wait. There is no better diversion from reality than the road.

Home is yin to the road's yang. The conceptual schism between the two is akin to that of the mind's left and right hemispheres, or that of order and chaos. You can't have one without the other. Home is static, stable, and studied—I know most every corner and get more intimate with the place as the clock ticks ahead. Surprises are few, but comforts are many. But you can get too comfortable. Such is the hazard of home.

The road, conversely, is impossible to know like home. Each bend holds the promise of the new, the unique, the unknown. Habit and routine take a backseat to the buzz of discovery, as mile markers and thoughts of all kinds punctuate the long distances driven.

You can get too precise in your daily routine. You can only gargle your name-brand mouthwash for exactly sixty seconds so many times before you want to kick the day-to-day to the curb. Waking leads to coffee leads to work to lunch to a workout or a daily application of facial cleanser or TV programming or prescription medication. Routine overwhelms everything else; you can actually feel habits cementing into timeworn modes of thought and existence that will be nearly impossible to change. Which brings us back to the relative chaos of the road. The opiate of perpetual motion can salve a soul.

It might sound like I want to take a vacation from myself. It's not entirely untrue. There is also the thought that external motion can provoke internal discovery. Life is a journey, and the road trip is a microcosmic symbol of the mortal trek toward enlightenment. Whatever.

My personal angle stems from the desire for a superlative freedom, for those intangible sensations that start in my gut and oscillate along the very center of my being. It's hard to get such primeval juices flowing from the comfort of a sofa, the gentle refrains of TV ads selling your soul into submission. But that's where these words are spilling out of my pen—a cozy dining table in a living room—as my right leg twitches, the rubber on the tip of my tennis shoe squeaking softly on the hardwood. Sure, home is nice. Home is where the heart is. Home sweet home. There's no place like home.

But there's no place like the road either. The predictability of home ultimately fuels the urge to roam. There's that burning desire to simply move. There's an allure of velocity that only velocity can placate.

There is nothing in life quite like cruising into a classic Western landscape, radio all the way up, windows all the way down, the sunshine and the beauty and the velocity! Velocity is all-important. Without movement, the road ceases to be. Velocity is the road.

The road calls, and I must listen. And why not? It beats sitting around at home all to hell.

The American road is an endless strip of neon-lit blacktop, lined with billboards, cactus, mountains, urban sprawl, toxic waste, and open space, at once desolate and inspiring and lonely and alive.

The road is also a temporary, ephemeral place. It pulses with activity with or without me, as life stories zoom by at eighty miles an hour. Motion is the norm; to move is to exist. The lack of motion is met with puzzlement and suspicion. Stopping is not a legitimate option.

I drive for hours in a meditative state. Then I think, "Well, I wonder what it's like to live here?" At some point, I realized that just about every last spot on the planet was home to somebody. It's the same old shit to somebody. What exactly the same old shit is depends on geography, but it is everywhere.

Except the road. Those fleeting periods of velocity are some of the purest feelings of freedom available. The road is just the place to get lost. And in my mind, that's a good thing.

Caffeine and long-distance driving are inseparable to me. Without coffee, it's doubtful I'd make it very far, mentally or physically. A cup of joe is the ignition for my imagination and inspiration.

I typically refill my travel mug every time I stop. If I chug sixteen ounces of coffee per tank of gas, there is very little chance I'll snooze. Between the caffeine and the sheer volume of fluid, my mind and bladder work hand in hand to keep me awake.

Another essential: music. Beauty is in the ear of the beholder, but the first rule of the road is that you can never have too much music. On a 5,000-mile journey, you could easily listen to 100 different albums and not repeat once. For those types of trips, a serious library is required. Or a well-stocked iPod.

I don't want to dawdle, but I don't want to rush either. Roadside motels are fine en route, but there better be something better at the end of the line. Greasy spoons provide sustenance, but it's best to have sandwich supplies and a steady stream of hot coffee.

Habit can evolve into a near science. Then I beg for a change, the phone to ring, an e-mail to arrive, anything...

But nothing happens. And it won't, not unless I can will it so. And the confines of routine cannot involve driving halfway across the country, unless you drive a large vehicle for a living. To make it happen, I must go.

But the wise traveler prepares. There are certain necessities. Clothes, and an organizational system for clean clothes, dirty clothes, and those clothes in between. That usually involves a large mothership bag that remains in the trunk, a satellite bag to bring toiletries and a change into motel rooms and friends' places, and a third bag for the stuff that's in need of a wash.

A full array of camping equipment is another must-have, to shave the lodging costs down and give opportunity to park the car and venture into the woods for a day or three.

Then there's the cooler, which sits in the backseat and occasionally hosts soft drinks and sandwich ingredients. Ice is kept to a minimum.

There's a backpack filled with books and notepads and pens and the like in the front seat, along with an assortment of compact discs with jazz, punk, and country songs. There's a laptop and a camera in the back.

Then there are the little things that suit one's tastes, maybe breath mints, drinking water, and marijuana...just don't get caught in the red states.

If you leave at the crack of dawn, it is an incredible feeling to rub your eyes at 9 AM and realize you are nearly 300 miles from home. It would take the pioneers weeks to make it this far. St. Louis to San Francisco was once a harrowing four-month journey. Today it's easy enough to do it in two days.

Indeed, the comfort of the couch and the mind-jelling television and the worn pathways of routine, the guaranteed paychecks and the fifteen-minute breaks, can coalesce into a prison.

APPENDIX: INFO, ETC.

State

**California Travel &
Tourism Commission**
800-862-2543
www.visitcalifornia.com

Major Convention, Visitors Bureaus, & Chambers

Los Angeles
800-228-2452
ww.discoverlosangeles.com

Anaheim/Orange County
714-465-8888
www.anaheimoc.org

Long Beach
800-452-7829
www.visitlongbeach.com

San Francisco
425-391-2000
www.sfcvb.org

Berkeley
800-847-4823
www.berkeleycvb.com

Oakland
510-839-9000
www.oaklandcvb.com

San Jose
800-726-5673
www.sanjose.org

San Diego
619-232-3101
www.sandiego.org

Sacramento
800-291-2334
www.discovergold.com

Santa Barbara
805-966-9222
www.santabarbara.com

Santa Cruz
800-833-3494
www.santacruz.org

Fresno
800-788-0836
www.fresnocvb.org

Napa Valley
707-226-7459
www.napavalley.org

Sonoma County
800-576-6662
www.sonomacounty.com

Monterey County
877-MONTEREY
www.montereyinfo.org

San Luis Obispo
800-634-1414
www.sanluisobispocounty.com

North Lake Tahoe
800-462-5196
www.gotahoenorth.com

Palm Springs
760-778-8415
www.palm-springs.org

Organizations

**California Hotel & Lodging
Association**
800-678-5780
www.calodging.com

**California Restaurant
Association**
800-765-4842
www.calrest.org

California Outdoors
(river outfitter organization)
www.caoutdoors.org

Wine Institute
(California winery organization)
www.wineinstitute.org

**California Ski Industry
Association**
415-543-7036
www.californiasnow.com

California State Parks
800-777-0369
www.parks.ca.gov

Pacific Crest Trail Association
916-349-2109
www.pcta.org

Transportation

**California Department
of Transportation**
(road conditions and closures)
800-427-7623
www.dot.ca.gov

**Los Angles
International Airport**
310-646-5252
www.lawa.org/lax

**San Francisco
International Airport**
800-435-9736 or 650-821-8211
www.flysfo.com

Amtrak
800-872-7245
www.amtrak.com

**Los Angeles County
Metropolitan
Transportation
Authority**
800-COMMUTE
www.metro.net

San Francisco Municipal Transit Authority
311 in SF or 415-701-2311
www.sfmata.com

National Parks & Monuments

Redwood State and National Parks
707-464-6101
www.nps.gov/redw

Lava Beds National Monument
530-667-8100
www.nps.gov/labe

Lassen Volcanic National Park
530-595-4444
www.nps.gov/lavo

Point Reyes National Seashore
415-463-5100
www.nps.gov/pore

Muir Woods National Monument
415-388-2595 (recorded message)
or 415-388-2596
www.nps.gov/muwo

Yosemite National Park
209-372-0200
www.nps.gov/yose

Pinnacles National Monument
831-389-4485
www.nps.gov/pinn

Sequoia and Kings Canyon National Parks
559-565-3341
www.nps.gov/sekin

Giant Sequoia National Monument
559-784-1500
www.fs.fed.us/r5/sequoia/gsnm.html

Channel Islands National Park
805-658-5730
www.nps.gov/chis

Cabrillo National Monument
619-557-5450
www.nps.gov/cabr

Death Valley National Park
760-786-3200
www.nps.gov/deva

Joshua Tree National Park
760-367-5500
www.nps.gov/jotr

INDEX

A

abalone, 165
Alabama Hills, 196
Alamitos Bay, 28, 82
Alembic, 125, 137
Alger Lakes, 215
Allen, Gracie, 23
Altamont Speedway, 101
Amargosa Opera House and Hotel, 237
Amboy, CA, 248
American Beauty, 91
Anaheim, CA, 41–42
Angel Dust, 91
Ansel Adams Wilderness Area, 204,
    207, 212, 221
Apple (birthplace), 101, 120
Aquarium of the Pacific, 80, 87
Arbuckle, Roscoe "Fatty," 21, 47, 52
artichokes, 164–65
Artist's Palette, 232, 242
Auburn, CA, 192

B

Baber, Melvyn, 231
Baby Blues Barbecue, 77, 87
Badwater, 232, 238, 241
Baker, CA, 224–26, 235, 248, 258
Bakersfield, CA, 150, 157, 186–87, 189
The Bakersfield Sound, 153
Ballerina Clown statue, 19
Banana Bungalow, 39
Barney's Beanery, 35, 53, 62
Barrio Boy (Galarza), 153
Batman, 28
Baum, L. Frank, 23, 56
Bay Bridge, 90, 96
Beach Ball, 83, 87
Beach Boys, 15
Beal, Art, 155
Beat Farmers, 15
Becket, Marta, 237
Bell, Claude, 16
Belly Flops, 166, 177
Belmont Shores, 82

Belushi, John, 60
Bennett Lane Winery, 141–42, 148
Beringer Vineyards, 142, 148
Beverly Hills, CA, 28
Bidwell Park, 160
Bigfoot hotspots, 102–3
Big Sur, CA, 116, 136, 151, 168, 169
*Big Sur and the Oranges of Hieronymus
    Bosch* (Miller), 153
Big Sur River Inn, 116, 136
Big Trouble in Little China, 91
The Birds, 90
Black Panther landmarks in
    Oakland, CA, 110–11
Blade Runner, 15, 28
Blair House Inn, 101
*Blood Meridian: Or the Evening Redness in
    the West* (McCarthy), 225
The Blue Beet, 83, 87
Bluff Creek, 102, 103
Blythe Giants (Intaglios), 33
Bodega, CA, 90
Bogart, Humphrey, 23, 56
Bolt's Antique Tool Museum, 161
Bombay Beach, CA, 230
The Booksmith, 121, 136
Border Field State Park and
    Border meetups, 40–41, 69, 70–73, 86
Borofsky, Jonathan, 19
Bothe-Napa Valley State Park, 144, 148
Bradbury Building, 28
Brannan's Grill, 139, 148
Bremer Family Winery, 140–41, 148
The Bridge, 91, 122
Bronson Canyons, 28
Brown, Divine, 28
Browning, Tod, 47, 52
Bubblegum Alley, 152
Buck Owens and the Buckaroos, 157
Bug Café, 201
Bukowski, Henry Charles, 23–24
Bun Boy Restaurant, 224
Bunny Museum, 30–31
Burgundy Room, 25, 55, 63
Burns, George, 23
Byck, Walter, 94

C

Cabazon Dinosaurs, 16
Calabasas, CA, 28
Calaveras County Jumping
    Frog Jubilee, 191
Caliente Tropics, 237
California Agriculture
    Resource Directory 2007, 173
California Citrus Growers Association, 184
California Coastal Commission, 82
California Desert
    attractions, happenings, and oddities,
        224–34, 238–39
    books to read, 225
    famous deceased people and
        cemeteries, 229, 236
    famous people, 223
    introduction, 222–24
    lodging, 236–37, 238
    movies and TV, 225, 232, 242
    music, 225
    restaurants/food, 224, 235
    stats and facts, 223
    to-do checklist, 225
    travelogue, the desert, 240–57
California Surf Museum, 67, 83, 86
California Uberalis, 91
Calistoga, CA, 109, 139, 144–45, 148, 149
Calistoga Inn, 109
Cambria, CA, 154–55
Camp Pendleton, 65, 68, 76
Candy, John, 23
Cannery Row, 165–66
Cannery Row (Steinbeck), 153, 157
Canseco, Jose, 119
Capote, Truman, 23
Captain Courageous (steer), 95
Captain Dutch's Sailboat, 167–68
Carlsbad, CA, 73–74, 86
Cartoon Art Museum, 92
The Casbah, 26–27
Cascades, 90
Cassady, Neal, 99
Castroville, CA, 164–65
Cathedral City, CA, 229, 234
Cave Store, 68–69, 86

Centennial Bulb, 89
Central California: The Coast
    and the Valley
    attractions, happenings, and oddities,
        152–63, 169–70
    books to read, 153
        famous deceased people and
            cemeteries, 156–59, 160
    famous people, 160
    introduction, 150–52
    lodging, 167–68
    movies and TV, 153
    music, 153
    restaurants/food, 164–66
    stats and facts, 151
    to-do checklist, 153
    travelogue, agriculture, 172–88
Chambers, Marilyn, 24
Chandler, Raymond, 15
Channel Islands National Park, 42–43, 44
Chaplin, Charlie, 196
Chateau Marmont, 60
Cheeta the chimpanzee, 223, 232
Chicano Park Murals, 19
Chico, CA, 159–60, 169–70
Chinatown (movie), 15
Cholame, CA, 158
Church Of Satan, 89
Cindy's Backstreet Kitchen, 144, 149
Citizen Kane, 153
Citrus Club, 125, 137
citrus industry, 182–86
City Lights Bookstore, 98, 124, 136
clams, 154
Cline, Pat, 146–47
Club Deluxe, 125, 137
Club Spaceland, 25
*COE the Good Dragon at the Center
    of the World* (JAI), 227
Coit Tower, 124
Colma, CA, 95–96, 126
Colorado Desert, 222
Colors, 15
Coltrane, John, 105
The Condor, 129, 137
A Coney Island of the Mind (Ferlinghetti), 91

Confessions of a Superhero
    (documentary), 49
Cool, Aaron, 151
Cool, CA, 151
Coppola, Francis Ford, 101
Cornerstone Gardens, 93
Cottonwood, 197
Cousteau, Jacques, 199
Crane, Bob, 23
Creedence Clearwater Revival, 153
Crescent City, CA, 109
Croce, Ingrid, 37
Croce, Jim, 37
Croce's, 37, 69
Crosby, Bing, 23
Crossroads Café and Tavern, 251, 254, 258
Cruise, Tom, 29–30
Crystal Pier Hotel, 40
Culver City, CA, 23, 28, 31, 62
Curly Redwood Lodge, 109
Cypress Lawn Memorial Park, 96

D
Darioush, 143, 148
Davis, CA, 162, 175
Davis, Sammy, Jr., 56
Dead Kennedys, 91
Dean, James, 158
Death Valley and
    Death Valley National Park,
    222–24, 232, 237, 238, 240–47, 258
Death Valley Junction, CA, 237
Defenestration, 92–93
Del Marcos Hotel, 237
Delta King Riverboat, 167–68
Dennis, Christopher, 49
The Depot, 184, 189
desert. *See* California Desert
Desert Memorial Park, 229
The Desert Sessions, 225
Desert Studies Center, 234
The Dharma Bums (Kerouac), 91
Dick's Place, 114
Die Hard 2, 232
DiMaggio, Joe, 96
Dirty Harry, 91, 101

Disney, Walt, 23, 56
Disneyland Resort, 41–42
Donner Memorial State Park, 195
Donohue Pass, 210, 211, 213
The Doors (band), 15
The Doors (movie), 225
Dr. Kenneth Fox's Giant Statues, 192
Dr. Seuss Collection and Trees, 20, 68, 86
Dracula and Freaks, 47, 52
Dragnet, 232
Drakes Bay Family Farm, 107
Dunsmuir, CA, 109

E
Earp, Wyatt, 96
earthquakes, 89, 191
East of Eden, 158
Eastwood, Clint, 101
Ebony Lady Salon, 111
Eggers, Dave, 105
Ehn, John, 18–19
Eight Immortals, 126, 137
826 Valencia, 104–5, 127, 137
Elbow Room, 126, 137
The Electric Kool-Aid Acid Trip (Wolfe), 91
Ellen Browning Scripps
    Memorial Park, 20
Emerald Bay, 194
Emerald Triangle: Humboldt, Mendocino,
    and Trinity Counties, 97–98
*An Emigrants' Guide to Oregon
    and California* (Hastings), 195
Encinitas, CA, 75
Esalen Institute Night Baths, 116, 136, 169
Escondido, CA, 20, 68, 86
Esquire Grill, 160
Evergreen Lodge, 202, 208, 221
Exeter, CA, 189

F
Fairbanks, Douglas, 21, 23
Fairfield, CA, 166, 175–77, 189
Faith No More, 91
Fanny Ann's Saloon, 173, 189
Farmer John Murals, 17–18, 52, 62
Farmer's Daughter Hotel, 39

Fash, Augie, 170
Felicity: The Center of the World, 227
Ferlinghetti, Lawrence, 91
Fields, W. C., 35, 56
Fine, Larry, 23
Fisherman's Wharf, 110, 124, 165
500 Club, 126, 137
Flying Burrito Brothers, 225
Forest Lawn Memorial Park, 23, 56, 63
Fort Bragg, CA, 114
Four Seasons Resort Aviara, 73–74, 86
Fourteeners (14,000-foot peaks), 191
Fox, Kenneth, 192
Frank, Rich, 145
Frankenstein, 28
Frank Family Vineyards, 145–46, 149
Frazee, Candace, 30–31
Free Festival, 101
Freeth, George, 78
Fresno, CA, 150, 179–81, 189
Fresno County, 151, 179–81, 184
Fresno (TV series), 153
Frolic Room, 25, 60, 63
Furnace Creek, 240
Furnace Creek Inn & Ranch,
    238, 242, 244, 247, 258

G
Gable, Clark, 23, 56
Galarza, Ernesto, 153
Ganda, 52, 62
Garberville, CA, 102–3
Garden of Memories
    Memorial Park, 157–58
Gaslamp Quarter, 26, 37, 69
Geisel, Theodore, 20
Gem Lake, 214, 215
Gem Pass, 214
General Sherman (tree), 191
Giant Artichoke, 165
Giant Rock, 233, 248, 250
*The Gilded Palace of Sin/Burrito
    Deluxe,* 225
Gilligan's Island, 28, 82
Gimme Shelter, 91
Gladiator, 196

Glendale, CA, 23, 28, 56, 63
Goat Rock, 90
goats, 108–9
The Godfather, Part II, 193
Golden Gate Park, 101, 127, 137
Gold Rush, 196
Good Vibrations Vibrator Museum, 100
Google (birthplace), 101, 120
The Goonies, 90
Grand Californian Hotel, 42
Grandma's All Natural, 181
Grant, Cary, 160
Grant, Hugh, 28
Grapes of Wrath (Steinbeck), 157
Grateful Dead, 90, 91
Grauman's Chinese Theatre, 48, 54, 57, 62
Greatest Hits, 91
Green Hills Memorial Park, 23–24
Greenlawn Cemetery, 157
Green Tortoise, 109
Griffith Park, 28
Grimes, Les, 18
Groveland, CA, 196, 201–2

H
Hagafen Cellars, 143, 148
Haggard, Merle, 153
Haight-Ashbury district, San Francisco,
    90, 123–24, 130–31, 134
Hammett, Dashiell, 91
Happy Days, 28
Harley Farms, 108–9
Hastings, Lansford, 195
Hayworth, Rita, 23
Hearst, William Randolph, 96
Hearst Castle, 155
Heidrick Ag History Center, 173, 189
Heinold's First and Last Chance Bar,
    98, 118–19, 136
Hemet Maze Stone, 33
Hemlock Tavern, 130, 137
Hermosa Beach, CA, 78, 87
Hermosa Cyclery, 78, 87
Herron, Willis, 234
Hetch Hetchy Reservoir, 208
Hewlett-Packard (birthplace), 101

High Sierra. *See* Sierra Nevada
and vicinity
Hills of Eternity Memorial Park, 96
Hog Island Oyster Company, 107
Hollywood, CA
attractions, 25, 28
Hollywood Boulevard, 46–60
lodging, 39, 47, 62, 63
nightlife, 25
restaurants/food, 35, 63
Hollywood Forever Cemetery, 21–22
Hollywood & Highland Center, 55, 63
Hollywood Roosevelt Hotel, 54, 63
Hollywood sign, 13
Hollywood Toys & Costumes, 51, 57, 62
Holmes, John, 24
Holy Cross Cemetery, 23, 96
Homegrown, 91
Home of Peace Cemetery, 96
Hoover, J. Edgar, 110–11
Hope, Bob, 223
Horace 8 and the Werewolves, 58–59
Hotel Cafe, 25
Hot Shots, 232
How the West Was Won, 196
Hubbard, L. Ron, 29–30
Hughes, Howard, 28, 83
Huntington Beach, CA, 82, 87
Hyperion, 111

I
Imperial Beach, CA, 64–65
Indio, CA, 231, 235
Ingleside Inn, 231
Inglewood, CA, 34, 62
The Integratron, 233, 248–50, 258
InterContinental Mark Hopkins Hotel, 100
International Surfing Museum, 82, 87
Inverness, CA, 107
Iron Door Saloon, 196
Ishi, 159

J
Jackson, Helen Hunt, 15
JAI, 227
James Dean Memorial Junction, 158

Jarvis, Kat, 139–47
Jedediah Smith State Park, 103
jelly beans, 166, 175–78
Jelly Belly Factory, 166, 175–77, 189
Jenner, CA, 90
Jerry's Famous Deli, 35–36, 56, 63
Jimmy Swaggart Prostitute Plaque, 231
John Barleycorn (London), 91
John Muir National Historic Site, 207, 221
John Muir's Grave, 207–8, 221
John Muir Trail, 204, 207, 209, 210–18
John Muir Wilderness Area, 204, 207
Johns, Howard, 225
Johnson, Albert, 246
Jones, Spike, 23
Josh Homme and Company, 225
Joshua Tree, CA, 226, 236, 239, 251, 258
Joshua Tree Inn, 229, 236
Joshua Tree National Park,
229, 239, 252–53, 258
Jumbo's Clown Room, 25, 51–52, 62
Juskiewicz, Joe, 208

K
Kansas City Barbecue, 27, 73, 86
The Karate Kid, 28
Karl, Nancy, 248–50
Kaufman, Andy, 35–36
Kelso Dunes, 234
Kerouac, Jack, 91
Keseberg, Lewis, 195
Keys View, 252
Kezar Bar and Grill, 122, 136
Kill 'Em All, 91
Kirkpatrick, John and Greg, 182–83
Klamath, CA, 95
Knight, Leonard, 227–28
Knight, Lora, 194
Knight, Ted, 23, 56
Knotts, Don, 23
Koip Peak Pass, 211, 214, 217
Kornell, Hanns, 145

L
La Jolla, CA, 38, 69, 86
La Jolla Cove, 68

Lake Elowin Resort, 202
Lake Sherwood, 28
Lake Tahoe, 192, 194, 199
Lake Tahoe, CA, 194
Landers, CA, 233, 258
Lantrip, Dean, 160–61
Lantrip's House of Ashtrays, 160–61
Lassen National Park, 113
La Super-Rica Taqueria, 164
Lavendar Lady (plant), 13
LaVey, Anton, 89
La Woman, 15
Lee Vining, CA, 200, 209, 219–20, 221
Legend of Bigfoot, 102–3
Lemmon, Jack, 23
Limbaugh, Rush, 160
Lindcove Ranch, 182–84, 189
Lindcove Research and
    Extension Center, 183, 189
Livermore, CA, 89
Lizard People below Los Angeles,
    32–33, 106
Loma Prieta quake, 90
Lombard, Carole, 56
Lombard Street, San Francisco, 89
London, Jack, 91, 98
The Lone Ranger, 196
Long Beach, CA, 28, 39–40, 44, 80, 87
Long Beach Harbor, 77, 78
Longboarder Café, 67, 86
The Longboard Restaurant & Pub, 82, 87
Longton, Stephanie, 142
Loomis Eggplant Festival, 199
Los Altos, CA, 101
Los Angeles and Southern California
    attractions, happenings, and oddities,
        16–25, 27–33, 40–44
    books to read, 15
    famous deceased people and
        cemeteries, 21–24, 28, 35–36, 37
    famous people, 28, 29–30, 51, 66
    introduction, 12–14
    lodging, 38–40
    movies and TV, 15, 28, 34, 35, 39
    music, 15
    nightlife, 25–27

restaurants/food, 34–38
stats and facts, 13
to-do checklist, 15
travelogue, beach cruising and
    surfing, 64–84
travelogue, Hollywood Boulevard,
    46–60
weather, 14
Los Angeles Harbor, 12, 77, 79, 80
Lost in Space, 232
Loud and Plowed and...Live!!, 15
Lovelace, Linda, 24
Lubanski, Steve, 30–31
Lucas, George, 101
Lugosi, Béla, 23
Lunnie, Kevin, 107–8
Lusty Lady, 124
Lyell Canyon, 210
Lynch, Randy and Lisa, 141

M
The Mad Greek, 235
Madison Bear Garden, 159–60
Madonna Inn, 167
Maiden Pub, 116, 136
Maitia, Danny, 187–88
Malibu Creek State Park, 28
The Maltese Falcon, (Hammett), 91
Manhattan Beach, 78
Manson, Charles, 90, 131
marijuana, 97–98, 173
Marina del Rey, CA, 77, 83, 86
Mars Attacks!, 34
Marshall, CA, 107
Martin, Dean, 23
Martinez, CA, 207, 211, 221
Marx, Chico, 23
M*A*S*H, 28
Mastodon Peak, 252
Matthau, Walter, 23
Maze Stone Park, 33
McCarthy, Cormac, 225
Melvyn's, 231
Mendocino, CA, 101, 113–14
Merced Fruit Stand, 178–79, 189
Metallica, 91

Midpines, CA, 201, 206–7
Miller, Henry, 153, 156
Modesto, CA, 101
Mojave Air and Space Port, 223, 232
Mojave Desert, 222, 223, 237
Mojave National Preserve, 234, 248, 258
monarch butterflies, 90
Mono Lake, 203, 215
Monroe, Marilyn, 23, 46, 164, 237
Monterey, CA, 150, 165–66
Monterey Abalone Company, 165
Monterey Bay Sailing, 168
Morrison, Jim, 19, 241
Mount Lassen, 90, 92, 113
Mount Rubidoux attack midgets, 33, 106
Mount Shasta, 106
Mount St. Helena, 142
Mount Whitney, 192, 196
Muir, John, 193, 206–8
Muir Lodge, 206–7
Murder She Wrote, 101
Murio's Trophy Room, 121–22, 124, 136
Musée Mécanique, 110, 124, 136
Museum of Jurassic Technology,
    31, 52, 62
Museum of Latin American Art, 80, 87
Mystery Spot, 106–7

N
Napa, CA, 148, 149
Napa Cellars, 139, 148
Napa Valley, 138–47
NASCAR, 141
National Date Festival, 235
National Steinbeck Center, 158
National Yo-Yo Museum, 169–70
Naval Ammo Depot, 82
Necromance, 27–29, 54, 63
Newport Beach, CA, 44, 77, 82–83, 87
Newport Beachwalk Hotel, 83, 87
New River, 255
Newton, Huey, 110–11
Nine Satanic Statements, 89
Nipton, CA, 237
Nitt Witt Ridge, 154–55
Nixon, Pat, 71

Noah Purifoy Outdoor Desert
    Art Museum, 226, 251, 258
Nob Hill, 100
North Beach, CA, 109
North by Northwest, 160
North Coast Brewing Company, 114
North Oakland Anti-Poverty Center, 111
Norton, Joshua, 95–96
Norton I, Emperor of the United States
    and Protector of Mexico, 95–96, 126
N.W.A. (band), 15

O
Oakland, CA, 96, 98, 100, 110–11, 136
Oakville, CA, 139, 148
Oasis of Mara, 253
Ocean Beach, CA, 40
Oceanside, CA, 65–68, 86
Oceanside Pier, 68
Oldenburg, Claes, 19
Old Trapper's Lodge, 18–19, 57, 63
Orbison, Roy, 23
Orbit In, 237
Oroville, CA, 159, 160–61
Owens, Alvin Edgar "Buck," 153, 157
Owens Valley, 196
oysters, 107–8

P
Pacifica, CA, 126
Pacific Grove, CA, 90
Palm Springs, CA, 46–47,
    62, 222, 223, 231, 236–37
Palm Springs Confidential:
    Playground of the Stars (Johns), 225
Palo Alto, CA, 101
Palos Verdes, 77, 78–79
Pappy and Harriet's Pioneertown Palace,
    230, 251, 258
Paradise Ridge Winery, 94
Parkfield, CA "Earthquake Capital
    of the World," 151
Parsons, Gram, 225, 229, 230, 236
Pasadena, CA, 30–31, 35
Patterson, Roger, 103
Paxton Gate, 105, 127, 137

Pescadero, CA, 108–9
Petersen, Patricia, 31
Peterson, Jon, 75–76
petroglyphs, 33
Pet Sounds, 15
Phillipe the Original, 36
Phoenix Hotel, 109
Pickford, Mary, 23
Pierce Brothers Westwood
    Village Memorial Park, 23
Pierce College campus, 18–19, 57
Pig 'n Whistle, 50, 54, 62
pink snow, 198
Pioneertown, CA, 230, 236, 251, 258
Pioneertown Motel, 230, 236, 251, 258
Pismo Beach, 154
Plagues & Pleasures on the Salton Sea, 225
Planet of the Apes, 232
The Player (Tolkin), 15
Point Lobos, 106, 163
Point Reyes National Seashore,
    107, 112–13
Pontiac Hotel, 109
Ponto State Beach, 75
Porno Grauman's, 24–25
Port of Long Beach, 13
Port of Los Angeles, 13
Potter Schoolhouse, 90
Price is Right, 39
Pulp Fiction, 15, 28
Purifoy, Noah, 17, 226, 251

Q
Queen Califia's Magical Circle, 20, 68, 86
Queen Mary, 38–39, 80, 81–82, 87

R
Racetrack, 243
Railroad Park Resort, 109
Ramble: A Field Guide to the USA
    (Peterson), 121
Ramona (Jackson), 15
Rancho Palos Verdes, CA, 23–24
Randy's Donuts, 34, 52, 62
Rappe, Virginia, 52
Ravenous, 193

Reagan, Ronald, 176
Rebel Without a Cause, 158
Red Cathedral, 243
Redick, Scott Durango,
    118, 122–23, 124–30
Redondo Beach, CA, 78
Red's Meadow, 209, 210, 211
Red Victorian, 109
Red Wind (Chandler), 15
Redwood National and State Parks,
    102, 111–12
Reed, Donna, 23
Reed, Virginia, 195
Reems, Harry, 24
Reiff, Mark, 155
Reiff's Gas Station House, 155
Rendezvous, 46–47, 62, 237
Reseda, CA, 28
Restaurante El Salvadoreño, 73, 86
Ritz-Carlton, Marina del Rey, 77, 86
Riverside County Fair, 235
River Street Inn, 196, 202
Rocking Stone, 198
Rodia, Simon, 16–17
Rogers, Roy, 236
Rombauer, Koerner, 145
Rosie the Ribeter (frog), 191
Roughing It (Twain), 203
R2's Arroyo, 232, 242

S
Sacramento, CA, 150, 156,
    160, 167–68, 172, 189
The Saint John Will-I-Am Coltrane
    African Orthodox Church, 105–6
Saint Phalle, Niki de, 20
Salinas, CA, 157–58
Salton City, CA, 255–56
Salton Sea, 223, 252, 254–55, 259
Salvation Mountain, 227–28
Sanamluang, 59, 63
San Andreas Fault, 113, 151, 252
San Diego, CA
    attractions, 19, 20, 31
    lodging, 40
    nightlife, 26–27, 69

Old Town, 31
restaurants/food, 37, 86
San Francisco and Northern California
attractions, happenings, and oddities,
92–107, 110–14
bars and pubs, 98–100
books to read, 91
famous deceased people
and cemeteries, 95–96
famous people, 90, 101
introduction, 88–92
lodging, 109
movies and TV, 90, 91, 101
music, 91
restaurants/food, 100, 107–9
stats and facts, 89–90
to-do checklist, 91
travelogue, sex, drugs, and
rock and roll, 116–34
travelogue, wine country, 138–47
San Jose, CA, 103–4, 136
San Luis Obispo, CA, 150, 152, 167
San Miguel Island, 43
San Onofre State Beach, 82
San Pedro, CA, 79–80
San Remo Hotel, 109
Santa Barbara, CA, 164
Santa Catalina, CA, 42, 43
Santa Cruz, CA, 106–7
Santa Monica, CA, 24, 35
Santa Rosa, CA, 94
Sardine Factory, 166
sardines, 165–66
Schulberg, Budd, 15
Schwarzenegger, Arnold, 160
Scientology, 29–30
Scott, Walter, 246
Scotty's Castle, 246
Seal Beach, CA, 82
Seale, Bobby, 110–11
The Sea of Cortez (Steinbeck), 158
sea otters, 163
Seau, Junior, 66
Senator Capitol Kitty, 156
Sequoia Brewing Company, 180, 189
Sequoia Grove Vineyards, 139, 148

Sequoia/Kings Canyon National Parks,
191, 192, 202, 204
Shatner, William, 196
Sheridan, Otto, 141
Shields Date Gardens, 235
Shoe Garden, 131
Shufelt, G. Warren, 32–33
Sideways, 143, 153
Sierra Nevada and vicinity
attractions, happenings, and oddities,
192–99, 203–4
books to read and maps, 193
famous deceased people
and cemeteries, 195–96
famous people, 196
introduction, 190–92
lodging, 201–2
movies and TV, 193
music, 193
restaurants/food, 199–200
stats and facts, 191
to-do checklist, 193
travelogue, in John Muir's
footprints, 206–20
Sierra Nevada Brewing Company, 159
Silver Strand, 64
Sinatra, Frank, 225, 229, 231, 234
singing dunes, 234
Six Rivers National Forest, 102
Skeletons in the Closet, 24, 52, 62
Ski Inn, 230
Slab City, CA, 227–28
Sly & the Family Stone, 91
SoCal Surf School, 65, 86
Soda Springs, CA, 196
Songs for Swingin' Lovers (Sinatra), 225
Sonny Bono Salton Sea National
Wildlife Refuge, 256
Sonoma, CA, 93
Spec's Twelve Adler Museum, 99
Speed, 232
Spin and Margie's Desert Hide-a-Way,
236, 254, 259
Springer, Curtis Howe, 234
Squeeze In, 200
SS Minnow, 82

St. Helena, CA, 139, 142, 144, 148, 149
Star Trek, 232
Star Wars, 101, 225, 232, 242
Steinbeck, John, 153, 157–58
Stephens, Clarence, 106
Stewart, Jimmy, 23
Stillman, Deanne, 225
Stovepipe Wells Village, 238
Straight Outta Compton, 15
Strauss, Levi, 96
Strolling Stones: The Mystery of Death Valley's Racetrack, 243, 244
Stuck in Lodi Again, 153
Studio City, CA, 35–36, 56, 63
Sunset Boulevard, 15
Sunset Inn, 201–2
Surfin Fire, 75, 86
Susie's Bar, 140, 148
Swaggart, Jimmy, 231
Swayne, Brooke, 65–66
Sweet Thursday (Steinbeck), 157

T

Tahoe Tessie, 199
Tate, Sharon, 23
Taxi, 35
Taylor's Refresher, 142, 148
Telos, the Last/Lost City of Atlantis, 106
Ten Point Program, 110, 111
Theodore Geisel Library, 20
Thompson, Hunter S., 99
Three Rivers, CA, 196
Thriftstore Allstars, 251–52
Tijuana, Mexico, 41, 69, 70, 71
Tiki-Ti, 25
Titus Canyon, 244
Toad Hollow, 162
Tolkin, Michael, 15
Tomales Bay Oyster Company, 107
TomKat Theatre, 52
Toomey, Matt, 200
Top Gun, 73
Top of the Mark, 100, 128, 137
Torrey Pines Gliderport, 38
Tortilla Flat (Steinbeck), 157

Tosca, 99, 129–30, 137
Tourist Club, 197
Tower23, 40
Tractor & Truck Museum, 173–74
Tracy, Spencer, 23
Trash Film Orgy, 160
travelogues
agriculture/Central California, 172–88
beach cruising and surfing/Southern California, 64–84
the desert, 240–57
Hollywood Boulevard, 46–60
in John Muir's footprints, 206–20
sex, drugs, and rock and roll/Northern California, 116–34
wine country/Northern California, 138–47
Travels with Charley (Steinbeck), 158
Treebones Resort, 168
Tremors, 196
Trestles, 82
Triangle Tattoo & Museum, 114
Tribute to Prostitutes Plaque, 102
Trinity River, 103
Trona Pinnacles, 232
Tropic of Cancer (Miller), 156
Tropic of Capricorn (Miller), 156
Troubadour, 25
Truckee, CA, 191, 195, 196, 197, 198, 200, 202
Tunnel Top, 100
Tuolumne Meadows, 209, 211
Tuolumne Meadows Lodge, 209–10, 221
Twain, Mark, 203
Twentynine Palms, CA, 236, 239, 253
Twentynine Palms: The True Story of Murder, Marines, and the Mojave (Stillman), 225
Twentynine Palms Inn, CA, 236

U

Uhebebe Crater, 238, 247
Ukiah, CA, 102
University Inn, 179, 181, 189
University of California, 20, 159, 183

V

Valdez Cave, 43
Valentino, Rudolf, 21
Van Tassel, George, 233, 248, 249, 250
Velaslavasay Panorama: Effulgence of the
    North, 20–21
Venice, CA, 19, 77, 87
Venice Beach Public Art, 19
Vernon, CA, 17–18, 52, 62
Vesuvio, 99, 124, 129, 136
Vibe Hotel, 39, 47, 55, 62
Victorian, 90
Vikingsholm, 194
Vintner's Collective, 142–43, 148
Visalia, CA, 182, 184, 189
Volcano, CA, 191
V Room, 80, 87

W

Wacko/Soap Plant, 29, 54, 63
The Waterfront (bar), 26
Waterfront Plaza Hotel, 118, 136
Waterworld, 232
Watman, Daniel, 41, 69–73
Watts Towers, 16, 52, 62
Waugh Lake, 214
Wave Organ, 94–95
Weed, Abner, 151
Weed, CA, 151
Weir, Ernie, 143
Welk, Lawrence, 23
West Hollywood, 39, 60
Westwood, CA, 23
Wetzel's Riverside Monster, 33
Whaley House, 31
What Makes Sammy Run (Schulberg), 15
Whisky a Go Go, 25–26
Whoa Nellie Deli, 200, 209, 219–20, 221
Willow Creek-China
    Flat Museum, 102, 103
Winchester, Sarah, 103–4, 120
Winchester Mystery House, 103–4,
    119–20, 136
Wine Country Inn, 139, 144, 148
wineries, 94, 139, 140–46, 148, 149
wines
Bennett Lane Maximus, 2002, 139, 144

Bremmer Family Claret, 2001, 141
Darioush Signature
    Cabernet Sauvignon, 2002, 143
Frank Famile Reserve
    Chardonnay, 2004, 146
Frank Family
    Cabernet Sauvignon, 2001, 147
Frank Family Napa
    Valley Chardonnay, 2004, 146
Melka Cabernet Sauvignon, 2003, 143
Napa Cellars Sauvignon Blanc, 2004, 147
Napa Valley Zinfandel, 2003, 139
Robert Sinsky Pinot Blanc, 2004, 144
wine production, 89
The Wizard of Oz (Baum), 56
Wolfe, Tom, 91
Wood, Natalie, 23
Woodland, CA, 155, 173, 189
Woodland Hills, CA, 18–19, 57, 63
Woodlawn Memorial Park, 95–96
Wool Growers, 187, 189
World's Largest Thermometer,
    234–36, 248, 258
Wyndham Oceanside Pier Resort, 67, 86

Y

Yahi people, 159
Yosemite Bug, 201, 220, 221
Yosemite National Park,
    192, 204, 206–18, 220, 221
Yoshi's, 100, 118, 136

Z

Zablosky, Dennis, 146
Zarki, Joe, 253
Zzyzx, 233–34